The Roaring Twenties

The Roaring Twenties

Other books in the Turning Points series:

Turning Points
IN WORLD HISTORY

The Roaring Twenties

Phillip Margulies, *Book Editor*

Bonnie Szumski, *Publisher*
Scott Barbour, *Managing Editor*

GREENHAVEN
PRESS ®

THOMSON

GALE

San Diego • Detroit • New York • San Francisco • Cleveland
New Haven, Conn. • Waterville, Maine • London • Munich

© 2004 by Greenhaven Press. Greenhaven Press is an imprint of The Gale Group, Inc., a division of Thomson Learning, Inc.

Greenhaven® and Thomson Learning™ are trademarks used herein under license.

For more information, contact
Greenhaven Press
27500 Drake Rd.
Farmington Hills, MI 48331-3535
Or you can visit our Internet site at http://www.gale.com

Cover credit: © Hulton/Archive by Getty Images
Library of Congress, 61, 177, 222
National Archives, 98

LIBRARY OF CONGRESS CATALOGING-IN-PUBLICATION DATA

The roaring twenties / Phillip Margulies, book editor.
   p. cm. — (Turning points in world history)
  Includes bibliographical references and index.
  ISBN 0-7377-1809-9 (lib. : alk. paper) — ISBN 0-7377-1810-2 (pbk. : alk. paper)
    1. Nineteen twenties. 2. United States—Politics and government—1919–1933.
3. United States—Social conditions—1918–1932. 4. United States—Social life and customs—1918–1945. I. Margulies, Phillip, 1952– . II. Series.
E784.R63 2004
973.91'5—dc22   2003049370

Printed in the United States of America

Contents

Foreword

Certain past events stand out as pivotal, as having effects and outcomes that change the course of history. These events are often referred to as turning points. Historian Louis L. Snyder provides this useful definition:

> A turning point in history is an event, happening, or stage which thrusts the course of historical development into a different direction. By definition a turning point is a great event, but it is even more—a great event with the explosive impact of altering the trend of man's life on the planet.

History's turning points have taken many forms. Some were single, brief, and shattering events with immediate and obvious impact. The invasion of Britain by William the Conqueror in 1066, for example, swiftly transformed that land's political and social institutions and paved the way for the rise of the modern English nation. By contrast, other single events were deemed of minor significance when they occurred, only later recognized as turning points. The assassination of a little-known European nobleman, Archduke Franz Ferdinand, on June 28, 1914, in the Bosnian town of Sarajevo was such an event; only after it touched off a chain reaction of political-military crises that escalated into the global conflict known as World War I did the murder's true significance become evident.

Other crucial turning points occurred not in terms of a few hours, days, months, or even years, but instead as evolutionary developments spanning decades or even centuries. One of the most pivotal turning points in human history, for instance—the development of agriculture, which replaced nomadic hunter-gatherer societies with more permanent settlements—occurred over the course of many generations. Still other great turning points were neither events nor developments, but rather revolutionary new inventions and innovations that significantly altered social customs and ideas, military tactics, home life, the spread of knowledge, and the human condition in general. The developments of writing, gunpowder, the printing press, antibiotics, the electric light, atomic energy, television, and the computer, the last two of which have recently ushered in the world-altering information age, represent only some of these innovative turning points.

Each anthology in the Greenhaven Turning Points in World History series presents a group of essays chosen for their accessibility. The anthology's structure also enhances this accessibility. First, an introductory essay provides a general overview of the principal events and figures involved, placing the topic in its historical context. The essays that follow explore various aspects in more detail, some targeting political trends and consequences, others social, literary, cultural, and/or technological ramifications, and still others pivotal leaders and other influential figures. To aid the reader in choosing the material of immediate interest or need, each essay is introduced by a concise summary of the contributing writer's main themes and insights.

In addition, each volume contains extensive research tools, including a collection of excerpts from primary source documents pertaining to the historical events and figures under discussion. In the anthology on the French Revolution, for example, readers can examine the works of Rousseau, Voltaire, and other writers and thinkers whose championing of human rights helped fuel the French people's growing desire for liberty; the French *Declaration of the Rights of Man and Citizen*, presented to King Louis XVI by the French National Assembly on October 2, 1789; and eyewitness accounts of the attack on the royal palace and the horrors of the Reign of Terror. To guide students interested in pursuing further research on the subject, each volume features an extensive bibliography, which for easy access has been divided into separate sections by topic. Finally, a comprehensive index allows readers to scan and locate content efficiently. Each of the anthologies in the Greenhaven Turning Points in World History series provides students with a complete, detailed, and enlightening examination of a crucial historical watershed.

Introduction: The Real Twentieth Century Begins

The 1920s are commonly remembered as a time of prosperity and frivolity wedged between two disasters, World War I and the great stock market crash of 1929. Its symbols are easy to recognize: short-haired young women in dresses with no waists, forbidden drinking at speakeasies, dance marathons, and the silent comedy of Charlie Chaplin. It was a time when gangsters used tommy guns and barbers picked up stock market tips from their customers. The wild behavior the period is famous for became part of the legend of the Roaring Twenties, a decadelong New Year's Eve party followed by a decadelong massive hangover called the Great Depression. The implication is that, ultimately, the twenties left no legacy. In the 1920s, Americans celebrated. In the 1930s, they cleaned up the mess and moved on.

The legend of the Roaring Twenties contains some truth. For most of the decade business was good and employment was up. More Americans than ever had the leisure time for experiments in what are now called lifestyles. It was a time of fads, when people—or at least newspapers, magazines, and films—focused a great deal of attention on matters of little importance. But far from leaving no legacy, the 1920s was an era of vast and permanent changes in the structure of American society and the outlook of American people.

The key to the legacy of the Roaring Twenties lies in its familiarity. In many important ways, today's society resembles that of the 1920s. Shopping in chain stores, mixing at nightclubs, flouting the authority of their parents, and making use of cars, telephones, and radios, the people of the 1920s seem closer to those of the twenty-first century than to those of the nineteenth. It was in the 1920s that America first became a brand-conscious society. The names of stores such as Woolworth, Macy's, and Kresge's and products such as Kleenex and Listerine embedded themselves deeply into each citizen's consciousness. It was in the 1920s that mass entertainment began to dominate the culture of the United States, as it now dominates the culture of the world. Tabloid newspapers and confession magazines appeared for the first time, purveying sex and violence in simple language with numerous photographs and illustrations. Silent-movie stars replaced debutantes and earls in the fantasy life of shopgirls, and magazines like *PhotoPlay* and *Screenland* began to document the daydreams, heartaches, and brand preferences of such screen idols as Clara Bow, Theda Bara, and Rudolph Valentino for the edification of the masses. Radios came into general use and began to broadcast music and sports events. These new mass-entertainment media began the process that would turn the whole country into a single audience for a single mass culture—the culture that America would eventually export abroad.

It was in the 1920s that America experienced what newspaperman Frederick Lewis Allen called "a revolution in morals," due in part to the increased personal freedom that access to telephones and automobiles afforded many people for the first time. Adolescents went from "courting" on the front porch a short distance away from their parents to "petting" in cars parked on country roads. Educated people began to speak with brutal frankness about sex, using the terms of Freudian psychology, which became fashionable in the 1920s. "Flappers," who cut their hair short, dressed in knee-length skirts, danced the Charleston, and shared the contents of illegal liquor in hip flasks with their boyfriends, came to symbolize the new woman of the 1920s. The abrupt change in attitudes and behavior surrounding youth and sexuality that occurred in the 1920s upset many people who saw a familiar world vanishing. The new moral codes of the 1920s were no passing fad. Like the movement toward brand consciousness and mass entertainment, this change in the pattern of social conduct continued after the 1920s ended and still exists today.

Many of the innovations that helped to revolutionize everyday life in the 1920s—automobiles, telephones, radio, chain stores, and skyscrapers—had arrived quietly during the preceding fifty years, one by one, like a series of stage props brought on before the show begins. But in the 1920s, the curtain rose abruptly on a transformed society. Looking back today, it all seems to have happened overnight. A pre-war world of mustachioed men and straight-backed women in corsets adhering to a genteel code of behavior that had held sway for a century gave way to a generation that knew exactly what it wanted to do with the tools the late nineteenth century had invented. A society that admired thrift, self-restraint, decorum, and do-gooding gave way to one that promoted consumption, publicity, salesmanship, and scientific management.

The Catalyst of War

In appearance, mood, and behavior, the society of the 1920s was a sharp break from everything that came before it. Yet, on close inspection, nearly all of the major elements of that society were in place before the twenties. How can this paradox be explained? A clue can be found in the architecture of the period before the war. Buildings in the early twentieth century were made with structural steel on the inside but covered on the outside with antique ornament. Modern industrial techniques were used to produce the illusion of a world that had already vanished. Thus Americans (and Europeans too) lived as if under an enchantment, not quite ready to admit how much their way of life had changed.

World War I put an abrupt end to the enchantment. In the bloodiest conflict humankind had ever known, the face of the twentieth century was brutally revealed. Beginning with cavalry charges by men with sabers in their hands and braids on their uniforms, the war soon turned out to be a thoroughly modern enterprise, a factory of death by mechanized troop transport, machine guns, barbed wire, airplanes, and tanks. The United States entered the war late (in 1917) and suffered far fewer casualties than the other major combatants. Its land and cities were untouched by the fighting. Yet for the United States, as for the nations of Europe, the war was a catalyst. It accelerated the modernization of the economy because the government encouraged corporations to work on a grand scale in the manufacture of armaments and supplies. Modern public relation techniques, which would be used to sell everything from Florida real estate to Ku Klux Klan membership in the 1920s, were pioneered during the teens in the sale of war bonds. The United States' experiment with the nationwide prohibition of alcohol, which resulted in so much defiant lawlessness during the 1920s, would not have occurred without the help of wartime idealism.

While the war was going on, the American people had supported it with patriotic fervor that led them to approve the imprisonment of anyone who opposed it. When it was over, public disgust for the war proved equally strong, especially when America's allies, France and England, imposed what many Americans saw as a cynical, land-grabbing peace on the vanquished in the Treaty of Versailles (1919). America expressed its discontent by rejecting the Versailles treaty, refusing to participate in the League of Nations (a failed predecessor to the United Nations), and insisting on an isolationist foreign policy that persisted until the attack on Pearl Harbor in 1941.

The decisions that led to World War I in Europe, and those that led to America's participation in it, had been made by men too old to fight, mouthing high-minded phrases about a "war to end war" and a "war to make the world safe for democracy." Young people did the fighting and the dying, in appalling numbers, and the survivors returned with a disillusionment that quickly spread to other parts of the population. The war was widely seen as a mistake, and the most respectable members of society were blamed for it. Thus, the disaster of World War I shamed the older generation and discredited their ideas. These ideas were summed up by historian Robert Sklar as a "genteel culture" that was "so ubiquitous a part of American culture it was like air—hard to see, describe or criticize." Its aim had been "to teach people how to behave, and to do so in the guise of disinterested benevolence—or of noble self-sacrifice."[1] According to Sklar,

> Most American wars destroyed the creative minds of their era, or swept them into practical tasks. . . . The First World

War is the only exception. It destroyed, instead, the official culture which waged and supported the war, smashed it like an old and brittle egg shell, and set free the creative life so long contained within.[2]

The American System

This startling new society had its basis in the growth of the American economy in the years after the Civil War, when unbridled capitalism held sway in the United States. Because skilled labor was scarce, American industry relied heavily on machinery and organization. It produced standardized goods in huge quantities. Although the United States was not the only country to use techniques of mass production, U.S. manufacturers developed them to such an extent that European observers called this method of production "the American system." The American system had disadvantages as well as advantages. Since large amounts of capital were needed to build the huge factories that supported it, the American system tended in the long run to reward a handful of big winners. Businesses too small to compete were bought out or forced into bankruptcy. The big winners—men like Andrew Carnegie, J.P. Morgan, and John D. Rockefeller—were able to use their money to influence senators, congressmen, and state government, distorting the American political process.

In the half century after the Civil War, the American system did great and terrible things. Since standardized production could quickly spread the use of a practical new device and make its inventor rich, the American system encouraged innovation, bringing forth the telephone, the reaping machine, the sewing machine, the phonograph, and the incandescent light. Through its capacity to produce goods in bulk and to reward large investments, the American system knit the vast young country together with communication wires and railroads, helping to settle the West and to build up mighty cities seemingly overnight. By rewarding the winners in a winner-take-all game, the American system created a tiny new class of rich industrialists who built marble palaces grander than the European aristocracy had ever been able to afford. At the same time, and in conspicuous contrast, it created hordes of low-wage workers and put children to work in mines and factories.

Early in the twentieth century, the American system was carried to its logical extreme with the advent of the assembly line, best exemplified by Henry Ford's giant automobile factory in Dearborn, Michigan. The largest, most complex, and most efficient the world had ever seen, Ford's factory had just one purpose: to produce a single car model in vast quantities at low cost. Each assembly-line worker stayed in one place for his entire shift, adding a part to the machine as it moved by. Ford's plant was so efficient that it could produce an automobile—until then a toy for the very rich—at a price that middle-class people could afford. Workers in Ford's plant did not have to know very much about making automobiles because each worker had to perform only a single task, in some cases a simple repetitive arm motion. Therefore, Ford did not have to spend much time training them, nor, in theory at least, did he have to pay them very much. Ford could even control the pace of their work, because everyone had to keep up with the assembly line. Workers were easier to replace than machinery.

Ford had a problem, though. His system depended on the cooperation of the workers. He had invested a lot of money into his plant, and in order for it to pay off, it had to be producing constantly. Anything that interrupted the flow of the assembly line—such as a union strike or worker sabotage at a critical point along the line—could bring the whole factory to a halt. Ford had to keep his workers happy, and in the beginning, they were not happy. The work was simply too dull and physically punishing. When Ford paid his workers the standard two-dollar-a-day rate for unskilled labor, an astonishing number of them quit. As economic historian J. Bradford DeLong points out:

> Ford's workers—sped up, automated, short-term, alienated, and about to quit—seemed obvious fodder for recruitment into the International Workers of the World [a radical union that had arisen in response to the low wages and harsh work-

ing conditions of the time], and Ford's profits were very vulnerable to IWW [International Workers of the World]-style wildcat action. Ford's solution was a massive increase in wages: to $5.00 a day for unskilled workers whose family circumstances and deportment satisfied Ford. By 1915 annual turnover was down to 16%, from 370% before the raise. Many to whom Ford jobs had not been worth keeping at $1.75 a day found the assembly line more-than-bearable for $5.00 a day. . . . Ford became a celebrity, and a symbol. This man was using the extraordinary productivity of modern manufacturing not (or not just) to make a fortune for himself, but to instantly raise his unskilled employees into the comfort of the middle class.[3]

Ford also shortened his workers' hours, giving them more leisure time in which to spend their money. Some people wondered what the workers would do with all this money. In the 1920s this question seemed to be answered by the enormous increase in attendance at sporting events and movies and the purchase of durable goods. When other employers reluctantly followed Ford's example, the spending power of ordinary people, and the industries created to feed their tastes, helped give rise to a whole new sector of the economy—the mass market. The American worker became the American consumer.

From Mass Production to Mass Consumption

Although increased wages did contribute to some changes in the 1920s, they were not the sole factor in the economic and cultural transformations of the period. Historians point to the way the problem of "overproduction" had gradually, during the period before World War I, led to changes in the way goods were sold. The productivity of American manufacturing was so great that finding new customers for products became a desperate matter. To meet this challenge, a new sector of the economy emerged around the art of persuasion. Chain department stores and grocery stores spread across the country. Advertising and public relations became major industries. Marketing occupied an increasingly important place in the American economy, and had important effects on the American mind. As cultural historian William Leach notes,

> Business pursued the imagination in a way no other group in U.S. history had ever done. It turned rapidly to new methods of marketing and to the dissemination of strategies of entice-ment—advertising, display and decoration, fashion, style, de-sign and consumer service. It reshaped the structure and char-acter of the work force as well, introducing . . . a new class of service workers (salespeople, waiters and waitresses, bellhops and desk clerks, etc.) at the beck-and-call of consumers and growing at a rate far in excess of any other workers.[4]

The new emphasis on marketing and consumption that characterized the American economy in the 1920s eventu-ally brought about changes in the production side as well, as manufacturers, on advice from merchandisers, began to re-design all sorts of products to increase their visual appeal and style. To induce well-off people to buy new products before the old ones had worn out, manufacturers turned to the con-cept of "style obsolescence." In the 1920s, for the first time, towels, fountain pens, wristwatches, and cars became fashion items—items that a self-respecting consumer should discard when trivial and nonessential "improvements" made them look old. The Model T Ford had been the same style year after year, available, so the joke went, "in any color so long as it's black." But what would happen to car sales, automak-ers wondered, when everyone had a car? Ford's competitor, the General Motors Company, applied the principles of style obsolescence by pioneering the idea of the "model year." Every year the company introduced cars in new styles and colors to appeal to the status-conscious consumer who wanted to keep up with the latest model.

With constant appeals to the appetites and anxieties of Americans of all classes, the new emphasis on selling and spending began to cause changes in the American character, helping to introduce what business historian Roland Marc-hand called a "consumption ethic,"[5] a new attitude that en-couraged people to buy things in order to feel better about themselves.

The Installment Plan: A New Way of Thinking

Of all the merchandising innovations that influenced the economy and culture of the United States in the 1920s, none contributed as much to the creation of a consumption ethic as the extensive use of "installment plan buying," the now familiar method of purchasing durable goods with a certain amount of money down and monthly payments thereafter. While the wealthy had been purchasing on credit for many years, the promotion of installment buying for a much wider range of people was an innovation of the automobile industry. The installment plan helped sell more cars by making them affordable to the middle class and eventually to many with relatively low incomes. Department stores adopted the idea, allowing people to buy on credit goods they could not have afforded up-front. In the 1920s, installment plan buying turned luxuries into "necessities" and filled the typical American home with wonderful electric gadgets: washing machines, vacuum cleaners, dishwashers, mixers, toasters, irons, space heaters, and refrigerators. By putting this machinery into the hands of average Americans, the installment plan changed the image of the ideal home from one where servants were summoned by bells to one in which an up-to-date housewife deployed labor-saving devices.

The installment plan also brought about a profound change in American ideas of right and wrong. To encourage people to buy on credit—to spend more money than they had—was to effect a moral reversal that is hard to comprehend today. For well over a hundred years Americans had been living by Benjamin Franklin's advice: "A penny saved is a penny earned." Not to live beyond one's means was the basic moral code of nineteenth-century capitalism, of the self-reliant, self-disciplined American middle class, and of everyone who hoped to rise in American society. Thrift was the virtue that had supposedly made men like Andrew Carnegie and John D. Rockefeller rich. It was the virtue extolled in stories and songs in the McGuffy readers used as the standard textbooks in American schools. It was the virtue preached to the poor, who were despised for their supposed tendency to throw away every dollar they made on instant gratification.

To discard this virtue and encourage people to "buy now, pay later" was a giant step toward the consumption-oriented society of today.

Sales and Publicity in the "Age of Ballyhoo"

Some writers called the new society the war unveiled the "Age of Ballyhoo," that is, of shameless sales promotion. Advertising reached unprecedented levels (levels it would not reach again until the 1940s) and people became aware of a new phenomenon—the "publicity stunt," an attention-grabbing event deliberately arranged to promote a product or company. Some of the bizarre fads the twenties are known for, such as dance marathons and flagpole sitting (long-running events in which individuals attempted to set records for sitting atop a flagpole), were done as commercial gimmicks. Others were driven by the new media's hunger for something to report.

People in the 1920s were conscious of the new place that public relations had in their society. In one of the best-remembered films of the period, *Safety Last* (1923), silent comedian Harold Lloyd scales the wall of a twelve-story building as a publicity stunt for a department store. A country boy trying to make good in the big city, the hero Lloyd portrays takes the path to success that many Americans were pursuing at the time: making good by becoming highly visible. The country boy becomes a promoter, a supersalesman.

In America before World War I, the salesman had been a suspicious character; he talked too fast, came from out of town, and might be a "flimflam" man, a con artist. In the 1920s the profession became respectable, and the salesman became an ideal for young men to emulate. Articles on salesmanship appeared in newspapers and magazines. Dale Carnegie, who would publish the book *How to Make Friends and Influence People* in 1936, was a popular lecturer in the 1920s, already instructing ambitious young executives on the importance of making a good impression—the importance, in short, of being *like a salesman*, whether or not one actually was one. At the same time, advertising perfected the technique of making people worry about the personal impression they made. A new medical condition, "halitosis," was invented to sell the mouthwash Listerine, and a new acronym, "B.O.," was coined to sell deodorant. Intentionally or not, such advertisements taught all kinds of people to think of themselves as salesmen, their success in life dependent less on inner qualities (like determination and grit) and more on the exterior qualities that formed the immediate impression they made on others.

The charge that the typical modern American has a salesmanlike personality—obsessed with appearances, conveniently adaptive to changing circumstances, shaped by the opinions of peers rather than by values inherited from parents—would be leveled many years later by sociologist David Reisman in *The Lonely Crowd* and by social critic Christopher Lasch in *The Culture of Narcissism*. Social historians like Lynne Dumenil would pinpoint the 1920s as the time when this personality type moved to the center of American culture.

New Media Create a New American Culture

Supported by increased income from advertisers and by new consumers with increased leisure, mass media (billboards, newspapers, magazines, radio, and movies) helped to create a new culture to fill the vacuum left by the genteel culture the war had discredited. The content of the new culture was the very opposite of genteel. Brash, vulgar, and irresistible, the media of the 1920s focused public attention on sports, movie stars, sex scandals, and murder. The media of the 1920s presented many new features that are familiar today. For example, they helped to make relatively trivial events, like the marriage between real estate tycoon "Daddy" Browning and his thirteen-year-old bride, Frances "Peaches" Heenan, seem worthy of the daily attention of millions of readers for months on end; they also greatly inflated the importance of more significant events like the first solo transatlantic airplane flight by Charles Lindbergh. In 1927 the media went wild over Lindbergh. Even the then-staid *New York Times* devoted fifteen pages to Lindbergh's feat, wondering in its editorial columns whether it just might be the greatest story in human history.

For long-running news stories, the media of the 1920s pioneered the now familiar method of soliciting the opinions of famous experts to help lend gravity to the proceedings and fill the gaps on days when there was nothing to report except some official's response of "no comment." One such story was the 1927 trial of Ruth Snyder and her lover Judd Gray. The two were convicted of murdering Ruth's husband Albert and were sentenced to death. Coverage of the trial, historian Gerald Leinwand notes, was especially significant for "the amazing concentration of celebrities, so-called experts, and commentators drawn in to comment, analyze, and interpret the human emotions and motivations of this ordinary couple who committed so heinous a crime."[6] Finally, the media of the 1920s helped to create a culture of celebrity by focusing public attention on a succession of famous names in sports, entertainment, crime, and politics, bringing individuals such as Babe Ruth, Louis Armstrong, Al Capone, Albert Einstein, and Mohandas Gandhi into the American home and everyday conversations. The media raised these subjects to the status of myth, but paradoxically they also democratized them, referring to them chummily by familiar nicknames and inadvertently implying that these assorted heroes and villains had one thing in common that was more important than the things that made them different—they were all famous.

The new mass culture of the United States in the 1920s might not have been uplifting, but it was unifying, because for better or worse it pushed itself right in everyone's face and belonged to everybody. Mass media and mass advertising appealed to the public as a whole. Rich and poor, highbrow and lowbrow, country boy and city slicker, all saw the same movies, listened to the same radio programs, read many of the same newspapers, and hummed the same show tunes.

Boom and Speculation

Consumers in the Age of Ballyhoo did not limit their purchases to cars and mouthwash. They bought the promise of success itself. The 1920s were rife with get-rich-quick schemes. The era witnessed many speculative bubbles, a phenomenon that often occurs in an economy running at full steam. Noticing that the prices of stocks, real estate, or commodities are going up, speculators buy with the plan of selling when prices are even higher. The law of supply and demand ensures that the more people buy, the faster prices rise. Investors congratulate themselves on all the profits they have made and buy even more. Speculative bubbles can puff up the price of anything from land to gold to tulips to levels far above the value of these items to the people who would actually use or keep them. They are called bubbles because eventually they burst. Anything that convinces enough people that from now on prices will fall can cause a downward spiral. Buyers become sellers, and selling forces prices down. Fortunes can be wiped out in a matter of hours.

The best-remembered and most consequential speculative bubble of the 1920s occurred in the stock market. The value of stocks rose to heights never seen before. More people than ever purchased stocks. Investment was made easier for them by the practice of "buying on margin." Buying on margin meant that at the time people bought stock shares, they had to pay only a fraction of the full price. It was the installment plan—buy now, pay later—applied to the stock market. When the price of the stock went up, often people could pay for their shares with the profits they had made on those very same stocks. This practice helped inflate the market, but it also made a very quick collapse possible because when prices went down, investors could raise the money they owed only by selling stock. That is just what happened during the several fateful days of the Wall Street stock market crash of 1929.

The stock market crash was immediately followed by a complete collapse of the U.S. economy, initiating a worldwide depression that lasted until the onset of World War II in the late 1930s. Historians today disagree about whether the crash caused the Great Depression, whether it merely triggered an economic breakdown that would have come anyway, or whether the timing of the crash and the Depression were simply coincidental. In any case, the contrast between the world economy before and after the stock market crash of 1929 was a stark one. Millions of people lost their jobs, wages and prices fell, and banks failed. Breadlines and homeless people living in shacks became a familiar sight in America's cities.

The Twenties Remembered

It usually takes ten or fifteen years for those who have lived through a given decade to look back on it with regret as something lost. The decade of the 1920s was an exception to this rule. It was available for nostalgia immediately. The stock market crash—and the grim worldwide depression it began—had closed the 1920s with such finality that few could doubt an era was over. Americans looked back with wonder on the period that had only just ended as a time from which they were now forever exiled. In 1931 reporter Frederick Lewis Allen published *Only Yesterday*, a history of the twenties. The intensity of many readers' nostalgia for the very recent past made Allen's book a best seller, and his work has had a powerful effect on both popular memory and serious scholarship about the 1920s ever since. Although his details were not all accurate, Allen was a remarkably astute observer. While giving fondly remembered trivia and fads their due, he recognized that matters of lasting consequence had taken place during the 1920s. He realized that the most important changes were the result not of the actions of great men but of those millions of people living in a new way, creating the American culture that exists today.

Notes

1. Robert Sklar, *The Plastic Age (1917–1930)*. New York: George Braziller, 1970, p. 3.

2. Sklar, *The Plastic Age*, p. 1.

3. J. Bradford DeLong, "The Roaring Twenties," chapter 13 in *Slouching Towards Utopia?: The Economic History of the Twentieth Century*, 1997. http://econ161.berkeley.edu/TCEH/Slouch_roaring13.html.

4. William Leach, *Land of Desire: Merchants, Power, and the Rise of a New American Culture*. New York: Pantheon Books, 1993, p. 37.

5. Roland Marchand, *Advertising the American Dream: Making Way for Modernity, 1920–1940*. Berkeley: University of California Press, 1985, p. 117.

6. Gerald Leinwand, *1927: High Tide of the Twenties*. New York: Four Walls Eight Windows, 2001, p. 248.

Chapter 1

The Rise of a Consumer Society

Turning Points

IN WORLD HISTORY

The Expansion of Giant Corporations and Mass Consumption

Donald R. McCoy

Through most of the 1920s the U.S. economy hummed. Factories produced goods in record-breaking quantities, and the average American's standard of living rose. Manufacturers had a more urgent need to sell their wares than ever before and paid more attention to merchandising, publicity, and sales—the business tools that persuade consumers to buy. Meanwhile, the average size of corporations expanded with the help of a business-friendly Republican government and a new legal ploy, the holding company, which helped corporations evade earlier restrictions on monopolistic business practices. In this article, historian Donald R. McCoy describes the elements that led to the prosperity of the 1920s. He points out that while hidden weaknesses in the economic engine led to a breakdown, its basic components would survive the depression of the 1930s. The country would continue to be dominated by supercorporations. Merchandising and advertising techniques aimed at the mass consumer would continue to shape American society.

McCoy, who died in 1996, was a distinguished professor of history at the University of Kansas. He was the author of several books, including biographies of Harry S. Truman, Alfred Landon, and Calvin Coolidge, as well as *Coming of Age: The United States During the 1920s and 1930s*.

Donald R. McCoy, *Coming of Age: The United States During the 1920s and 1930s*. New York: Penguin, 1973. Copyright © 1973 by Donald R. McCoy. Reproduced by permission of the Literary Estate of Donald R. McCoy.

In a time of relative tranquility the United States was more prosperous than ever before. The average industrial workweek declined from 47.4 hours in 1920 to 44.2 hours in 1929. There was a 13-percent increase in the real wages of industrial workers between 1922 and 1929, and many factory employees enjoyed new fringe benefits. The average unemployment rate was 3.7 percent between 1923 and 1929, compared with 6.1 percent between 1911 and 1917, which was a fairly prosperous period itself. . . . Most of this resulted from the jump in gross national product from $73,300,000,000 in 1920 to $104,400,000,000 in 1929, in terms of 1929 prices. Equally significant was the 50-percent leap in the quantity of manufacturing production between 1922 and 1929.

There were many reasons for the expanded production of the 1920's. One was the rising efficiency of American industry. Production was increasingly harnessed to mechanization and more effective power modes, and the assembly-line method, pioneered by [car manufacturer] Henry Ford in 1915, was applied in growing numbers of factories. The industrial efficiency movement, associated with the names of Frank Gilbreth and Frederick W. Taylor, moved into high gear to cut down on wasted time and motion by workers. It led to better plant layout and use of manpower, with the result that the index of man-hour productivity rose from 44.6 in 1920 to 72.5 in 1929. Increasingly professional plant managers, men trained to do their jobs, took the places of the owners' relatives and heirs. Business consolidation probably contributed to efficiency by eliminating marginal producers. And one cannot overlook the role of new inventions that boosted production as well as expanded the variety of commodities for sale.

Transportation was another important component of increased production and distribution. . . . Surfaced roads under state control grew from 350,000 to 662,000 miles between 1919 and 1929. By the end of the 1920's it was clear that although rail and water traffic still dominated commercial transportation, they had lost their monopoly. Buses and trucks could compete in prices and often speed with trains and go places that railways could not reach; trucks had an

ter advantage over the cheaper water transport in
in where they could travel. Aviation was the other
....sportation development. A novelty at the beginning of the decade, by 1929 there were thirty-eight domestic operators carrying 162,000 paying passengers and flying
seventy thousand ton-miles of express and freight.

A New Role for Sales and Advertising

The heightened efforts to create a buyer psychology also
helped to produce the prosperity of the 1920's. Salesmanship
rose to new levels as a career. It was widely proclaimed as one
of the easiest ways to make money in a decade when the earn-
ing of money seemed the highest goal. Articles on salesmanship appeared in newspapers and magazines with great frequency, and salesmanship courses entered the academic
curriculum. The emphasis was not so much on serving the
customer as on convincing him of the advantages of the wares
that one had to sell. Thus the proprietor and the clerk became salesmen, and old-line salesmen became supersalesmen.

Salesmanship was reinforced by advertising, which, already a big business, became a bigger business during the
1920's. An increasing proportion of newspaper and magazine space was devoted to advertising copy as the modest,
even staid advertisements of the prewar era burgeoned into
large, eye-catching testimonials to the efficacy of this, the
low cost of that, or the status-raising properties of this and
that. The old colorful advertising curtains still remained in
vaudeville houses, but filmed advertisements flooded the
screens of the rapidly growing number of motion-picture
theaters. Commercials quickly became an integral part of
radio programming. Increasing numbers of roadside billboards extolled the virtues of the various products to be
found just down the pike or around the bend. Sloganeering
rose to previously unreached heights as a way to capture the
public's attention and favor. "They Satisfy" was all one had
to say about one brand of cigarettes, and for those who were
not thus satisfied, the advice was "Reach for a Lucky instead
of a Sweet." "Halitosis" and "B.O." became household terms
along with the names of the products that could prevent

such social offenses. Ballyhoo seemed to receive the impri-
matur of many churches, which adopted techniques of salesmanship and advertising in their proselyting. Bruce Barton
expressed this convergence of church and mammon when he
wrote in his best-selling book, *The Man Nobody Knows*, that
Jesus "would have been a national advertiser today."

If the methods were increasingly available to produce,
transport, and sell commodities, the goods themselves were
becoming more attractive to buyers. A choice of colors was
available in many products. Variety was the watchword,
whether applied to automobiles, vegetables, or clothes.
Moreover, new products were turned out in increasing
abundance. A greater variety of fabrics was found on the
market as rayon became a commonly used material and as
celanese came into production. Many items were geared to
the vastly increasing use of electricity in the home, such as
radios, electric irons, vacuum cleaners, and even by the late
1920's refrigerators, washing machines, and electric razors.
There were plenty of other new products including cello-
phane, cigarette lighters, Pyrex cooking utensils, various
Bakelite goods, and lacquers, which testified to the fast-
paced technological advances in industry. . . .

The Growth of Super Corporations

Another essential ingredient of the phenomenal economic
spurt of the 1920's was the growth of the super corporation.
Increasingly American business was conducted by large organizations. It was the giant corporation that mainly exploited
the earth and the forests, both at home and abroad, for the
raw materials necessary for manufacturing; it was the super-
corporation that did the manufacturing, distributed the products to consumers, and even financed the operations. More
and more, consumers were to use as parts of their everyday
vocabulary the names of Standard Oil, A&P, Westinghouse,
General Motors, United States Steel, Bell Telephone, East-
man Kodak, Bank of America, and similar firms.

By 1929 the largest two hundred corporations possessed
about 20 percent of the nation's wealth and almost 40 percent of business wealth. This was attributable in part to ex-

pansion of corporate business with its total assets rising from $262,000,000,000 to $336,000,000,000 between 1926 and 1929 alone. The share of total corporate net income for the wealthiest 5 percent of corporations grew from 76.73 to 84.34 percent between 1919 and 1929. Their rise was also due to an increased number of recorded mergers, which in manufacturing and mining mounted from 438 in 1919 to 1,245 in 1929. Contrary to widespread belief, however, the number of corporations, and of business concerns, did not decrease during the 1920's. The total of American business concerns jumped from 1,711,000 in 1919 to 2,213,000 in 1929. What was happening was a grand expansion of private enterprise in response to a rising market and easier financing. More and more Americans were entering business to take their chances. What was also happening was that the supercorporations were profiting the most, gaining a larger share of the market and therefore the wealth.

It is not surprising that the greatest benefits went to the biggest businesses. They had the resources to expand operations vastly and to make them efficient and to produce and market new commodities. With mass methods of exploitation, purchasing, production, advertising, and distribution, the giant corporations could hold down their costs. With their research departments, they could put out new products and improve old ones. Most of the increase in American patents issued for inventions was accounted for by corporations, as between 1921 and 1929 the number of patents that they had received almost doubled. Large corporations could also staff their operations with specialists in various phases of business instead of relying on family skills or jacks-of-all-trades. At least as important, supercorporations could, by themselves or in conjunction with others, move toward controlling their sectors of the economy.

There were two basic ways to accomplish this dominance. One method was to control the whole industrial process, including the extraction of raw materials, the fabrication or refinement of products, and their distribution to wholesalers and even retailers. This pattern of vertical integration was well established before the war in the petroleum industry and was increasingly seized upon by other large corporations during the 1920's. Another method commonly employed, and by no means at variance with the one described above, was to join with supposedly competing firms to regulate an entire industrial segment. This could be carried out in several ways. Illustrative of one pattern, United States Steel was so dominant in its sector of the economy that it could usually force other steel firms to adhere to common price, labor, and marketing practices. Another method was the use of interlocking directorates whereby a group of industrial executives would turn up sitting on each other's boards of directors, thereby forming a superdirectorate for a number of related industries. There was also the holding company, which by 1929 became the prime method of economic concentration, with ninety-four of the largest ninety-seven industrial corporations being such organizations. Under this method one gigantic corporation would possess the controlling interest in two or more operating corporations. Holding companies sometimes grew to bewildering proportions, as with Samuel Insull's electric-power empire, which included 111 companies organized in twenty-four layers of operation between Insull and the companies actually distributing power. Often a holding company could gain control through shrewd business maneuvering of properties of tremendous value. One of the best examples of this was the railway complex directed by O.P. and M.J. Van Sweringen. Using $500,000 of their own money and another $500,000 from some associates, the Van Sweringen brothers were able to obtain control of ten railroads holding more than 29,000 miles of track.

The trade association was another major technique of arranging business matters to the satisfaction of industrial leaders. This method was encouraged by the Department of Commerce under Herbert Hoover's guidance. It was seen as an effective way to minimize cutthroat competition in industries that were not dominated by holding companies, huge leading corporations, or interlocking directorates. The objective of the trade association was to organize firms engaging in a common industrial activity so that they would exchange information that would allow them to keep their

ine, standardize tools, measurements, and product
shapes, and to take advantage of the latest techno-
ivgicai, managerial, and distributive techniques. Some two
thousand of these associations already existed by 1920, and
hundreds more came into existence by 1929. Although they
were criticized as being in violation of antitrust laws, the Republican attorneys general of the 1920's rarely acted against
trade associations, and when they did, the Supreme Court
held that associational activities were legal so long as they
were not aimed at increasing prices.

Easy Credit

The last essential ingredient of the prosperity of the 1920's
was easy financing. As the largest corporations grew, they
had more money in their pockets to invest, and increasingly
they financed their own operations and sometimes those of
other firms. Yet the growing financial independence of supercorporations did not hinder the expansion of traditional
lenders. Bank assets jumped from $48,000,000,000 to
$72,000,000,000 between 1919 and 1929. Proportionately
more dramatic was the rise during the same period in the assets of savings-and-loan associations from $2,000,000,000 to
$12,000,000,000, and the assets of America's life-insurance
companies shot up from $7,000,000,000 to $17,000,000,000.
Obviously, plenty of money was available for lending, at reasonable rates, and it was borrowed at a previously unheard-
of volume, especially by small businesses. Moreover, corporations, to finance their activities, not only took from their
expanding assets but borrowed substantially as well. The
amount of corporate stock grew from $76,000,000,000 to
$186,000,000,000, and the amount of corporate debt in-
creased from $58,000,000,000 to $88,000,000,000 between
1922 and 1929. The mass consumer was also well financed,
expanding his buying capacity well beyond his mounting income. Between 1919 and 1929 the amount of consumer non-
farm credit grew from $32,000,000,000 to $60,000,000,000,
thanks to the liberality of loans from banks, savings-and-loan
companies, insurance concerns, loan companies, and merchants. "Just a little bit down and a small monthly payment"

increasingly became the American way of buying
fore of financing one's dreams and the country's p

A New Economy Produces a New Mass Consumer

Few of the ingredients of the prosperity of the 1920's were
new, for most of them had been developed before 1920.
What was new was the frequency of their use and the recognition of them as forming the bases of a new, even revolutionary economic system. All together they signaled the
domination of the economy by giant corporations that were
producing for the mass consumer. Thereby a greater variety
of standardized goods could be produced more cheaply. Ide-
ally, the advantages of the mass-production-consumption
system were tremendous. The large corporations could
more efficiently and profitably coordinate their operations
and maintain mass employment at wages and salaries sufficient to provide the mass consumer with the wherewithal to
buy their goods and services. Market and employment stability would make the mass consumer a better credit risk so
that his purchasing power could be supplemented with
larger loans and more installment buying than ever before.
The resultant prosperity would theoretically beget more
prosperity as industry and creditors could expand, thereby
providing additional jobs, higher income, and further credit.

It was all so logical and seemed to be working. No wonder that by 1929 most Americans believed that prosperity
would be permanent. That they were wrong, however,
should not obscure the fact that the basic components of the
economy of the 1920's would survive. Giant corporations
would continue to dominate, and the customer, for whom
they produced, would still be the mass consumer. The supercorporations would still seek more efficient methods of
production and distribution, and all, producers and consumers alike, would continue to believe in the efficacy of
salesmanship, advertising, technological improvement, and
organizational expertise.

The Installment Plan Changes American Values

Sharon Murphy

Advertisers for a wide variety of durable goods urged consumers to "Buy Now, Pay Later!" in the 1920s. Installment-plan buying was not a new phenomenon, but the scale on which it was practiced in the 1920s was unprecedented. Installment-plan buying helped drive the growth of the economy in the 1920s while working a permanent change in American values. People who had been brought up to practice self-restraint and to delay their gratification were for the first time encouraged to spend money they had not yet earned. Sharon Murphy is a graduate student and instructor in American history at the University of Virginia.

After several decades of urbanization and industrialization, post–World War I America was marked by a rapid increase in the availability of mass-produced commodities. For the growing middle-class population, the twentieth century American dream had become based on the acquisition and consumption of this rising tide of commodities. Economic historians like Martha Olney have described this period as a consumer durables revolution, characterized by an increase in both the average household expenditure for durable goods and the amount of installment credit issued to help pay for these goods.

A critical precursor to this revolution was a transformation of the prevailing consumer attitudes towards incurring debt, and particularly a removal of the stigma against buying on installments. The idea of being in debt had always been looked down upon by the American public, yet the expan-

Sharon Murphy, "The Advertising of Installment Plans," *Essays in History, Volume 37*. Charlottesville: University of Virginia Press, 1995. Copyright © 1995 by the University of Virginia Press. Reproduced by permission.

sion of the market for consumer durables depended upon an increase in credit transactions. The birth of the automobile installment finance company in 1919 provided the foundation for this transformation, creating a successful example of installment selling in a major industry.

The catalyst to this change, however, lay not in the mere availability of installment credit but in the selling of the concept of debt through advertising. During the 1920s, businesses increasingly utilized advertising as a method not only to sell their products, but also as a means to convince the American public to buy on installments. Both the quantity and the quality of advertisements which mentioned installment plans rose significantly during this period, particularly in local publications. By 1929, these advertisements reflected the general acceptance of installment buying as a way to finance consumption and demonstrated that this shift in attitudes had reached its completion.

The Origins of Installment Buying

Installment buying is a specific method of purchasing goods on credit, distinct from other forms of credit such as loans or credit cards. Unlike a loan which entails a direct exchange of money from one party to another, these transactions always involve a transfer of wealth in the form of goods or services. A partial payment may be made at the time of the sale but full payment is deferred until some future date. In contrast with credit card purchases, an exact schedule of payments is enumerated at the time of the sale. The remainder owed is paid in specific quantities at successive intervals.

Installment buying most commonly occurs in conjunction with the sale of durable goods. The Department of Commerce defines a durable good as any household product that can be used, on average, for three years or more. Durable goods are often divided by economists into major and minor durables. [According to historian Thomas Juster] major durables are goods "characterized by relatively long service lives, by the existence of commercial markets in which the services of similar assets [can] be purchased, and by unit costs high enough so that purchase with borrowed funds [is] a common method of acquisition." Goods such as automobiles and automobile parts, furniture, household appliances, radios, phonographs, and pianos fall into this category. Minor durables are defined as all other durable goods, such as china and tableware, house furnishings, jewelry, books, maps, and some toys. . . .

Overall, selling on installments was a very limited practice prior to the Civil War. It was confined primarily to goods which could be easily resold and the terms of payment tended to be rather stringent. It was a privilege enjoyed only by those customers with good credit histories and with income levels high enough to ensure the ability to meet the contract terms. As a business method, installment selling proved to be highly profitable for those retailers who chose to utilize it.

At the end of the nineteenth century, however, retailers of lower grade commodities began to extend installment credit to lower income families who were higher credit risks. The practice became commonly used by the poorest families who began to buy the necessities required for everyday living on installments. This was particularly true in cities like New York, where peddlers sold goods on installment to the rising tide of immigrants. Many of these peddlers took advantage of the immigrants by delivering products of much poorer quality than what was originally selected or by greatly overvaluing the goods. Although the idea of being in debt had always been looked down upon, it was at this time that the negative reputation of installment buying was intensified. No longer a privilege reserved for the upper classes, it became "symbolic of poverty, prodigality, [and] gullibility" [according to credit expert Rolf Nugent].

Automobile Financing Makes the Installment Plan Commonplace

This was still the prevailing attitude towards installment buying in 1919 when General Motors created the General Motors Acceptance Corporation (GMAC), the first automobile installment finance company. This organization was originally developed in response to the large seasonal fluctuations which automobile sales experienced. Before closed cars became popular, automobile sales occurred primarily in the spring and summer. There were several months when assembly lines ran at full capacity, and then long periods when they were practically dormant and large numbers of workers had to be laid off. The car manufacturers wanted to remedy this problem by building up inventories during the slower months and then selling them off during the peak season. They expected this surplus to be stored by the individual dealers, but these dealers lacked the capital necessary to fund this storage. The solution to this problem came with the development of the sales finance company which provided the capital essential to maintain these inventories.

Eventually, these companies expanded into automobile installment finance companies for middle- and lower-middle class consumers. Without credit, a customer needed to save enough cash to cover the full price of the car. That was impossible for most Americans. As Olney noted, in order to purchase an automobile with cash during this time period, a typical American family would have to save for almost five years. With the spread of credit between 1919 and 1929, the percentage of households buying cars on installment more than tripled, rising from 4.9% to 15.2%. The creation of GMAC accounted for a large portion of this increase. In 1925, GMAC was three times larger than its nearest competitor, financing almost half of all installment purchases of automobiles that took place in that year.

With this dramatic increase in the installment selling of automobiles came the expansion of this technique into the markets for other major durable goods. According to credit expert Rolf Nugent, the success of automobile installment plans "tended to remove the stigma which installment selling had acquired at the hands of low-grade installment merchants in the 1890s." In fact, credit was used in the purchases of up to 90% of major durable goods by the end of the 1920s. Average purchases of major durable goods rose from 3.7% of disposable income between 1898 and 1916 to 7.2% between 1922 and 1929. Accompanying this rise in purchases of durables was a drop in the personal savings rate, from 6.4% of disposable income in the former period to 3.8% in the latter.

Advertising Changes Consumer Attitudes Toward Debt

This rise in installment purchases of major durable goods was contingent on a fundamental transformation of consumer attitudes towards incurring debt. In a report commissioned in 1926 by the American Bankers Association, economist Milan Ayres commented, "During the nineteenth century the things that a self-respecting, thrifty American family would buy on the installment plan were a piano, a sewing machine, some expensive articles of furniture, and perhaps a set of books. People who made such purchases didn't talk about them. Installment buying wasn't considered quite respectable." The change in the popular attitude towards installment buying which primarily occurred between the years 1922 and 1929 was therefore imperative to this revolution in consumer durables. . . .

The number of advertisements which mentioned installment plans did not really begin to increase until about 1922. Although GMAC had been created in 1919, the change in the popular perception of installment buying was initially very gradual since many customers still remained wary of making purchases on credit. By 1922, however, the overwhelming success of installment buying in the automobile industry began to attract manufacturers and dealers of other major durable goods. A boost was given to installment sales of furniture, pianos and sewing machines, but a major portion of the increase in installment selling can be traced to new products just entering the market or older products which had previously avoided offering installment plans. These goods included phonographs, washing machines, electric refrigerators, vacuum cleaners, and radio sets. This rise in installment sales was reflected in the steady increase in advertisements which mentioned the availability of installment plans, especially after 1922. . . .

There were several ways in which advertisements during the 1920s tried to sell the idea of installment buying to the

American public. One way was to appeal to the traditional sentiments that had originally made installment buying unattractive. An advertisement in 1920 [in the *Richmond Times-Dispatch*] for a New Edison phonograph called its budget plan "a real thrift idea. It helps you purchase your New Edison without paying spot cash and without increasing your monthly allowance for enjoyment." A similar advertisement for Pettit and Company furniture stores stated, "Buying home furnishings on credit at Pettit's is a thrifty habit. The easy weekly installments are like savings put in the bank, that pay big dividends in happiness and service." Thus, these advertisements tried to show that there was no contradiction between incurring debt and the time-honored American virtue of thrift.

Advertisers also endeavored to elevate the reputation of installment buying in other ways. Several businesses used the adjective "dignified" to describe their installment plans and one furniture company even called itself "The House of Dignified Credit." Other advertisements went even further by attempting to convince the purchasers that they would actually save money by buying on installments. Bloomberg-Michael Furniture Company said that its "plan enables you to save at least 25% in your purchase and gives you the benefit of extended time." This advertisement did not, however, explain exactly how installment buying would save the consumer money.

Equating installment buying with thrifty ideals softened popular fears of the practice. By incorporating the traditional economic values of the average, middle-class American into their descriptions of installment plans, advertisers depicted installment buying as a practice which aided consumers in their attempts to make frugal purchases. Paying in installments was characterized as the modern equivalent of saving money in the bank. By placing installment buying in a traditional context, advertisers helped consumers adjust to the notion of paying a small down payment with the remainder to be paid in easy weekly or monthly installments. . . .

Advertisers also emphasized the convenience of buying on time. As many advertisements explained, the consumer could use the product while it was still being paid for, rather than having to save over several years and being deprived of current enjoyment. These advertisements introduced and played on new ideas of leisure and pleasure. They encouraged customers to "ride as you pay" or "play as you pay." For just "a small amount down" you could "get want you want now." Rather than waiting to buy a new refrigerator or baby carriage, retailers "are making it easy to get these things, right now when you need them" [according to an ad in the *Richmond Times-Dispatch*]. These advertisements played upon the rising consumption ethic by which Americans increasingly desired to buy goods immediately rather than postponing their purchases until enough money had accumulated in the bank. Customers were told that they should not wait to obtain the commodities they desired, nor did they have to wait any longer. The availability of installment plans made it possible for them to fulfill these desires almost instantly. . . .

"Nearly Everyone" Prefers to Pay Later

By the end of the decade, the wholly positive portrayals of installment plans reflected the complete transformation in consumer attitudes. Words like "convenient," "low-cost," and "easy" continued to be used in the descriptions of payment plans. Additionally, the image of joyful dealers who "welcome business on the General Motors deferred payment plan" [the words of an ad in the April 1929 issue of *Good Housekeeping*] was still a common sight. Advertisements of this time period went one step further, however, demonstrating that buying on installments had become a permanent aspect of the twentieth-century American dream.

One of the most telling examples of an advertisement which fully reflected the completion of this transformation in consumer attitudes was a LaSalle automobile advertisement from a 1928 issue of *Good Housekeeping*. In mentioning the available installment plan it poignantly stated, "If you prefer to buy out of income, as nearly everyone does today, the General Motors plan is very liberal." At this point, the journey from a world in which customers were expected to pay with cash and were discouraged from buying on installments, to a world in which salesmen actually encouraged the use of installment plans was complete. Customers who made purchases on installments were no longer depicted as a minority group deviating from the normal course of action. It was now the people who insisted on paying in cash who seemed overly traditional and backward looking. As historian Frederick Lewis Allen commented in 1931, "People were getting to consider it old-fashioned to limit their purchases to the amount of their cash balances."

By the end of the 1920s, installment plans had become the primary way for a middle-class family to attain a piece of the American dream. People who had formerly shied away from acquiring debt now accepted installment buying as a means to finance modern consumption. This transformation in consumer attitudes resulted from a gradual change in the depiction of installment buying in advertisements. Retailers increasingly utilized this medium in order to convince consumers to buy on installments, both influencing and reflecting popular perceptions of this practice. By the eve of the Great Depression, they had intimately linked installment buying to the attainment of the American dream.

The Mass Media Promotes Consumption as the Solution for Dissatisfied Workers

Lynn Dumenil

Cultural critics often remark that modern America (and indeed, much of the developed world) is highly status conscious. People define themselves by the things they own and constantly fret about their appearance, as if they themselves were brand-name products that needed to be sold. In the 1950s, sociologist David Riesman labeled modern Americans as "other-directed," obsessed with the opinions of friends, neighbors, and coworkers, in contrast to the "inner-directed" Americans of the nineteenth century, who were more concerned about their morality and character. Historians who agree with Riesman—including Lynn Dumenil, the author of the following article—often point to the 1920s as the time when the "other-directed" personality made its first appearance. By the 1920s, millions of people were working in highly specialized, unsatisfying jobs for large corporations. Addressing these workers' anxieties, lecturers such as Dale Carnegie began to tell office workers that they could achieve success through the creation of a beguiling personality. Meanwhile, mass advertisers warned that positive "first impressions" could be assured only with the purchase of the right products.

The following selection describes the development of this focus on personal image and the consumer culture in the United States. Dumenil argues that workers who increasingly found themselves in routine jobs with little autonomy turned to consumption and recreation to find satisfaction. Lynn Dumenil is a professor of American history at Occidental College. She is the author of *The Modern Temper: American Culture and Society in the 1920s* and *Freemasonry and American Culture*. She is also the coauthor of *America: A Concise History*.

Clearly, it was the middle class for whom the consumer culture had the most import in the 1920s, an import that went beyond having the income to participate in expanded recreational opportunities and to acquire the material products that rolled off the assembly line. Scholars have identified a behavioral and value shift embodied in the emergence of a new social type. In *The Lonely Crowd* (1950), David Riesman contrasted the nineteenth-century middle-class character type, "inner-directed," with the twentieth-century "other-directed" individual whose life was organized by keeping tuned in to the impressions and opinions of others. [Sociologist] Leo Lowenthal posited a shift from individuals geared to the Horatio Alger values of the nineteenth century that emphasized "production" to people attuned to the consumer values of the twentieth. [Historian] Warren Susman characterized the shift as linked to changing perceptions of the self, with the nineteenth-century emphasis on character giving way to a twentieth-century obsession with personality. "The vision of self-sacrifice began to yield to that of self-realization." [Historian] Jackson Lears has identified this concern with personality as part of therapeutic ethos, a widespread trend in twentieth-century middle-class culture that pervaded religion, social sciences, success ideology, and advertising, and concentrated on self-expression and self-realization through consumption and leisure.

Although there are significant differences between these schemas, they all point to a fundamental cultural change arising from the emergence of a modern, organized society. For many of the new middle class, especially men, because they were the ones who expected to remain in the workforce permanently, work was becoming intrinsically less meaningful, while at the same time rising prosperity, consumer goods, and increased leisure time offered new venues for meaning: one could seek satisfaction and definition in the personal realm of leisure and consumption. Other factors influenced both men and women. . . . The increasing pluralism of America's cities helped to challenge Victorian cultural hegemony and promote alternative visions of leisure and sociability. The expansion of the corporate national economy eroded local ties and propagated bureaucracy, specialization, and routinization, helping to undermine the individual's sense of community and autonomy. Similarly, urban mass society underlined the individual's fragile status in an anonymous society and compounded a sense of fragmentation. Although many Americans sought to root themselves in religion, mounting secularization further contributed to a search for secular forms of salvation.

All of these factors were in place before the 1920s, of course, but that decade helped to cement the trends. The decline in voting and the widespread indifference to reform . . . signaled a rejection of civic responsibility and a shift to the private and the personal. Although prosperity was not universal, the flood of consumer goods, made more accessible by installment buying, did provide more Americans than ever with the delights and perils of conspicuous consumption. Moreover, the continued expansion of the mass media and commercial entertainment, most notably the increased importance of advertising and movies, reflected and reinforced the thrust of the consumer culture toward leisure and consumption.

While consumption and participation in leisure-time pursuits constituted the basic conditions of a consumer society, equally important was a shift in values, in the ways in which Americans interpreted their society and circumstances. These values were scarcely universal or uncontested, for here as in many other arenas where Americans faced the new modern culture, individuals diverged in their response to social changes. One clear and important pattern emerges in the messages of the purveyors of mass culture—advertising agents, moviemakers, popular writers, and the like—who articulated the therapeutic ethos. They offered consumption and leisure as partial antidotes to the dilemmas of the modern world and promoted the cultivation of personality and other direction as the key to the individual's success and satisfaction in a mass society.

Many observers in the 1920s were insistent in their denial that success or even individuality must be sacrificed in the new white-collar business world. This was particularly evident in success books and schemes of the decade that modified the older tradition of success ideology identified with Horatio Alger. Nineteenth-century success stories posited hard work, sobriety, thrift, and restraint as the keys to personal and business good fortune. And invariably the success in mind was that of the old middle class—material rewards, civic virtue, and personal autonomy. By the 1920s, there was a subtle shift. Reflecting in part the popularization of Freudian thought, an important theme became the subconscious, which one writer described as "an infinite storehouse of intelligence and power" that man could draw upon to "supply his needs and wants." This idea of being able to marshal one's innate ability through exercise of will emerged in articles and books and was also popularized by agencies such as the Pelman Institute of America, whose advertisements in popular magazines offered "Scientific Mind Training." Pelmanism promised that it "awakens the giant, the superman, within you; it enables you to *realize your true self*, to become the man or woman you have dimly felt all along that you ought to be." Similarly, Frenchman Emile Coué took the country by storm by urging the daily invocation of a simple mantra: "Day by day, in every way, I am getting better and better." These approaches reaffirmed the possibilities for success, even in the modern corporate structure, by offering up-to-date techniques of realizing individual potential.

Perhaps the most famous success guru was Dale Carnegie. In the twenties, Carnegie was well known in business circles, and toured the country giving speeches and teaching businessmen how to speak, to present themselves, and to manage people. His best-seller *How to Win Friends and Influence People* was not published until 1936, but its ideas had already gained currency in the 1920s. The chapter titles are themselves revealing: "Fundamental Techniques in Handling People," "Six Ways to Make People Like You," "Twelve

Ways to Win People to Your Way of Life." The key to success as it emerged in Carnegie's work was the manipulation of others, presentation of self, and an acute consciousness of impressions.

Although these proponents of success certainly directed themselves toward men and occupational mobility, they also promised a more fulfilling personal life as well. This blurring of the lines between qualities needed for work and those needed for leisure meant that, unlike the Horatio Alger tradition, the more modernized success formulas encompassed women as well as men. The question behind them was not just how to live in the business world but how to live in the modern world.

Many other forms of popular culture addressed the same questions and pointed to the same reorientation of the culture. The managers and editors of the Book-of-the-Month Club, founded in 1926, offered a complex message. On the one hand, as [historian] Joan Shelley Rubin argues, the books the editors chose to feature were often those in keeping with the traditional genteel culture's emphasis on "character," such as Marjorie Kinnan Rawlings' *The Yearling* or Clarence Day's *Life with Father.* But the BOMC's promotion techniques—its advertisements and newsletters—decidedly reflected the newer emphasis on the self and personality and assured the book buyer that he could be "completely informed about *all the interesting new books.* He knows about them and can talk about them." The BOMC, in Rubin's words, "promised to cure the floundering self's social distress by enabling subscribers to convey the instant and favorable impression required for success in a bureaucratic, anonymous society."

The message that one could purchase what one needed for personal growth and success permeated the advertising industry. Advertising itself mushroomed in the twenties. Estimates are that in 1914 the volume of advertising stood at $682 million; by 1929 it had grown to $2,987 million. Although radio would become important toward the end of the decade, the most significant advertising medium was the mass magazines, whose circulation had exploded in the early twentieth century, so that by 1929 they were selling 202 million copies. Even the most cursory examination reveals the consumer culture orientation of magazine advertising: large and, as the decade progressed, colorful photographs of products and, increasingly, of individuals enjoying the products. As a car manufacturer summed it up, in a lushly colored scene of the countryside: "You find *a Road of Happiness* the day you buy a Buick." Advertisements like these repeatedly depicted the satisfactions of leisure and the products that created or enhanced leisure.

Beyond a mere glorification of consumption and leisure, advertising agents were often self-consciously "apostles of modernism," as [historian] Roland Marchand put it. In hawking their various products, they sought to associate their clients' good with the modern era, with fashion, style, and progress. But on a different level, admen—and the majority were men—revealed a darker side of modernity and sought to sell their products by addressing consumers' anxieties occasioned by the modern world, and in particular sought to soothe the embattled self: "Adopting a therapeutic mission, advertising provided comforting reassurances to those who anxiously watched the institutions of their society assume a larger, more complex, and more impersonal scale."

The advertisement of products for jangled nerves were the most obvious example of the therapeutic model in advertising. Post Bran Flakes' picture a harassed businessman was captioned: "Too Busy to Keep Well!" The text began: "We Americans, what a hurly-burly race we are! Getting up by the alarm clock; racing through our meals; hurrying from this appointment to that as though our lives depended on it." The resulting poor health and constipation, however, happily could be cured by eating Post Bran Flakes regularly. Examples concerning poor energy, health, and nerves could be repeated endlessly. And other products, not directly related to health, also played on the same theme of the stress accompanying the modern world. On a relatively subtle note, an advertisement for tourist tents celebrated outdoor leisure, and announced: "A Million Brain Workers Will Soon Want Tents" because "auto camping is the fastest-growing sport in

The Adman in 1920s Fiction

The sheer amount of advertising increased sharply enough in the 1920s to make critics and novelists take notice. Stephen Fox describes the adman of the fiction of the 1920s.

"The chief economic problem today," said [advertising executive] Stanley Resor, "is no longer the production of goods but their distribution. The shadow of overproduction, with its attendant periods of unemployment and suffering, is the chief menace to the present industrial system." In this situation, advertising increasingly seemed a necessary part of the industrial process, one of the standard costs like labor and raw materials, instead of an afterthought tacked on if the manufacturer could afford it. Now fifty years beyond his old associations with snake oil and consumption cures, the adman could regard himself as a regular guy, just another businessman. In popular fiction of the 1920s, the adman often appeared as the hero: the copy cub who at the last minute writes a brilliant ad, snares the client, and gets the promotion and the girl.

If not exactly a hero, George F. Babbitt did offer unconscious testimony to the new power of advertising in American life. Sinclair Lewis sometimes referred to himself as a former adman ("at least they used to let me write publishers' advertising"). He made advertising a large presence in *Babbitt*, a best-seller of 1922. Not a conventionally religious man, Babbitt believed in the God of Progress and the Great God Motor. He sold real estate and composed his own ads: "Course I don't mean to say that every ad I write is literally true or that I always believe everything I say." But he did trust most of the advertising he saw. The big national brands oriented him to the universe, offering the outward evidence of inner grace. "These standard advertised wares—toothpastes, socks, tires, cameras, instantaneous hot-water heaters—were his symbols and proofs of excellence; at first the signs, then the substitutes, for joy and passion and wisdom."

Stephen Fox, *The Mirror Makers: A History of American Advertising and Its Creators.* New York: William Morrow, 1984.

the world, because it is based on freedom, economy and common sense." Hammermill Bond was more explicit. A color ad featured two businessmen on a busy street, with one declining an invitation because "I'd get fired." The text bemoaned that it was "the same old story of the nose on the grindstone. No time for play. No time for anything but work. And no time then to make a success of himself. Always to busy grinding—grinding. A slave routine work." The imaginative solution to this grind was simple: preprinted office forms that would relieve men of "details and free themselves for advancement."

Another advertising theme that seemed directed at the plight of the individual in modern mass society was the personal approach, the tendency to include "you" in the text. As Roland Marchand has argued, advertisements, inspired by tabloid journalism's and movie matinees' phenomenal success, created mini-dramas of the consumer's life and solved them with products ranging from face creams to batteries. Other techniques of personalizing consumption included the celebrity endorsement, which linked movie stars and sports figures to ordinary Americans in shared consumption, and the advent of company spokespersons such as Betty Crocker, who humanized the corporate image. All of these techniques aimed at reassuring consumers that they had connections to their purchases, that they could exercise some control even in a mass society.

Perhaps the clearest indication of advertising's concern with the fragile self was the extraordinary emphasis ads placed on the opinions of others as vehicles for personal and business success, a theme especially evident in ads for toiletries. Mouthwash, deodorants, cosmetics, and perfumes were scarce products at the turn of the century, but by the 1920s they had become a major industry, with large advertising campaigns that accounted for the second most advertised range of products, next to food. Deodorant manufacturers took their small discreet advertisements off the back pages and used full-page ads to address "The Most Humiliating Moment in My Life." Cosmetics manufacturers surrounded women with mirrors and underlined the centrality of fashionable and youthful appearance in striving for personal fulfillment. Listerine publicized and more or less invented the fear of halitosis, "the unforgivable social offense," and promised to keep its users on "the safe and polite side." The Listerine campaign was especially revealing of the other-directed sense of the self conveyed in advertising, because, as [historian] Vincent Vinikas has noted, the users of mouthwash "had to be so attuned to appeasing others that they would routinely engage in a practice, the results of which were, from the user's perspective, virtually imperceptible." Certainly not all ads played on consumers' anxieties and insecurities, or promised antidotes to the various ills of modern society, but these themes were pervasive and point to the importance of advertising in shaping the contours of the personality-oriented consumer culture.

Equally significant were the movies. Modern films began to emerge shortly before World War I. As movies shifted from nickelodeons, with primarily a working-class audience, to photoplays, they became more sophisticated and also began to attract the middle class. As they moved into middle-class districts, their numbers expanded, with the twenties witnessing significant growth. As theaters became part of the chain-store phenomenon, firms like Loew's and First National Exhibitor's Circuit started the process of consolidating movie distribution. Theater architecture was also transformed: movie houses became palaces, large buildings, seating up to several thousand, sometimes air-conditioned, and increasingly luxurious. In the teens the firm of Balaban and Katz of Chicago started the trend that would culminate in such flights of fancy as Los Angeles' Grauman's Chinese "palace" and the Egyptian "temple." The decor was often geared to specific movies. A review in *The New York Times* reported that for the premier of *The Thief of Bagdad* (1924), the theater had assumed "a thoroughly Oriental atmosphere, with drums, ululating vocal offerings, odiferous incense, perfume from Bagdad, magic carpets and ushers in Arabian attire, who during the intermission made a brave effort to bear cups of Turkish coffee to the women in the audience." The exotic, glamorous settings for the films underlined their appeal: they were not merely entertainment, but an escape from the mundane, workaday world.

If movies as recreation represented an antidote to the modern world, their content further offered a variety of messages appropriate to the consumer culture. Some films (most noticeably those of Douglas Fairbanks in the late teens) directly addressed the issue of the degradation of work. As [cultural historian] Lary May has pointed out, many of these movies featured a white-collar worker frustrated by the confines of meaningless work. Thus, one caption described the hero: "his boundless energy is trapped at a desk in a button factory." The solution to the dilemma was never to change work itself—but to find meaning in leisure. "The heroes in Fairbanks' films," May notes, "discover new energy through boxing, tumbling, fencing, or gymnastics." Fairbanks was one of the first major stars whose personal life became the subject of intense public interest. As an "idol of consumption," Fairbanks promoted the new leisure not only in films but also in real life. In articles, speeches, and books, he propounded a new leisure ethic: "We read so much of work and success that someone needs to preach the glory of play."

In the 1920s, Fairbanks' films shifted to another way of challenging the older Victorian traditions of restraint associated with the work ethic and "character." He often played foreigners, tanned, robust, vibrant. These roles emphasized not only physicality but escape into an exotic world. A poster for *The Thief of Bagdad* that did justice to the tone of the movie portrayed him astride a magnificent winged horse, his sword upheld, as he streaked across the sky, with the minarets and mosques of Bagdad in the background. Fairbanks' physical grace and vibrancy evoked sexuality, but kept eroticism in check; far more explicit was the sensation of the decade, Rudolph Valentino. Valentino became synonymous with the role he played in *The Sheik*, a character of aggressive physicality and smoldering passion, unfettered by the restraint of "civilization." Appropriately, "Ben-Allah," in his biography, *Rudolph Valentino: His Romantic Life and Death* (1926), repeatedly insisted that the key to the box office idol's success was personality. "With nothing but his personality to sell,

Valentino sold it, and at a price that but few have done in the history of the world." Both in their films and personality, stars like Fairbanks and Valentino emphasized charm, youth, and physical expressiveness, thus helping to set the tone for an updated version of masculinity, as well as for the new cultural emphasis on self-expression, leisure, and personality.

At the opposite end of the spectrum, away from the daring exploits and desert romances, were the vastly popular comedies featuring stars like Charlie Chaplin, Harold Lloyd, and Buster Keaton. But they, too, with their ironic humor and visual gags, offered challenges to older notions of order, restraint, and propriety. In some cases, the characters that screen comics played came up against machines or the bureaucratic world and made wry comments on the individual's plight in urban mass society. Harold Lloyd in *Safety Last* (1923) played a not too successful clerk in a department store. In an effort to achieve a promotion and impress a young woman, he devises an advertising stunt: a human fly to climb up the side of the store's building. The stuntman is delayed by a run-in with a policeman and Lloyd's character must go up—hindered by a variety of hair-raising obstacles, including being caught by an appropriate symbol of modern times, a huge clock. He finally succeeds and wins the girl. As [professor of cinema studies] Robert Sklar has commented: "One could hardly ask for a more graphic satire on the theme of 'upward mobility.'"

Another movie addressed upward mobility in modern times more directly, and is a perfect exemplar of the confluence of consumption, personality, and success. In *Skinner's Dress Suit* (1925), a white-collar husband is ground down by his monotonous job. He punches a clock and commutes to suburbia to a wife who spends above her means and buys on the installment plan. One of her purchases was dance lessons. The film's denouement is an office party, staged at an Arabian-theme nightclub, where the Skinners' skill at the new dances brings the husband to the attention of his boss. As Lary May concludes: "Now his employer promotes Skinner away from his desk, for they realize he has a personality that can sell goods. . . . In the age of cooperation, personality is a commodity that will advance one up the ladder."

The films of Cecil B. De Mille further illustrate the linkage between consumption, personality, and success. in contrast to D.W. Griffith, a leading director of the prewar years whose films aimed at shoring up Victorian values, De Mille embraced new values. Many of his films depicted modern marriage. His characters remake themselves into more modern individuals in order to find ultimate happiness in updated marriages. Films such as *Foolish Wives* and *Male and Female* are particularly striking in the way in which they portray women's identity as inseparable from the clothes and cosmetics that adorn them. . . . De Mille's films further suggest the trend toward privatization, with individuals looking for satisfaction increasingly in the personal sphere, and achieving it through consumption, leisure, and self-expression.

Finally, the first talkie, *The Jazz Singer*, suggests the way in which movies reflected and reinforced the consumer culture. The film centers on the character Jack Robin, played by Al Jolson. He is a second-generation New York Jew whose father, a cantor wedded to Jewish orthodoxy, wants his son to follow in his footsteps. Jack wants to use his voice in a more secular way; he is a jazz singer. He rejects the old world for the new and embarks on his entertainment career, in the process becoming estranged from his parents. When he returns to New York and is about to be featured in a major show at the Winter Garden, he discovers that his father is dying and that the synagogue will have no cantor for Yom Kippur, the day of atonement, a central Jewish holiday. On his deathbed, the old cantor urges his son to sing Kaddish [prayer of mourning]. But if Jack fulfills his Jewish and filial duty, he will miss the opening of the show, and his big chance. In the play the movie was based upon, Jack sings Kaddish for the synagogue and the play ends. Family, ethnicity, and religion triumph together. In the movie, Jack fulfills his familial obligation. He sings Kaddish, but he returns to the Winter Garden the next night, where he has his big chance and sings "Mammy" to an approving audience that includes his mother.

The film offers many messages. One clearly is a story of assimilation. Jews can be Americans and pursue their individual goals but still be loyal children. But the film is also an unintentional reminder of the various threads that went into the fabric of the emerging consumer culture. Jack is a Jewish entertainer, albeit an Americanized one, who sings in blackface. As many scholars have noted, one of the functions of blackface was to offer whites a mask that allowed them to be more expressive than the Victorian norm permitted whites. The meaning of Jews, another outsider group, donning blackface is beyond our story here, but *The Jazz Singer* does suggest that both African American and immigrant performers helped influence the contours of the new culture. More overtly, the film's message is significant in that Jack's career choice was one that put him at the center of consumer culture: he is an entertainer, a *jazz* singer. Jack's character is exuberant, when he sings, he emotes, he dances, he has personality, he is an exemplar of the reorientation of culture, toward the new, the modern that Hollywood so often celebrated.

The Automobile Transforms America

Frederick Lewis Allen

Henry Ford did not invent the automobile, but he made it affordable by introducing highly efficient assembly-line production on a scale never before attempted. By 1925 Ford's plants were producing a completed car every ten seconds. The result of Ford's efforts, and those of the other car manufacturers who followed his example, was a true revolution whose effects first became visible in the 1920s. Once a rich man's toy, in the 1920s the automobile became a necessity for the average family.

As journalist and historian Frederick Lewis Allen writes in the following excerpt from *The Big Change*, the millions of automobiles that were purchased during the 1920s permanently altered the American landscape. New paved roads and a roadside economy of motels, gas stations, roadhouses, and roadside amusements grew up to serve a new market of car owners. The automobile made commuting between jobs easier, vastly expanding the suburbs around cities. It helped end the isolation of farm communities and create a more unified, sophisticated, and urban culture in the United States. It even transformed crime, introducing the drive-by shooting and the getaway car. Finally, the automobile, which President Woodrow Wilson had once bemoaned as the source of class conflict and "socialistic feeling," become a powerful yet peaceful force for democratization, giving a sense of pride and independence to the average American. Frederick Lewis Allen was an influential figure in scholarship about the 1920s. *Only Yesterday*, his first account of the period, appeared in 1931, while memories of the 1920s were fresh. Combining nostalgia with serious analysis, it sold widely and has served to flame debate about the decade ever since.

In the year 1906 Woodrow Wilson, who was then president of Princeton University, said, "Nothing has spread socialistic feeling in this country more than the automobile," and added that it offered "a picture of the arrogance of wealth." Less than twenty years later, two women of Muncie, Indiana, both of whom were managing on small incomes, spoke their minds to investigators gathering facts for that admirable sociological study of an American community, *Middletown.* Said one, who was the mother of nine children, "We'd rather do without clothes than give up the car." Said the other, "I'll go without food before I'll see us give up the car." And elsewhere another housewife, in answer to a comment on the fact that her family owned a car but no bathtub, uttered a fitting theme song for the automobile revolution. "Why," said she, "you can't go to town in a bathtub!"

This change in the status of the automobile from a luxury for the few to a necessity for the many—a change which, as we shall see, progressively transformed American communities and daily living habits and ideas throughout the half century—did not come about abruptly. It could not. For it depended upon three things. First, a reliable, manageable, and not too expensive car. Second, good roads. And third, garages and filling stations in profusion. And all these three requirements had to come slowly, by degrees, each reinforcing the others; a man who had tried to operate a filling station beside a dusty rural road in 1906 would have speedily gone bankrupt. But it was during the nineteen-twenties that the impact of the change was felt most sharply from year to year.

The Automobile Before the 1920s

When Woodrow Wilson spoke in 1906, and for years thereafter, the automobile had been a high-hung, noisy vehicle which couldn't quite make up its mind that it was not an obstreperous variety of carriage. It was so unreliable in its performance, so likely to be beset by tire blowouts, spark-plug trouble, carburetor trouble, defects in the transmission, and other assorted ailments, that a justly popular song of the time celebrated the troubles of the owner who "had to get under, get out and get under." The country doctors who in increasing numbers were coming to use the little brass-nosed Fords of the day had to be students of mechanical as well as human pathology. Each car had a toolbox on the running board, and tourists were accustomed to carrying with them blowout patches, French chalk, and a variety of tire irons against that awful moment when a tire would pop, miles from any help. One had to crank the engine by hand—a difficult and sometimes dangerous business. All cars except the limousines of the wealthy were open, with vertical windshields which gave so little protection against wind and dust to those in the back seat that dusters and even goggles were widely worn; and a gust of rain would necessitate a frantic raising of the folding top and a vexatious fitting and buttoning of the side curtains.

Roads were mostly dusty or muddy, with no through routes. Even as late as 1921 there was no such thing as an officially numbered highway. In that year the *Automobile Blue Book* warned those who proposed to drive from Richford, Vermont, to Montreal: "Chains on all four wheels absolutely essential in wet weather." And it advised tourists in general that "where mountain roads, sandy stretches, and muddy places are to be met with, a shovel with a collapsible handle" might prove very useful. At the time when Wilson spoke, panicky horses were still a hazard for the driver in remote districts, and speed limits set by farmer-minded local officials were sometimes low indeed: my personal memory tells me—unbelievably but I think reliably—that in tranquil Holderness, New Hampshire, the original legal limit was six miles an hour.

Design Improvements Pave the Way

Ford's energetic driving down of prices helped to make the automobile more popular, but equally responsible were a series of vital improvements: the invention of an effective self-starter, first designed by Charles F. Kettering and installed in the Cadillac in 1912; the coming, within the next two or three years, of the demountable rim and the cord tire; but above all, the introduction of the closed car. As late as 1916 only 2 per cent of the cars manufactured in the United States were closed; by 1926, 72 per cent of them were.

What had happened was that manufacturers had learned to build closed cars that were not hideously expensive, that did not rattle themselves to pieces, and that could be painted with a fast-drying but durable paint; and that meanwhile the car-buying public had discovered with delight that a closed car was something quite different from the old "horseless carriage." It was a power-driven room on wheels—storm-proof, lockable, parkable all day and all night in all weathers. In it you could succumb to speed fever without being battered by the wind. You could close its windows against dust or rain. You could use it to fetch home the groceries, to drive to the golf club or the railroad station, to cool off on hot evenings, to reach a job many miles distant and otherwise inaccessible, to take the family out for a day's drive or a weekend excursion, to pay an impromptu visit to friends forty or fifty miles away, or, as innumerable young couples were not slow to learn, to engage in private intimacies. One of the cornerstones of American morality had been the difficulty of finding a suitable locale for misconduct; now this cornerstone was crumbling. And if the car was also a frequent source of family friction ("No, Junior, you are *not* taking it tonight"), as well as a destroyer of pedestrianism, a weakener of the churchgoing habit, a promoter of envy, a lethal weapon when driven by heedless, drunken, or irresponsible people, and a formidable convenience for criminals seeking a safe getaway, it was nonetheless indispensable.

Furthermore, a car was now less expensive to maintain than in the days when the cost of successive repairs might mount up to a formidable sum each year. And it could be bought on easy payments. The installment selling of cars, virtually unknown before World War 1, spread so rapidly that by 1925 over three-quarters of all cars, new and old, were being sold this way.

Over these same years more and more roads had been paved, as public officials discovered that appropriations for

Automobile sales boomed during the 1920s as manufacturers began building more reasonably priced models.

highway surfacing were no longer considered mere favors to the rich; and garages and filling stations had multiplied.

The result of all these developments was a headlong rush to buy cars on the part of innumerable people to whom the idea of becoming automobile owners would have seemed fantastic only a few years before. In 1915 there were fewer than 2½ million cars registered in the United States. By 1920 there were more than 9 million; by 1925, nearly 20 million; by 1930, over 26½ million.

The Automobile Reshapes the American Landscape

So it was that the years between 1918 and 1930 introduced to America a long series of novelties which are now such familiar features of the American scene that one might think we had always had them: automatic traffic lights, concrete roads with banked curves, six-lane boulevards, one-way streets, officially numbered highways, tourist homes, and tourist cabins; and lined the edges of the major thoroughfares with that garish jumble of roadside services and businesses that [urban planning critics] Benton Mackaye and Lewis Mumford called "road town"—roadside diners, hot-dog stands, peanut stands, fruit and vegetable stalls, filling station after filling station, and used-car lots.

Meanwhile an antidote to the increasing snarl and confusion and frustration of traffic through the built-up areas of the East was already in preparation. For a generation the officials of Westchester County, New York, had been disturbed by the polluted condition of the little Bronx River and by its tendency to flood, and had been planning to restrict and control its flow while making it the chief attraction of a long strip of parkway—which almost incidentally would contain a through automobile road. When this road was opened to the public in 1925, motorists and traffic commissions and regional planners happily saw in it the answer to their prayers: an ample highway, with traffic lanes separated at intervals, uncluttered by local traffic, winding through a landscape undefaced by commerce. On such a highway one could make time most agreeably. Other parkways, wider and straighter, were thereupon built, both in Westchester County and elsewhere; existing through highways were rebuilt to by-pass towns along their way; so that by August, 1931, Mackaye and Mumford, writing in *Harper's*, could announce that it had at last been recognized that the automobile was less like a family carriage than like a family locomotive, and also could look forward prophetically to a now-familiar scene. The time would come, they predicted, when a motorist with a long drive before him would ease into the fast traffic on a "townless highway" and presently would be spinning along "with less anxiety and more safety at 60 miles an hour than he used to have in the old road-town confusion at 25." When that day came, they said, the automobile would have become "an honor to our mechanical civilization and not a reproach to it."

In 1931 those days had not yet arrived. There was still no Merritt Parkway, no Pennsylvania Turnpike; there were no butterfly intersections; there was no such majestic combination of separate lanes of traffic as would be seen by the mid-century at Cahuenga Pass in Los Angeles, where no less than fourteen lanes were to run side by side. Already motor busses had arrived in quantity, but the progressive ripping up of trolley tracks had only begun. Already motor trucks were taking freight business away from the railroads, but there was still no such vast and humming all-night traffic of trucks, truck tractors, and semi-trailers between our great cities as later years were to bring. And that perfect symbol of our national mobility, the residential trailer, was only just appearing: the first trailer had been built in 1929 by a bacteriologist, for vacation use, but these houses on wheels were not to arrive in force until the mid-thirties. Yet already the pattern of the automobile age had been set.

No such startling change in the habits of a people could have taken place without having far-reaching social effects. Let us glance at a few of them.

The Expansion of the Suburbs

1. It developed the motorized suburb. Where a suburb had previously been accessible by railroad, but had been limited in size because of the difficulty of reaching the station from any place more than a mile or so away from it, it grew with startling speed, as real-estate subdividers bought up big tracts of property and laid out Woodmere Road and Edgemont Drive and Lakeside Terrace, suitable for English-cottage-type or Spanish-villa-type or New-England-salt-box-type (or, later, ranch-type) houses with attached garages; where the children would have the benefit of light and air and play space, and their parents would have the benefit of constant battles over the policies of the local school board; where the wife would gulp down her coffee at 7:52 to drive her husband to the 8:03 train before driving her children to school and doing the family errands.

In a suburb which had previously been inaccessible by railroad the same phenomenon took place with only a slight variation: the earner of the family drove all the way from his almost-rural cottage to his place of work—and worried about the parking problem in the city. . . . And as more and more people whose living was dependent upon work at the center of the city fled to the leafy outskirts, urban planners began to be concerned about the blighted areas around the center of the city, where land values were falling and a general deterioration was manifest.

Business Moves Away from Main Street

2. The coming of the automobile age brought other changes too. It caused a widespread shift of business, and of economic and social importance, from the railroad town to the off-the-railroad one; from the farm that was four miles from a railroad station but had poor soil to the fertile farm that was twenty or fifty miles from rail; and from the center of the small city to its outskirts.

The hotel on Main Street, that had formerly been the one and only place for the traveling salesman to stop, lost business to the tourist camp on Highway 84. In due course this tourist camp was transformed into a new kind of roadside hotel, which offered overnight privacy—and sometimes luxury—without having to carry the economic load of high land value and of maintaining a restaurant and other public rooms. The shops along Main Street lost business to the new Sears Roebuck store at the edge of town, with its ample parking lot. City department stores, becoming painfully aware of their dwindling appeal to commuters, opened suburban branches to catch the out-of-town trade. And by the mid-century, shopping centers were beginning to be developed out in the open countryside, where the prime essential of parking space would be abundant.

The big summer hotel lost business, as the automobile opened up to a vast number of people the opportunity either to range from motel to motel or to have their own summer cottages, to which they could travel not only for the summer, but even for occasional week ends at other times in the year, by wedging the family into a car that bulged with people, suitcases, and assorted duffle. In resort after resort a pattern of change was repeated: the big hotel on the point, or at the beach, or on the hilltop was torn down, while the number of cottages in the neighborhood of its site doubled, tripled, quadrupled; and meanwhile the Friday afternoon traffic out of the city to various points, beaches, and hilltops became denser and denser. The trunk manufacturers lost business to the suitcase manufacturers, and the express companies languished.

During the single decade of the nineteen-twenties, railroad passenger traffic was almost cut in half; only commuter traffic held up. (In the outskirts of New York, the next two decades were to witness a decline even in railroad commuter traffic, as the new parkways, bridges, and tunnels into Manhattan swelled the number of commuters by bus and by private car.)

A Never-Ending Parking Problem

3. The automobile age brought a parking problem that was forever being solved and then unsolving itself again. During the early nineteen-twenties the commuters who left their cars at the suburban railroad station at first parked them at the edge of the station drive; then they needed a special parking lot, and pretty soon an extended parking lot, and in due course a still bigger one—and the larger the lot grew, the more people wanted to use it. New boulevards, widened roads, and parkways relieved the bottlenecks at the approaches to the big cities—and invited more and more cars to enter. At the end of the half century the question, "Where do I park?" was as annoyingly insistent as it had been at any time since the arrival of the automobile.

Highway Fatalities and Farm Life

4. The new dispensation brought sudden death. During the nineteen-twenties the number of people slaughtered annually by cars in the United States climbed from a little less than 15,000 in 1922 to over 32,000 in 1930; eighteen years later, in 1948, it stood at almost exactly the 1930 figure. As cars had become more powerful, and roads had become more persuasively straight and smooth, and speeds had increased, the shocking death toll each week end had led to the more cautious licensing of drivers and inspection of cars, to the multiplication of warning signs along the roadsides, and to the study of the causes and cures of death on the highway by such organizations as the National Safety Council and the

Automotive Safety Council. But meanwhile youngsters had learned to play "chicken," and hot-rod enthusiasts had taken to the road; and many older drivers, after a few drinks, found it easy to persuade themselves that they should overtake and pass that damned old creeping car at the crest of a hill, and even the most sedate motorist sometimes fell asleep at the wheel—and now the accidents that took place, while less frequent, were more lethal. So that at the turn of the half century one could still predict with reasonable certainty that a holiday week end would bring several hundred men, women, and children to an abrupt and gory end.

5. Along with the telephone, the radio, and the other agencies of communication, the automobile revolution ended the isolation of the farmer. In 1900 Ray Stannard Baker, describing a wave of prosperity among the farmers of the Midwest, had said that when a farmer did well, the first thing he did was to paint the barn; the second was to add a porch to his house; the third was to buy a piano; and the fourth was to send his children to college. By the mid-twenties the purchase of a car was likely to come even before the painting of the barn—and a new piano was a rarity. The widening use of the tractor was enlarging farms; and with the aid of the profusion of scientific information which was made available through the publications and county agents of the Department of Agriculture, the farmer was becoming less and less a laborer by hand, using rule-of-thumb methods, and more and more a businessman of the soil, an operator of machines, and a technologist. No longer, now, when he visited town, was he a rube, a hayseed, whose wife and daughters looked hick in calico. . . .

A New Personal Freedom

6. The automobile broadened geographical horizons, especially for people who had hitherto considered themselves too poor to travel. One could still find, here and there, men and women who had never ventured farther from home than the county seat, but their number was dwindling fast. For now the family who had always stayed at home on their day off could drive to the lakes or the shore, and on their vaca-

tion could range widely over the land, see new things, engage in new sports, meet new people. Even their daily radius of activity lengthened startlingly: by the nineteen-forties it might be a matter of routine for a rural family to drive ten or fifteen miles to do their shopping, twenty or thirty to see the movies, fifty to visit a doctor or dentist.

Furthermore, the automobile weakened the roots which held a family to one spot. Always a mobile people by comparison with the peoples of Europe, now Americans followed the economic tides more readily than ever before, moving by automobile—and before long by trailer—wherever there might be a call for construction workers, or fruit pickers, or airplane mechanics. Sober intellectuals were wont to deplore the growing American restlessness and to praise the man who was rooted to the land where he and his forefathers had been born and bred; but the automobile suited the American genius. For that genius was not static but venturesome; Americans felt that a rolling stone gathers experience, adventure, sophistication, and—with luck—new and possibly fruitful opportunities.

A New Pride

7. The automobile revolution engendered personal pride. When I say this I am not thinking of the envy-in-reverse of the man or woman who revels in having a finer model of car than the neighbors can afford, but of something less readily defined but no less real. Someone has said that the Asiatic, long accustomed to humiliation at the hands of the lordly white European, will endure it no longer after he has once sat at the controls of a tractor or a bulldozer. Similarly the American who has been humbled by poverty, or by his insignificance in the business order, or by his racial status, or by any other circumstance that might demean him in his own eyes, gains a sense of authority when he slides behind the wheel of an automobile and it leaps forward at his bidding, ready to take him wherever he may personally please. If he drives a bus or a huge truck trailer his state is all the more kingly, for he feels himself responsible for the wielding of a sizable concentration of force.

Growing Cities Provide the Market for a Consumer Economy

Howard P. Chudacoff

At the very outset of the 1920s, government statisticians noted that a demographic shift had taken place: There were now more Americans living in urban than in rural settings. While the U.S. Census Bureau's definition of "urban" was very broad—it included towns of only twenty-five hundred inhabitants—America was becoming an urban nation. Driven by economic pressures, a massive migration from farm to town and from small towns to major cities continued throughout the 1920s. Americans in the 1920s believed that city life represented the future. In the following selection, historian Howard P. Chudacoff describes the urbanization of the United States and the expansion of consumerism in the developing cities. Chudacoff teaches history at Brown University. His writings include *The Evolution of American Urban Society, How Old Are You?: Age Consciousness in American Culture*, and *The Age of the Bachelor: Creating an American Subculture*.

The 1920 federal census marked a milestone in American history: its figures revealed that a majority of the nation's people (51.4 percent) now lived in cities. Of course this revelation, like other historical watersheds, can be misleading: Massachusetts and Rhode Island had been predominantly urban long before 1920. Moreover in 1920 a city was defined as a place inhabited by at least twenty-five hundred people—hardly a rigorous criterion. Nevertheless the 1920 tallies were symbolically important. In 1890 the Census Bu-

Howard P. Chudacoff, *The Evolution of American Urban Society*. Englewood Cliffs, NJ: Prentice-Hall, 1981. Copyright © 1975 by Prentice-Hall, Inc. Reproduced by permission.

reau had signaled the end of America's youth by announcing that the frontier no longer existed. Now, thirty years later, the figures confirmed that the nation had evolved into a mature, urban society. The city, not the farm, had become the locus of national experience.

Urban Growth Brings an Urban Way of Life

The traditional, agrarian way of life, with its slow pace, moral sobriety, and self-help ethic, had been waning ever since urbanization accelerated early in the nineteenth century. To be sure, by the 1920s the demise was far from complete. Several social-reform movements and much political rhetoric looked nostalgically backward to the simple virtues of a fancied past. But everywhere signs pointed to an urban-industrial ascendance. A precipitous drop in commodity prices after 1920 spun small farmers into economic distress. Convinced that there was a better life elsewhere, millions gave up the land during the twenties and poured into Atlanta, Memphis, Detroit, Chicago, Denver, and Los Angeles.

Agrarian depression was only part of a broader development. All forms of primary economic activity—mining and other extractive industries as well as agriculture—were receiving a diminishing share of national wealth while tertiary activities—retail and service establishments—were mushrooming. These latter functions created an ever larger white-collar, urban middle class that became increasingly influential in local and national affairs. At the same time, some critics added a disdain for rural society to a general cynicism toward social conventions and business. Edgar Lee Masters' *Spoon River Anthology* (1915), Sherwood Anderson's *Winesburg, Ohio* (1919), Sinclair Lewis's *Main Street* (1920), and Thomas Wolfe's *Look Homeward Angel* (1929) assaulted the drabness of village and small-town life. The term "hick" became a widely used derogatory adjective, equating something clumsy or stupid with the farm. Much of the contempt for rural life represented a larger revolt against what writers called Puritan moralism—a revolt reflected in the popularization of the writings of Austrian psychoanalyst Sigmund Freud. But the debunking of the sturdy yeoman and small-town folkways also underscored a cultural shift that accompanied the city's rise to numerical superiority.

During the 1920s urbanization took place on a wider front than ever before. Maturing industrial economies boosted the populations of many areas, particularly steel, oil, and automobile centers such as Pittsburgh, Cleveland, Detroit, Akron, Youngstown, Birmingham, Houston, Tulsa, and Los Angeles. New commercial and service activities primed expansion in regional centers such as Atlanta, Cincinnati, Indianapolis, Kansas City, Minneapolis, Portland, and Seattle. The most exceptional growth, however, occurred in resort cities. Between 1920 and 1930 the population of Miami ballooned from 29,571 to 110,637. As the prime beneficiary of the Florida real-estate explosion of the twenties, Miami attracted thousands of land speculators and home builders. A citrus-crop failure and two disastrous hurricanes punctured the boom in 1927, but the expansion of warm-climate cities continued: Tampa and San Diego doubled their populations during the twenties.

A new spurt in construction, the biggest since the 1880s, accompanied the urban population growth. Wartime restrictions and high prices for materials had virtually halted construction of new residences between 1917 and 1918. After the war many cities faced acute shortages as workers who had arrived to man the war industries, and returning servicemen looking for employment swelled demands for housing. By 1919, however, construction costs began to drop while rents and sale values on existing buildings continued to rise. This situation triggered a frenzy of construction that lasted for seven years. New houses and buildings in fast-growing cities could be sold for substantial gains, and many buyers and renters, profiting from the general prosperity of the age and from new forms of credit, could afford the inflation. For example, in the decade after World War I builders erected one hundred thousand bungalows in Chicago and its environs, thousands of two- and three-story apartment houses in outlying neighborhoods, and a string of taller, luxury apartments along the city's north and south lakefronts. . . .

As in the past most new construction occurred at the edges

of cities. As the automobile made outer areas of cities more accessible, speculators started another epidemic of town building, a mania that had spurred urban growth for two and a half centuries. Between 1920 and 1930 suburbs around Los Angeles, Milwaukee, Atlanta, Cleveland, Detroit, and Buffalo doubled and redoubled in population. Among the most rapidly growing suburbs were Elmwood Park, Berwyn, and Wilmette near Chicago; Beverly Hills and Inglewood near Los Angeles; Grosse Pointe and Ferndale near Detroit; and Cleveland Heights and Shaker Heights near Cleveland. [Scholars] Charles N. Glaab and A. Theodore Brown have noted that of thirty-eight towns incorporated in Illinois in the 1920s twenty-six were around Chicago or St. Louis; of thirty-three incorporations in Michigan twenty-two were on the outskirts of Detroit; and of fifty-five in Ohio twenty-nine were Cleveland suburbs. The majority of these were residential communities for the middle and upper classes. A large number, however, were industrial suburbs, places such as East Chicago and Passaic, where industries had moved to take advantage of cheaper land and taxes and where factory wage earners constituted a fifth or more of the population.

Occasionally, as in the past, investors overextended themselves and when the boom broke they were left with too much vacant land and too many debts. The crash of 1929 transformed Burbank, California and Skokie, Illinois into temporary ghost towns, cruel reminders of over zealous optimism. Usually, however, the middle- and upper-middle-class families who populated most new suburbs provided a solid financial base and assured their future existence.

The proliferation of urbanization around the fringes of big cities created new attitudes of political independence. Throughout the nineteenth century suburban areas had eagerly sought to unite with the city nearby in order to receive municipal services such as water, gas, and fire protection. By the turn of the century, however, many people who were fleeing to the suburbs began to balk at paying high city tax rates, especially when they believed their tax money was supporting a corrupt political machine. Thus, although they still needed some of the municipal services, many suburbanities tried to preserve political independence for their communities. In 1910 Oak Park, Illinois residents rejected amalgamation with Chicago. Thereafter it became increasingly difficult for big cities to annex nearby towns. As one suburban editor reasoned, "Under local government we can absolutely control every objectionable thing that may try to enter our limits— but once annexed we are at the mercy of city hall."

Yet suburbs remained economically dependent upon cities. More than ever before suburban commuters rode automobiles, trolleys, or the electric interurban railroad to work in the city. And more than ever before adjacent towns were satellites of large urban centers connected by ever expanding transportation and commercial networks. These networks formed metropolitan districts—regions that included a city and its suburbs. The concept of metropolitanism had been recognized as early as 1854, when by an act of the state the city of Philadelphia absorbed all of Philadelphia County. In 1910 the Census Bureau gave the concept official recognition by identifying twenty-five areas with central-city populations of over two hundred thousand as metropolitan districts, and another nineteen with over one hundred thousand in the central city as emerging metropolises. By 1920 the total of metropolitan and near-metropolitan districts had grown to fifty-eight, and together they contained two thirds of the nation's urban population. By 1930 there were ninety-three cities with populations over one hundred thousand. The rise of urban America had climaxed; the genesis of metropolitan America was underway.

Skyscrapers Begin to Dominate Downtown

While new towns sprouted around the edges of cities, a new type of building began to dominate the central districts. The decade of the twenties was the age of the skyscraper. Between 1920 and 1926 the value of land in cities with populations above thirty thousand increased twentyfold. Suburban expansion accounted for much of this increase, but rising rents for offices and stores in central business districts also contributed considerably. Yet the demand for prime locations outran the inflation of rents. This demand, coupled with falling construction costs after 1921 and technological advances in electrical and structural engineering, prompted builders to erect ever taller structures. Cities across the country revoked height restrictions, and new buildings began to protrude above earlier skylines. By 1929 editors of *The American City* could count 377 buildings at least twenty stories tall. Although New York claimed nearly half of them, Syracuse, Memphis, and Tulsa also boasted of their own. These buildings quickly became objects of urban boosterism. For example, the cluster of skyscrapers at one of Birmingham's intersections prompted local enthusiasts to dub the location "the South's most developed downtown corner." Just as lavish hotels and railroad stations had symbolized the prosperity and refinement of nineteenth-century cities, skyscrapers represented progress in twentieth-century cities. Cleveland's 52-story Terminal Tower, Chicago's 36-story Tribune Tower, and New York's 102-story Empire State Building galvanized civic pride and presented a bold image to outsiders.

The Makeup of the Urban Population Changes

As business districts expanded horizontally and vertically, the surrounding residential cores began to experience a change of ethnic and racial composition. World War I shut off the flow of foreign immigration that had streamed into cities in earlier years. After the war a feverish urge for national unity merged with latent prejudices and fears to fuel sentiment for restricting immigration. Support for an end to free immigration had been building since the 1880s among urban reformers as well as unions and nativist conservatives. By 1919 humanitarians who had formerly opposed restriction were willing to admit that the melting pot had not worked and that many immigrants—particularly those from southern and eastern Europe—stubbornly resisted assimilation. Labor leaders, fearful that a new flood of unskilled aliens would depress wages, looked at the high postwar unemployment rates and increased their longstanding support for restriction. At first businessmen opposed the rising clamor out of self-interests: they hoped that a new surge of foreign workers would not only aid industrial expansion but also cut wage rates and curb unionization. But by 1924, when Congress was debating whether to close the doors more tightly, many industrialists were willing to support restriction because they discovered that mechanization and native migration from farm to city enabled them to prosper without foreign-born labor.

Congressional acts of 1921, 1924, and 1929 successively reduced the numbers of immigrants who could be admitted annually. A system of quotas, ultimately based on the number of descendants from each nationality living in the United States in 1890, severely limited immigrants from southern and eastern Europe, the very groups who had clogged urban cores since 1880. The laws left the doors open only to Western Hemisphere countries. Mexicans now became the largest foreign group entering the country. Many came to work in the fields and vineyards of the Southwest, but others streamed into the region's booming cities. By 1930 Mexicans constituted sizable segments of the populations of El Paso, Los Angeles, San Antonio, and Tucson. Like the Europeans who preceded them, these "new-new" immigrants were poor and unskilled, and they sought jobs and housing in inner-city districts.

The bulk of new inner-city residents, however, consisted of white and black native Americans, pushed off the farms by hard times and lured to the cities by hope for a more certain existence. During the 1920s rural population in the United States declined by almost a million. In the Midwest scores of thousands of farm families and, particularly, young, single people sought their fortunes in nearby regional centers or headed toward the cities of southern California. (The refrain to a popular song might well have been revised to read, "How ya gonna keep 'em down on the farm after they've seen Des Moines?") Larger movements occurred in and out from the South. Many whites moved northward to work in the automobile plants around Detroit, in the steel mills of Pittsburgh, and in various industries in New York, Chicago, and Cincinnati. Many more whites pushed into nearby cities in the South. After lagging behind the rest of the nation for nearly a century, the South now became the most rapidly urbanizing region in terms of proportionate population growth. Memphis, Atlanta, and Chattanooga experienced extraordinary expansion. The epitome of southern urbanization was Birmingham, Alabama. A burgeoning steel-making center in the late nineteenth century, Birmingham developed a diverse industrial, commercial, and service economy in the 1920s. This expansion attracted workers and their families from all over the South, who boosted the population of the metropolitan area from 310,000 to 431,000 during the decade (the population of the city proper was 260,000 by 1930). Smaller cities, many of them created by textile companies who had left New England to take advantage of cheap southern labor and readily available hydroelectric power, also helped boost the urban population of the South to thirteen million by 1930.

The most visible contingents of native migrants from World War I onward were the millions of blacks who moved into northern and southern cities. Pushed off their tenant farms by failures in the cotton fields and lured by jobs in labor-scarce cities, hundreds of thousands of black families packed up and boarded the trains for Memphis, New Orleans, Chicago, Detroit, Cleveland, and New York. When the war cut off the influx of cheap foreign labor, some companies began to hire blacks, sending recruiters south to promise instant wealth to potential migrants in much the same way that railroads and industries had recruited laborers in Europe a generation or two earlier. By 1920 four fifths of the country's blacks residing outside the South lived in cities. During World War I Chicago's black population increased by fifty thousand, almost doubling in two years—in 1920 only one of every seven blacks in Chicago had been born in Illinois. . . .

City Plus Suburb Equals Metropolis

As in previous eras cities stood in the center of economic change. City dwellers, now constituting a majority of the country's population, more than ever provided workers and consumers for expanding industry and related services. Following population patterns the urban economy now became a metropolitan economy, a system of interdependence between an urban nucleus and its contiguous regions. Industry began to decentralize. Mechanization and assembly-line production reduced the number of workers needed to manufacture an item but also increased the desirability for deploying production on one floor rather than in the multistory lofts common in the nineteenth century. Thus beginning before 1900 but occurring more and more frequently in the 1920s, factories moved from urban cores to suburbs, where large tracts of land were cheaper. At the same time a separation of production from management was underway. A number of firms retained or acquired offices in central business districts while building factories farther away in suburbs or even in other cities. Transportation between offices and factories via streetcars or highways and communication over the telephone made this separation possible.

Retailing also followed a pattern of centrifugal dispersion, particularly in the larger cities. Outlying secondary business centers around major intersections and streetcar-transfer points grew rapidly during the twenties. Neighborhood banks, movie theaters, office buildings, branches of major department stores, and chain stores such as Woolworth's, Kresge's, A&P, and Walgreen's brought the amenities of downtown to the periphery and suburbs. In Chicago corners at Lincoln and Belmont Avenues and Lawrence and Halsted, Sixty-third and Halsted, and West Madison and Crawford Streets became bustling business centers where land values reached ten thousand dollars per front foot by 1928.

The twenties witnessed the birth of the country's suburban shopping centers. In 1922 Jesse C. Nichols, a Kansan well versed in land economics, built the Country Club Plaza Shopping Center as the commercial hub of his huge real-estate development in Kansas City. A few years later Sears Roebuck and Company began to build stores in outlying districts to reap sales from growing suburban populations. The major proliferation of shopping centers occurred after World War II, but decentralization was well underway in the 1920s. Doctors, saloon-keepers, restauranteurs, and independent merchants followed clients and customers into expanding residential areas until business districts speckled every quadrant of a city's map. Downtown was still the focus of activity, but in many places its eclipse was imminent.

City Dwellers Provide the Market for a Consumer Economy

The proliferation of commercial and service establishments in the cities reflected the rise of a mass-consumer economy on a national level. American industrialists during the twenties utilized mass-production techniques to market commodities that practically any family could afford. Aided by advertising and by new forms of consumer credit, producers and promoters created a democratized materialism. A dizzying array of comforts and luxuries now dangled within reach of most consumers—washing machines, vacuum cleaners, refrigerators, radios, canned goods, lamps, cigarettes, and automobiles. Installment buying ("a dollar down and a dollar forever") made acquisition possible. And advertising—an expanding professional service—made acquisition desirable by celebrating consumerism in the popular media: newspapers, pulp magazines, radio, billboards, and motion pictures. "You have to *create* a demand for a product," lectured one advertising man. "Make the public want what you have to sell. Make 'em pant for it."

Most advertising campaigns were directed at urban consumers, particularly at the expanding middle class, because these were the people who had money to buy new products—or at least to make a down payment. Between 1920 and 1929 farmers' share of the national income dropped from 16 percent to 9 percent while industrial and service incomes, most of which went to urban households, mushroomed. Moreover the proportion of urban dwellings wired for electricity rose from 10 percent in 1920 to over 50 percent in 1930, whereas even at the later date very few farmhouses had electricity. Thus most household appliances, vanguards of the new materialism, could be sold mainly to urban families. . . .

Another type of consumption basically supported by city dwellers was the expanding range of leisure activities. A mania for sports, movies, radio, and fads gripped every city in the nation. In 1923, 300,000 fans attended the six-game World Series of baseball between the New York Yankees and the New York Giants. In 1926 the attendance of 130,000 at the first Jack Dempsey–Gene Tunney heavyweight championship prize fight in Philadelphia broke all records. But the return bout the next year shattered the newly set marks: 145,000 spectators jammed Soldier Field in Chicago, paying $2,650,000 to view the contest—even though many seats were so far from the ring that thousands were unable to see Tunney win.

Spectator sports were only half the attraction. Each week millions of enthusiasts filled tennis courts, golf links, and beaches. During the banner years from 1927 to 1929 weekly movie attendance reached an estimated 110 million people (a number almost equal to the nation's total population). Many moviegoers were country folk who streamed into the Bijou on Main Street in a thousand towns and villages. But many more were city dwellers who stood in line for one of the six thousand seats in Roxy's in New York or for the luxury of one of the Balaban and Katz movie palaces in Chicago. In 1922 three million homes had radios; in 1930 twelve million. By the latter date radio production had become a billion-dollar industry. Stations sprouted in hundreds of cities and became sources of community pride. To prevent chaotic expansion the federal government in 1927 created the Federal Radio Commission, which distributed broadcasting licenses and frequencies among 412 cities. A dizzying succession of games and other fancies passed through the cities. During 1922 and 1923 the Chinese game of mah jong was the rage. A new pastime, the crossword puzzle rose in 1924. Newspapers boosted sales by printing daily puzzles, and crossword-puzzle books broke into the best-seller lists. At the end of the decade fun seekers were adopting miniature golf as their newest diversion. By 1930 thirty thousand courses had filled empty lots in scores of towns and cities. . . .

Cities Gain Political Power

The growing importance of the city on the national scene was . . . reflected in the expanding relationships between municipal functions and the federal government. Many of these relationships dated from the latter half of the nineteenth century. For example, the federal government had the constitutional responsibility for such activities as maintaining a postal service and improving waterways and harbors, and cities had always sought federal assistance in these areas. Congress extended these responsibilities during and after World War I when it pumped funds into the construction of highways, airports, and even some housing. Increasingly, federal contracts and payrolls sustained a share of urban work forces—although the proportions were still small and many of the funds were filtered to the cities through the states. At the same time, several metropolitan areas had grown so large and complex that they rivaled the states of which they were parts for influence in the federal system. New York, Chicago, Philadelphia, Los Angeles, and Detroit—each with a population over one million by 1930—were rising above the screen of state government, which had formerly intervened between municipalities and Washington. These metropolises and the thirty-two others whose 1930 populations ranged between 250,000 and one million, were economically and politically powerful enough to constitute a third, urban partner to traditional federal-state relationships. When the economic crash of 1929 and its ensuing depression wiped away urban self-sufficiency, the lines of assistance and communications that had been stretched between cities and the federal government in the 1920s became the framework for the structure of government activities that was built in the 1930s.

Chapter 2

Prohibition Transforms the Nation

Turning | Points

IN WORLD HISTORY

How Prohibition Became Law

David E. Kyvig

In 1918 Congress passed the Eighteenth Amendment, which prohibited "the manufacture, sale or importation of intoxicating liquors." The Volstead Act, passed a year later, provided a precise definition of "intoxicating liquors" and gave the U.S. Treasury Department responsibility for enforcing the law. Today it is common to think of Prohibition as a movement of naive bluenoses. Yet it was pushed by an alliance that joined the most conservative and the most progressive forces of its day. While religious leaders in the rural South led the nation in imposing Prohibition on a state-by-state basis, their drive to achieve national Prohibition by constitutional amendment would not have been possible without the reform-minded temper of the Progressive Era, the desire of northern manufacturers for a sober workforce, and the high moral ambitions occasioned by America's entry into World War I. In this selection, David E. Kyvig describes the events that led to the passage of the Eighteenth Amendment. Kyvig, a professor of history at Northern Illinois University, has written extensively on the Prohibition era and on the history of constitutional law. This excerpt is from his book, *Repealing National Prohibition*.

The crusade to abolish the use of alcoholic beverages through an amendment to the Constitution hit the United States like a whirlwind in the second decade of the twentieth century. In November 1913 the Anti-Saloon League of America first publicly appealed for a prohibition amendment. By January 1919, scarcely five years later, Congress had approved and forty-four state legislatures had ratified the Eighteenth Amendment, which proclaimed:

1. After one year from the ratification of this article the manufacture, sale, or transportation of intoxicating liquors within, the importation thereof into, or the exportation thereof from the United States, and all territory subject to the jurisdiction thereof for beverage purposes is hereby prohibited.

2. The Congress and the several States shall have concurrent power to enforce this article by appropriate legislation.

3. The article shall be inoperative unless it shall have been ratified as an amendment to the Constitution by the legislatures of the several States, as provided in the Constitution, within seven years from the date of the submission hereof to the States by the Congress.

A tremendously significant social reform affecting the lives of millions had suddenly become part of the nation's rarely altered basic law.

Proponents of the so-called dry law faced little organized resistance as they marched to their triumph. Only brewers, distillers, and other commercial interests made strenuous efforts to block the reform. Individuals and groups offended by the challenge to their ethnic cultural traditions or by the limitation of their right to choose what to drink objected to the national liquor ban, but they lacked the channels and agents to give their protest focus and strength. New opposition to the Eighteenth Amendment began to form, however, in the midst of the prohibitionist victory in response to the law itself, the manner of its adoption, and the political assumptions upon which it was based. The reaction against this important constitutional innovation, therefore, can only be understood in light of the circumstances of national prohibition's creation.

The Prohibition Movement Had a Long History

The Eighteenth Amendment was the product of a century-long temperance crusade, the early-twentieth-century progressive environment, and a temporary spirit of wartime sacrifice. Various historians of the reform have tended to emphasize one or another of these factors. However, it is hard to imagine national prohibition being adopted without all three interacting.

The temperance movement's long and rich history began early in the nineteenth century as clergymen, politicians, business leaders, and social reformers became concerned about American society's increased drinking. They appealed for moderation in the use of intoxicants in the interests of health, morality, and economic well-being. From the start, evangelical Protestant churches stood in the forefront of the antiliquor movement. These churches felt that intemperance seriously interfered with their soul-saving mission because it destroyed man's health, impaired his reason, and distracted him from the love of God. Intemperance also undermined society by producing poverty, crime, and unhappy homes; this conflicted with the church's obligation to create a Christian social order. Finally, sobriety was considered to be the foundation of economic success and political liberty—visible signs of God's grace. For all of these reasons, evangelical Protestants became increasingly militant temperance agitators as the nineteenth century wore on.

In the mid-1820s the Reverend Lyman Beecher and others started urging total abstinence. They had come to believe that even moderate use of liquor started people on the downward path to drunkenness. The argument that intemperance was a disease preventable only by complete avoidance of spirits became a crucial article of the prohibitionist faith. Never again would moderate liquor consumption satisfy most temperance reformers; the complete elimination of intoxicants became their goal.

By the 1840s, temperance advocates had been disappointed several times by the results of crusades to win individual abstinence pledges, and they began asking for statutory curbs. Initial efforts in Massachusetts to confine the sale of alcoholic beverages within taverns and in New York to establish local option—the right of a community to ban the sale of intoxicants within its boundaries—proved unsuccessful. Next came the first attempt at statewide prohibition, the Maine law of 1851 which outlawed the manufacture or sale of "spiritous or intoxicating liquors." A dozen states quickly followed suit, but for the moment the movement had abated. The Maine law and others imitating it were repealed before the end of the 1850s. Then, for a time, the turmoil of the Civil War diverted reformers.

A new wave of temperance agitation began with the formation of the Prohibition party in 1869 and the Women's Christian Temperance Union in 1873, two organizations which put prohibition at the top of a list of desired social and political reforms. By the 1880s their efforts had helped make prohibition a vital issue in many states and territories. Five states adopted prohibitory legislation during the eighties, though only Maine, Kansas, and North Dakota retained their laws for long. The rising tide of populism soon overshadowed and pushed aside the antiliquor crusade. Although once again aborted, the crusade for enforced temperance at this time recorded one significant achievement: the creation in 1893 of the Anti-Saloon League.

The Anti-Saloon League proved the most single-minded and politically effective of all dry organizations. Established by men willing to confine their efforts solely to temperance reform, the league operated as a nonpartisan pressure group. Recognizing that whenever two political parties or two factions of the same party competed with approximate equality the support of a relatively small unattached group could be crucial, the league sought to demonstrate that it controlled enough votes to make the difference between election and defeat, thereby gaining candidates' acceptance of its program in return for its endorsement. Drawing its support primarily from the evangelical Protestant churches, the Anti-Saloon League became a political force to be reckoned with by the early twentieth century.

From Local Law to Constitutional Amendment

Prior to 1913 the Anti-Saloon League and its allies in the temperance campaign concentrated on winning local option elections and obtaining state statutes or constitutional amendments barring liquor sales. Nine states and many communities by then had adopted some sort of prohibition, though generally their laws allowed the continued sale of beer and wine and often permitted residents to mail order distilled spirits for their own use from outside the dry district. (Only half of the twenty-six states which instituted prohibition laws before 1920 went "bone-dry," banning alcoholic beverages totally.) Encouraged by such signs of progress as six state prohibition laws since 1907 and congressional passage early in 1913 of the Webb-Kenyon Act, a long-sought federal statute against transporting liquor into states that wished to block its entry, the Anti-Saloon League declared in November 1913 that it would seek a federal constitutional amendment providing for nationwide prohibition.

An amendment to the Constitution obviously appealed to temperance reformers more than a federal statute banning liquor. A simple congressional majority could adopt a statute but, with the shift of a relatively few votes, could likewise topple one. Drys feared that an ordinary law would be in constant danger of being overturned owing to pressure from liquor industry interests or the growing population of liquor-using immigrants. A constitutional amendment, on the other hand, though more difficult to achieve, would be impervious to change. Their reform would not only have been adopted, the Anti-Saloon League reasoned, but would be protected from future human weakness and backsliding.

"Although the Eighteenth Amendment would probably never have materialized except for the [Anti-Saloon] league," observed James H. Timberlake, a perceptive historian of the prohibition movement in the 1910s, "it is equally certain that the league would never have attained its success had not temperance reform been caught up in the progressive spirit itself." Progressivism and prohibition were, in his view, closely related middle-class reform movements seeking to deal with social and economic problems through the use of governmental power. They drew on the same broad base of support and moral idealism, and they proposed similar solutions to society's ills. Examinations of temperance campaigns in such varied states as Texas, Washington, Tennessee, New Mexico, Virginia, California, and Missouri support Timberlake's conclusion that "prohibition was actually written into the Constitution as a progressive reform."

The Impact of Progressivism

Progressivism, the reform spirit which gripped the United States in the early twentieth century, involved a variety of impulses, some parochial, some national, some complementary, some independent, some innovative, and some conservative. The various strands of progressivism were united, however, at the level of basic assumptions. Sensitive to the upheavals caused by the rapid industrialization and urbanization of America, progressives rejected the populist response of opposing modernization and instead sought to impose an order on the emerging society which would be consistent with their own values and interests. Far more optimistic than the preceding generation about man's capacity to solve problems and mold a satisfactory world, progressives believed that their goals could be reached by creating the proper laws and institutions. Whether the particular task into which they plunged was raising the quality of life for the urban working class, conserving natural resources, establishing professional societies and standards, improving governmental morality, democracy, and services, or controlling business practices, progressives repeatedly displayed their unshakable confidence that legal and bureaucratic instruments could be found which would permanently uplift that aspect of their environment. "They believed," as Ralph H. Gabriel put it, "that man, by using his intellect can re-make society, that he can become the creator of a world organized for man's advantage."

From the progressive viewpoint, temperance arguments made sense. In a modern society, liquor both reduced men's efficiency and spawned a multitude of social, political, and economic evils. Such a phenomenon should be reformed or outlawed for the common good. It is wrong, suggests Paul A. Carter, to think of prohibition as "exclusively the work of moralizing Puritans compensating for the repressions of their own harsh code in a spurious indignation at the pleasure of their neighbors." In his study of progressivism within the Protestant churches, the so-called Social Gospel movement, Carter found "thousands of sincere and not particularly ascetic folk who believed that they fought liquor, not because it has made men happy, but because it has made men unhappy." He concluded that "the dry crusade spoke the language of social and humanitarian reform—and had the profoundest kinship with the Social Gospel."

Arguments in behalf of national prohibition by the Reverend Charles Stelzle, a Presbyterian Social Gospeler and ardent prohibitionist, suggest some reasons why liquor reform appealed to many progressives. Stelzle, in a 1918 book, *Why Prohibition!*, held that banishing alcohol was essential for the material advancement of American society. Drinking, he asserted, lowered industrial productivity and therefore reduced wages paid to workers; it shortened life and therefore increased the cost of insurance; it took money from other bills and therefore forced storekeepers to raise their prices in compensation; and it produced half of the business for police courts, jails, hospitals, almshouses, and insane asylums and therefore increased taxes to support these institutions.

Stelzle held that the burden of these social and economic costs for the whole society outweighed any individual right to use intoxicants and legitimized the restriction of personal liberty. "There is no such thing," he wrote, "as an absolute individual right to do any particular thing, or to eat or drink any particular thing, or to enjoy the association of one's own family, or even to live, if that thing is in conflict with the law of public necessity." Anti-prohibitionists would charge drys with insensitivity to individual rights and liberties, but this was not the case. Prohibitionists simply felt that social betterment outweighed other factors. . . .

Businessmen and manufacturers often favored prohibition in the belief that it would increase industrial efficiency and reduce accidents. They felt that drinking even a small quantity of alcohol impaired a worker's mental and physical faculties, made him more careless, and lessened his productivity. Following the lead of the railroads, a number of firms, including the Henry C. Frick Company and the American

Sheet and Tin Plate Company, forbade their employees to drink alcohol either on or off the job. Other companies strictly prohibited drinking during working hours. Inevitably, many businessmen turned from their individual efforts to enforce sobriety to the attempt to achieve abstinence through law. Their enthusiasm for prohibition had a deep tint of self-interest but clearly shared the progressive attitude that rational men should use the power of the state to promote the general good as they understood it.

Not all progressives felt it wise to banish intoxicants. In particular, eastern urban progressives who represented alcohol-using ethnic groups opposed antiliquor legislation. Yet for the most part, prohibition upon the same broad base of support as the other progressive reforms. . . .

The Impact of World War I

The entry of the United States into World War I produced an atmosphere in which enthusiasm for prohibition accelerated. The need to sacrifice individual pleasure for the defense and improvement of society became a constant theme. The war centralized authority in Washington, loosening restraints on activity by the federal government. The importance of conserving food resources became apparent, and drys seized the opportunity to emphasize the waste of grain in the production of alcoholic beverages. Finally, the war created an atmosphere of hostility toward all things German, not the least of which was beer.

Called into special session to declare war in April 1917, the new Congress adopted temporary wartime prohibition as a measure to conserve grain for the army, America's allies, and the domestic population. The Lever Food and Fuel Control Act of August 1917 banned the production of distilled spirits for the duration of the war. The War Prohibition Act of November 1918 forbade the manufacture and sale of all intoxicating beverages of more than 2.75 percent alcohol content, beer and wine as well as hard liquor, until demobilization was completed. Although some regarded these measures merely as ploys to speed the imposition of national prohibition, they reflected the depth of concern generated by the war and the prevailing belief that alcoholic beverages ought to be sacrificed under the circumstances. . . .

Congress Votes for Prohibition

By 1917 so many congressmen were prepared to vote for a constitutional amendment that the doubters found themselves brushed aside. On August 1, 1917, by a vote of 65 to 20, the Senate approved an amendment prohibiting the manufacture, sale, transportation, import, or export of intoxicating liquors. The House, after revising the resolution to specifically grant state and federal governments concurrent power of enforcement, approved it 282 to 128 at the end of one afternoon's discussion on December 17. Senate acceptance of the House alterations on December 22 sent the proposed Eighteenth Amendment to the state legislatures for their consideration.

Partisanship was notably absent from congressional action on prohibition in 1917. The Anti-Saloon League had asked legislators, whatever their positions on other issues, to endorse national prohibition in return for its support. This pressure apparently influenced many individual congressmen without having any noticeable effect on either major political party. In the Senate, 29 Republicans and 36 Democrats voted for the resolution; 8 Republicans and 12 Democrats voted against it. In the House, 137 Republicans, 141 Democrats, and 4 independents supported the proposed amendment, while 62 Republicans, 64 Democrats, and 2 independents stood opposed. More than a decade would pass before the major parties adopted distinguishable positions on the liquor question.

Some Senate opponents of the amendment, rather than attacking it outright, had sought to sabotage the proposal by requiring that it be ratified by the states within seven years. They assumed that the twenty-six states which by then had adopted total or partial prohibition laws would not be joined by ten other states in ratifying the amendment within that time span. This proved a major miscalculation. By January 16, 1919, little more than a year after the amendment was placed before the state legislatures, it had been fully ratified.

The lop-sided vote of Congress in submitting the resolution, and the rapid ratification of the Eighteenth Amendment by state legislatures provides an indication of the wide acceptance of the prohibition concept. In only thirteen months, forty-four state legislatures gave the proposal their endorsement, making it one of the most rapidly approved of all amendments. The absence of a direct national referendum or reliable public opinion survey makes it impossible to judge precisely the degree of popular support for the new law. Yet the very requirements for a constitutional change—approval by two-thirds of each house of Congress and ratification by the legislatures of three-fourths of the states—suggests that the assent of a major portion of the body politic and not just the enthusiasm of an aroused minority was involved. Confirmation can be found in the results of referendums on statewide prohibitory measures held in twenty-three states during the five years preceding ratification of the Eighteenth Amendment. The issues voted upon differed in detail, as did the circumstances surrounding each election. Nevertheless, only in California and Missouri did voters persistently reject prohibitory legislation by wide margins, in both states doing so more than once. In three close elections, Ohio voters twice turned down and then adopted statewide prohibition. In Iowa and Vermont state prohibition was narrowly defeated. But in eighteen other states, majorities ranging from 52 percent in Colorado up to 73 percent in Utah and 76 percent in Wyoming approved varying degrees of prohibition. While votes on state measures ought not to be considered as identical to endorsement of a national law, these returns provide impressive evidence that liquor bans enjoyed broad support in the 1910s.

The Volstead Act

The adoption of the Eighteenth Amendment did not complete the creation of national prohibition. One of the most critical steps followed. The constitutional decree needed enforcement legislation to become effective. Congress in 1919 approved a strict enforcement act drafted by the Anti-Saloon League's general counsel, Wayne Wheeler, but known by the name of its sponsor, the chairman of the House Committee of the Judiciary. Andrew J. Volstead of Minnesota. The Volstead Act established procedures and agencies for enforcement and, in its most controversial section, defined intoxicating beverages as any containing more than one-half of one percent of alcohol. The .5 percent provision—advocated by the Anti-Saloon League and other militant drys—surprised considerable numbers of persons who assumed that, as had been the case with many state laws, only distilled spirits would be banned. Even beer and wine were outlawed under the terms of the Volstead Act.

President Woodrow Wilson, a temperance advocate but an opponent of prohibition, maintained an absolute neutrality toward the Eighteenth Amendment as it progressed through Congress and the state legislatures. Wilson disliked the drys' use of the continuing technical state of war as an excuse to implement prohibition even before the amendment was due to become effective on January 17, 1920, and gave this as his reason for vetoing the Volstead Act on October 27, 1919. Only a month before, however, the president had collapsed while campaigning for the Versailles peace treaty, and he was in no condition to fight for his beliefs regarding prohibition even if he had been willing to risk his little remaining political capital in such a battle. Congress immediately overrode the presidential veto by a vote of 176 to 5 in the House and 65 to 20 in the Senate. The Volstead Act, with its extreme program for implementing national prohibition, became law.

A brief summary can only hint at the rich history of the crusade which led to the passage of the Eighteenth Amendment and the Volstead Act. Nevertheless, it should make several points apparent. The idea of incorporating prohibition into the Constitution to protect against a legislative reversal arose only in the final stages of temperance agitation. The banning of liquor had long been discussed, trials had been undertaken on the local and state level in many parts of the country, and extensive support had accumulated. Progressive attitudes regarding the purpose and possibility of reform reinforced earlier temperance notions and created new sympathy for a dry law among those who previously had little interest in it. A wartime atmosphere of self-sacrificing patriotism provided a final boost. A righteous spirit of reform carried national prohibition into the Constitution of the United States. . . .

National prohibition took effect at midnight, January 16, 1920, one year after ratification of the Eighteenth Amendment. America entered the new age quietly, accepting the law as a great step forward or as a *fait accompli* and in either case believing that its reversal was quite out of the question. The following morning the *New York Times* reported, "John Barleycorn [an informal expression for alcohol] Died Peacefully At The Toll of 12." Had Mr. Barleycorn been in a position to reply, he might have chosen Mark Twain's famous response, "The reports of my death are greatly exaggerated."

Prohibition Contributed to the Rise of Organized Crime

Michael E. Parrish

In 1919 the Volstead Act gave the U.S. Treasury Department responsibility for enforcing the Eighteenth Amendment's ban on the manufacture, sale, and importation of intoxicating beverages. However, the same Congress that passed the Volstead Act over President Woodrow Wilson's veto refused to appropriate the money needed to enforce it. Throughout the decade, "wets" (those against Prohibition) drank in open defiance of the law and of the "drys" (those in favor of Prohibition). Millions of ordinary Americans became willing coconspirators with the gangsters and rumrunners who traded in liquor. As University of California history professor Michael E. Parrish argues in this excerpt, defiance of Prohibition was a powerful influence on the cultural changes of the 1920s. It also helped make organized crime a permanent feature of the American scene.

The prohibition movement, which finally achieved national political success during World War I with the adoption of the Eighteenth Amendment and the Volstead Act, was one of the most durable social crusades in the country's history. Beginning in the colonial period, upper- and middle-class citizens attempted to limit the consumption of spirituous drink to what they called "responsible and respectable persons." They condemned drunkards to the stocks or required them to wear the stigma of the letter D. Despite frequent legislation, however, the American nation remained, in one historian's memorable phrase, "the alcoholic republic"—a

Michael E. Parrish, *Anxious Decades: America in Prosperity and Depression, 1920–1941*. New York: W.W. Norton & Company, Inc., 1992. Copyright © 1992 by Michael E. Parrish. All rights reserved. Reproduced by permission of the publisher.

country notorious for its heavy consumption of hard cider, rum, and corn whiskey. . . .

For the drys [those who supported Prohibition], passage of the Volstead Act began the millennium. They expected the measure to elevate the nation's moral tone, increase its productivity, reduce crime and political corruption, and protect the hearth. [Navy] Secretary [Josephus] Daniels declared the saloon "as dead as slavery." [William Jennings] Bryan [celebrated Populist leader and Prohibition advocate] said "the man who peddles liquor, like the man who sells habit-forming drugs, is an outlaw." As "the virtue of the country asserts itself," the Great Commoner predicted, the number of citizens with a fondness for beer and hard drink would "constantly decrease."

Few anticipated massive resistance to the law and the Constitution. The first chief of the enforcement division in the Treasury Department, John F. Kramer, vowed that "this law will be obeyed in cities, large and small, and in villages, and where it is not obeyed it will be enforced. . . . We shall see that it [liquor] is not manufactured . . . sold, nor given away, nor hauled in anything on the surface of the earth or under the earth or in the air." Congress, however, gave Kramer only $2 million to achieve his goals. . . .

The Futility of Enforcement

Despite the optimism of Daniels and Bryan, the virtue of the country failed to assert itself over the next thirteen years. Federal officers charged with implementing Kramer's pledge soon discovered that it was no easier to enforce the Volstead Act in New York City, Chicago, or New Orleans in 1925 than it had been to collect a federal tax on whiskey in western Pennsylvania in 1794, to return a fugitive slave from Boston to Charleston in 1854. . . . Unless the national government secured the active support of important local elites for its programs or was prepared to employ to the fullest its own fiscal and coercive resources, it could never hope to prevail against united local resistance. The bitter struggle to dismantle racial segregation in the South during the 1950s and 1960s demonstrated this proposition just as did the failure to enforce prohibition between 1920 and 1933.

At its peak strength near the end of the decade, the Treasury Department fielded about three thousand prohibition agents. They were paid on average $2,500 a year to close down an illegal industry whose income probably reached $2 billion annually. In a pinch, these prohibiton sleuths could call on the Coast Guard, customs, and immigration officials for assistance, but even if every one of them had been a model of zeal and integrity (10 percent were fired for corruption between 1920 and 1930), they faced the staggering task of damming the flow of intoxicating drink that reached thirsty consumers through smuggling, diversion, and illicit stills. From the perspective of rumrunners and bootleggers, America had been blessed with twelve thousand miles of coastline and borders; alcohol was readily available in hundreds of legal products ranging from perfume to antifreeze; breweries continued to manufacture gallons of "near beer" that awaited enrichment; and home-brewing gear could be purchased at most local hardware stores for less than $10. When it came to defying the Volstead Act, the imagination and ingenuity of those breaking the law knew few bounds; the resources allocated to enforcement remained pathetically small.

By all accounts, diversion and redistillation of alcohol intended for industrial and commercial purposes constituted the single largest source of illegal liquor sold to Americans between 1920 and 1933. Illicit distilling ran a close second. Even when the federal government tightened its licensing system after 1930, an estimated ten to fifteen million gallons of alcohol, once destined for hair tonics, cosmetics, and paint, turned up in the bootleggers' inventory each year. Sometimes it was called Scotch whisky, sometimes "Kentucky Tavern" or "Pebble Ford," which prohibition agents in Detroit discovered had been concocted from "Parisienne Solution for Perspiring Feet, 90 Per Cent Alcohol." Although not widespread, wood-alcohol poisoning from liquor made by incompetent or greedy bootleggers became a grim reality. Thirty-four people died from such poisoning in New York City during a brief four-day period in 1928. Throughout the decade, doctors and coroners saw cases of impoverished drinkers felled by Sterno, while the more affluent succumbed to crudely distilled corn mash, squash, and potatoes. According to legend, one skeptical buyer took his bootlegged purchase to a chemist, who reported to him after analysis: "Dear sir, your horse has diabetes."

Whether operated by amateurs for home consumption or by professional criminals for a wider market, the illicit still that produced pure grain alcohol became another ubiquitous source of cheer. In some Northern cities, entire neighborhoods were major centers of production; the mash vat and the three-spout copper still replaced sewing machines as the basic tools of sweated labor. A single such operation on Chicago's South Side or in the Great Dismal Swamp could turn out two hundred gallons of alcohol a day. Cut with a little California or New York grape juice, water, juniper drops, and glycerine, it could bring from 2 to 4 cents an ounce, depending on the market. Manufacturers of corn sugar did a booming business in the twenties as their output rose in some cases sixfold to meet the demand of moonshiners, home brewers, and the mob.

Smuggling by land and sea, although it did not account for the bulk of the nation's illegal liquor, became the most romantic form of entrepreneurship. Caravans of trucks laden with Canadian whiskey roared down the back roads of Vermont, New York, Minnesota, and Washington to bring shipments of liquid contraband to patrons in speakeasies from Boston to Seattle. Similar traffic, specializing in tequila and mescal, poured across the U.S.-Mexico border from Texas to California. . . .

The forces of law and order recorded a few notable victories during the decade. In the first two years of enforcement, the federal government initiated 3,500 civil and 65,000 criminal actions under the Volstead Act and won about 60 percent of these cases. Prohibition agents smashed 172,000 illegal stills in 1925 alone. Two agents, Izzy Einstein and Moe Smith, became celebrities because of their innovative methods. When the roly-poly Izzy nearly froze to death outside a notorious speakeasy while waiting for an illegal shipment to arrive, his sidekick carried him into the place, pounded the

bar, and demanded: "Give this man a drink! He's jus
bitten by a frost." When the kindly bartender obliged, they
arrested him and closed down his establishment. The team of
Izzy and Moe made four thousand arrests in five years and
seized five million bottles of illegal liquor worth $15 million.
But for every illicit still they destroyed, probably nine continued to operate. Four out of every five shipments from
Canada, Mexico, or the West Indies eluded federal agents. At
the conclusion of Izzy and Moe's crime-busting campaign,
any thirsty citizen could still buy a drink in most major American cities about one minute after stepping off the train.

Some states, notably New York and Wisconsin, showed
their defiance by repealing all local laws that supplemented
the Volstead Act. . . .

Barons of Booze

The deepest irony of prohibition arose not from the desire
to impose virtue through repression, but from the success
and power that flowed to many ethnic Americans who became the beneficiaries of the very laws intended to limit
their cultural influence. German-Americans had long dominated the American beer market. The Irish had operated saloons and pubs from San Francisco to Boston. Prohibition
now delivered a $2 billion illegal industry into the hands of
an underworld dominated by second-generation Italians,
Jews, and Irish, who faced far less discrimination in this line
of work than in the more reputable middle-class professions
of law, medicine, accounting, and teaching. The mortality
rate might be high and job security low, but the opportunities for quick riches proved very attractive.

Crime became a highly organized big business in these
years when the local purveyors of prostitution and gambling
discovered they could reap huge profits by controlling on a
regional basis the manufacture and distribution of illegal alcohol, too. The ingredients for entrepreneurial success were
very simple: a dependable source of supply and a steady, pre-
dictable number of brothels, restaurants, and speakeasies
where customers consumed it. The police could not be
counted on to protect the means of production and no civil

court would enforce these business contracts, so professional criminals devised their own methods for defending markets and safeguarding profits. Like the businessmen of an earlier era who struggled to bring order to the fledgling railroad, petroleum, and meat-packing industries, the barons of booze hated competition and cherished monopoly, even when the latter could be imposed only through the muzzle of a sub-machine gun.

The Torrio-Capone gang of Chicago emerged as the prototype of the new criminal organization specializing in the business opportunities created by the Volstead Act. A few months after prohibition became the law of the land in 1920, one of Chicago's leading mobsters, James "Big Jim" Colosimo, was shot to death by a gun-toting hoodlum from Brooklyn, Frankie Yale. It is likely that Yale had been hired by Colosimo's own partner in crime, Johnny Torrio, who wished to overrule the boss's decision not to expand from brothels and gaming into bootlegging. The flowers had barely wilted on Big Jim's casket when Torrio took charge of the opera-

Police inspect brewing equipment discovered during a raid. An extensive underground liquor market emerged during Prohibition.

tions, imported additional firepower from New York, and began lining up new clients for his growing business.

Torrio's ambitions infuriated the city's other gangs, especially those run by the Irish, but Johnny had struck it rich with one of his Brooklyn imports—a heavyset twenty-three-year-old Italian with a love of opera, a taste for good cigars, and a real flair for mayhem and murder. On his business cards, Alphonse "Al" Capone listed his occupation as "secondhand furniture dealer," but as Torrio's lieutenant and later his partner, he specialized in protecting the organization's Canadian pipeline and making certain that Chicago's hotels, brothels, and speakeasies gave their product a fair deal with the competition. When other gangs failed to respect the Torrio-Capone territory, they faced swift retaliation—beatings, a hail of bullets, bombings.

In the first four years of prohibiton, until the Italian-dominated Torrio-Capone mob consolidated its control over Chicago, the city witnessed over two hundred gang-related killings, an average of almost one a week. In November 1924 the Capone forces eliminated Dion O'Banion, an archrival with good political connections, who had made the fatal mistake of having Torrio picked up by the police on bogus charges. The Irish boss was gunned down outside his flower shop. The fallen gang leader's grieving widow described O'Banion as an ordinary family man who was never late for dinner and loved to tinker with the radio. Along with thousands of other mourners, Capone sent a huge wreath of flowers for the casket, but he was very blunt when speaking to reporters about how O'Banion had failed to respect the bootleggers' code of fair competition. "His head got away from his hat," Al told them. "Johnny Torrio taught O'Banion all he knew and then O'Banion grabbed some of the best guys we had and decided to be boss of the booze racket in Chicago. . . . It was his funeral.". . .

Just a Businessman

Befitting a wealthy Italian businessman who found himself often locked in combat with the city's older Irish power structure, Capone voted Republican, and his soldiers made certain that the party of Coolidge and Hoover swept Cicero [Illinois] on election day. The irony of this situation was no doubt lost on the stalwart Republicans downstate in Illinois, who fervently supported prohibition. If Cicero's mayor strayed too far from the Capone interests, however, he risked being kicked down the steps of city hall. Unreliable council members and newspaper editors were bought off, beaten up, and run out of town.

Despite his unsavory reputation for violence and corruption, Capone became something of a folk hero to many who resented prohibition and felt themselves to be social outcasts. Like heavyweight champ Jack Dempsey, "the Manassa Mauler," Capone came from the wrong side of the tracks, a scrapper, who had battled his way to the top of the booze business. Now he lived as well as the upper-class big shots who had gone to Princeton, ran the brokerage houses on LaSalle Street, and looked down on ethnic minorities. Capone could afford to dine where they did, buy his clothes from the same tailors, and drive a Cadillac—bulletproof, of course.

Reporters covered the details of Capone's public and private life with the same zeal accorded movie stars. They hung on his words as if he were a candidate for governor. In Chicago, Capone usually received as much press as Mayor Thompson and only a bit less than the elusive running back for the University of Illinois, Harold E. "Red" Grange. Although Calvin Coolidge might wince at the idea, Al Capone embodied the spirit of free enterprise and the power of the market; he was a perverse symbol and parody of America's business culture. "If people didn't want beer and wouldn't drink it," he once observed, "a fellow would be crazy for going around trying to sell it. I've seen gambling houses, too . . . and I never saw anyone point a gun at a man and make him go in. . . . I've always regarded it as a public benefaction if people were given decent liquor and square games."

The Balance Sheet

The epidemics of gangland violence generated by prohibition brought forth new demands for the modification or repeal of the Eighteenth Amendment. The Reverend Billy Sunday had called liquor "God's worst enemy . . . Hell's best friend," but from the perspective of others, the efforts to eradicate its use had created even more terrifying allies of the devil. At decade's end, especially as the nation slid into economic depression, a great many Americans questioned whether the costs of the "noble experiment" did not exceed the benefits. Was the open saloon really a greater menace to society than the Capone mob? Had the old liquor monopolies not been replaced by new, criminal ones? Were urban politics less or more venal as a result? Were the social problems attributed to hard drink—unemployment, poverty, family violence—now under control?

As the answers to these and other questions became increasingly problematic, popular support for national prohibition eroded. Herbert Hoover, whose political career in the twenties had included support for the Volstead Act, signaled the change in public mood. In the wake of the negative findings of the Wickersham Commission, he promised more efficient enforcement by placing the Prohibition Bureau under the supervision of the Justice Department and raising the civil service requirements for its agents. A year later, as the nation's economic fortunes worsened, Hoover, a Quaker who loathed alcohol and the saloon, endorsed repeal.

More than half a century after its demise, scholars continue to debate the costs and benefits of the "noble experiment." Congress, some point out, never appropriated sufficient money to ensure effective enforcement. It preferred a symbolic crusade to a real one by choosing to pay lip service to the forces of righteousness while maintaining a flow of liquor to the unrepentant. But more than fiscal conservatism, a lack of political will, or hypocrisy explains this gap between congressional rhetoric and resources. In both monetary and legal terms, the true costs of effective national enforcement would have been astronomically high, including a large increase in police and judicial personnel along with perilous consequences for constitutional rights. The nation would face this dilemma again in the 1980s, when engaged with the far greater social menace of heroin and cocaine.

In the short run, prohibition proved a boon to boat operators, firearms manufacturers, auto dealers, ethnic mobility, and undertakers. But the workingman's corner saloon shut its door for a decade, to be replaced by the elegant speakeasy that catered especially to a middle-class and upper-class clientele. Except in rural areas where high-grade moonshine or "white lightning" had always been available, the quality of liquor available to the lower classes, never high to begin with, deteriorated further. Like the impact of many other Republican policies during the decade, the burdens of prohibition fell heavily on economic and racial minorities.

For all their defects and contradictions, some students argue, the Eighteenth Amendment and the Volstead Act changed for the better the nation's drinking habits. We became, according to this theory, a more sober society after prohibition when per capita consumption of hard liquor declined significantly in favor of beer and wines. But it is not altogether clear that these changes arose solely because of prohibition and the legal stigma attached to drinking. As before, the American public officially denounced drunkenness and alcoholism in the twenties, but the press still reported mirthfully on intoxicated celebrities riding through the streets of New York atop taxis and taking a 3:00 A.M. dip in one of the city's public fountains. Americans probably drank less hard liquor after prohibition for a variety of reasons unrelated to the Volstead Act—greater affluence following World War II, changing status expectations, the spread of medical knowledge, and new dietary habits.

The historical and sociological connection between organized crime and prohibition is far less problematic. Without the considerable economic resources and managerial experience generated by the traffic in illegal alcohol, the mob could not have developed its nationwide network of influence or branched out into other lucrative activities. Shortly before his problems with the Internal Revenue Service began, Capone almost realized his ambition to create a national crime cartel and his organization had begun to invest in reputable enterprises of all kinds, including banks and real estate firms. The expansion of vice and the bureaucratization of crime flourished long after the Anti-Saloon League had passed from the scene.

The Legacies of Prohibition

Norman H. Clark

The Eighteenth Amendment, prohibiting the trade in liquor, was repealed by the adoption of the Twenty-first Amendment in 1933. Most people came to remember Prohibition as a misguided effort at social engineering, a "noble experiment" that completely failed. In this selection historian Norman H. Clark argues that Prohibition was in many ways a success, with lasting effects that were not undone by repeal. One of Prohibition's main targets had been the old-time saloon, and the saloon did disappear. Although a highly visible section of the population flouted the law, per capita consumption of alcohol declined and never returned to its former levels. Instead of remaining the purview of drunk and violent saloongoers, drinking became associated with a sophisticated, urban lifestyle. Clark is the author of *The Dry Years: Prohibition and Social Change in Washington* and *Deliver Us from Evil: An Interpretation of American Prohibition*.

In *The Dry Decade*, published in 1931, Charles Merz explained that the Repeal Movement had become a nullification of federal legislation and official morality. He described it as a rebellion on the part of many people who finally refused in any way to honor a law held almost universally in contempt. Merz compared this rebellion, as the wets [those who opposed Prohibition] had for years compared it, with the reaction of Americans, especially in the South, to the Reconstruction laws which reformers carried through Congress after the Civil War. This is to a degree a useful analogy, for it reveals a certain similarity in the efforts of Americans to suppress racism and intemperance. But at best it has a narrow validity. There is surely little to be learned from comparing racism to drinking or drunkenness, and surely history has no need for another shaky analogy.

It is true that Charles Merz did not work this particular analogy very hard. But he did, at least by implication, suggest that because the efforts to suppress racism and the efforts to suppress intemperance were both failures, Americans should have learned from the history of the one experience what to anticipate from the other. This is the unfortunate distortion. Though racism has not been suppressed, slavery is dead; this is surely because of the Antislavery Movement, and since 1865 racism has been measurably diminished in American society. Though intemperance has not been abolished—and there is here no further implied comparison—the movement against it did abolish the saloon, and this in turn has made the public drunkard at least less common than he was during the nineteenth century and something less of a social hazard. There is every reason to believe, as we have seen, that even with their inadequacies, the various state dry laws and the Volstead Act [which provided for the enforcement of Prohibition] were, in part, causes of the substantially reduced consumption of alcohol among Americans.

What is unfortunate, then, is that many people have come to explain both Reconstruction and Prohibition as decades of experiment and failure, as periods when the efforts of misguided reformers were abandoned to a historical slag pile by a disillusioned society whose values were inconsistent with sustained repression. It would be nearer the truth to explain that while the American experiences with racism and intemperance were in most ways dissimilar, neither racism nor intemperance was, or now is, necessarily incompatible with American values. But the institutional structure of racism before the 13th Amendment [which outlawed slavery] and the institutional stimulation of public drunkenness before the 18th Amendment were incompatible with the values of the societies which ratified those changes.

Drinking in a Saloonless Society

A distinctive mood of the new society—the society which repealed the 18th Amendment—was shaped by the feeling that in a saloonless society, public drunkenness would never again approach the proportions of a social crisis. . . . This widespread feeling made the success of the Repeal Movement possible. And while the repealers themselves were often eager to assist their state governments in designing laws to prevent the return of the "old-time saloon," few of them expressed any enduring anxiety about the less dramatic forms of intemperance. After the [stock market] Crash of 1929, Edgar Kemler wrote in *The Deflation of American Ideals* (1941) that the traditions of "proper" behavior sustained by the older society seemed irrelevant to hard times and to hard economic decisions which would shape the future of the nation. To Kemler's friends, at a time of great distress, these traditions seemed even to be a barrier against effective social action. "Proper" men like Woodrow Wilson and Herbert Hoover had failed because they had arrogantly mixed their personal ethics with political and economic objectives, because they had determined to "lift men to higher things," and because their vision was thus distorted by "self-righteousness and moral superiority." To a good New Dealer [adherent of Franklin D. Roosevelt's "New Deal" social programs], according to Kemler, high moral indignation was the sure sign of political bankruptcy; it made significant social reform quite impossible.

With the repeal of Prohibition, Kemler wrote, "sin was returned to the jurisdiction of the churches where it belongs." Thus liberated from the institutional moral restraints of the pietist republic (this was a conspicuous liturgical triumph), New Dealers were free to refine the agency-society without confusing morality with the techniques for relief, recovery, and reform. It seemed beautifully efficient. The agency-society was in control, not the churches or the families, and there could finally be truly objective analyses of social problems and truly scientific solutions. In this confidence, New Dealers like Kemler disdained both the ideals and the lifestyles of their predecessors. They talked openly with prostitutes, used shocking vocabularies, drank cocktails. They tried to show that a liberated comportment—an honest surrender to impulse, a self-generous indulgence, an identity of individual wants and needs—was an essential characteristic of the scientific and civilized man. The Volstead Act, as did the Mann Act, became the butt of jokes. The implications of both were not ideals with which a liberated person cared to associate himself. This was the legacy of the raised eyebrow, the snicker, the sneer—at someone's abstinence.

Drinking Takes On New Meaning

Even before repeal, drinking had become the comportment of protest, the existential identity of the individual against the system. The defiant rebel with his pocket flask had become an almost irresistible symbol of dignity, courage, manhood, and liberation from hypocrisy and pigheaded repression—a symbol which could elevate drinking into a sacrament of true individualism. After repeal, advertising specialists brought to these symbols an increasingly delicate and effective illumination. The techniques were necessarily subtle, for after 1933 the Federal Alcohol Control Administration was severely sensitive to obvious associations in advertising copy of liquor or beer to women, children, health, sex, religion, or group drinking which might even seem "excessively convivial." Accordingly, ad copy of the 1930s suggested a hearty masculinity by associating drink with the horse race, the hunt club, the vigorous sportsman, the daring adventurer. They showed drinking as integral to the fashionable life—to the world of the wealthy, the proud, the elite. These associations, rising from values essential to conspicuous consumption, projected a new linkage of images which—like the saloon-based images of a previous generation—were seared into the American mind until they became coordinates for a new American conscience.

Drinking Man and Drinking Woman After Prohibition

Drinking man was the man of physical action and triumph, distinguished in his masculinity and in the demonstration of its symbols. Drinking man was keenly aware of his uniquely complex individuality; he nurtured it, guarded it, exercised it, polished it. His indulgences were deep, yet honest, always consistent with health and spiritual equilibrium. His impulsiveness was mature and humane and firmly true. He was not a man who would ever beat his, or anyone's, wife or children. He was never irresponsible. His life was never overshadowed by loneliness, which in the society of social atoms was a grievous affliction. By the fact and the style of his drinking, he could attract not only sexual partners but loyal friends. Drinking man was a man's man, intelligent, discreet, always thoughtfully sensitive to the possibilities of lifestyle

Drinking Declined During the Prohibition Era

Due to the attention the media gave to the speakeasies and the urbanites who defied Prohibition, it is widely believed that the Eighteenth Amendment led to an increase in drinking. However, sociologist Joseph R. Gustfield argues that total consumption of alcohol declined during Prohibition.

It would be fair to say . . . that Prohibition did affect drinking behavior. . . . The total consumption of alcohol did drop. Even after the upsurge following the initial effects of the act, it still remained well below the rates of consumption in the pre-Prohibition years. It is also the case, however, that hard drinking was apparently substituted to some degree for beer, especially in those urban groups that represented high-income levels. Its greatest impact in eradicating drink was thus on the working classes, and, paradoxically, coinciding as it did with the shift of morals in the general prosperity of the 1920's, it may well have increased the hard and excessive drinking among precisely those groups that had in the past been pace-setters and style-setters. As may often happen, Prohibition was least effective in curtailing the drinking among precisely those groups that were most clearly visible to the mass media of communication.

Joseph R. Gustfield, "Prohibition: The Impact of Political Utopianism," in *Change and Continuity in Twentieth-Century America: The 1920s*, eds. John Braeman, Robert H. Bremner, and David Brody. Columbus: Ohio State University Press, 1968.

in the new urban era. Drinking woman was her own person, liberated yet compassionate, firm-minded, yet ready to yield to the proper stimulation. She knew, as though intuitively, the symbolism of intimacy and of intimate experience which could be carried with the raised glass. Thus Drinking American was warm, friendly, convivial, physically attractive, distinctively upper-middle or upper-class in taste, demeanor, and comportment.

In an easy passage, advertising values became movie values. Achievements in romantic love became the most common Hollywood theme; gangsters and cowboy heroes found individual, rather than social, fulfillment; the immediate gratification of wants became stylish and fashionable. In the plotlines of the 1930s, it was usually the clowns and fools and villains who got drunk—or who did not drink at all. For the good people, drinking was the symbolic action suggesting sexuality, a finely sharpened identity, a cool sophistication. But even more significantly, the movie star cults were becoming lifestyle cults. Around stars such as James Cagney, Clark Gable, Tyrone Power, Greta Garbo, Jean Harlow, Mae West, and Humphrey Bogart this cultism carried the potential of a new and startling institution: People could *learn* a lifestyle—not at home or at church, but at the movies. This was becoming a revolution of extraordinary dimensions.

Women learned from Garbo how to embrace, how to express sexual anguish, how to dress, how to drink, and how to smoke. From Mae West they learned smartly and wittily how to defy convention. The Reverend John J. Cantwell, Catholic Bishop of Los Angeles, expressed a militant dismay when he saw that "talking pictures" could actually "teach" a "philosophy" which could undermine "the sanctity of the home." Hollywood's response to the Legion of Decency was the Production Code for purity, which may have kept Greta Garbo and Mae West out of some movie-set bedrooms but which also may have encouraged the directors of their films to invest their styles of taking a drink or of holding a cigarette with an even more unnerving symbolism. Women imitated their movements, their gestures, their aura of liberation and individual freedom.

And so with the masculine heroes, Gable, Power, Bogart—one cannot imagine them *not* drinking. They drank convivially, in pleasant cocktail lounges or at elegant cocktail parties where one might escape from the urban-industrial world of anxiety and high personal tension. Or they drank in barrooms, hardly distinct from old-time saloons, where the overtones of sexuality could reveal the constantly libidinous core of American drinking. Or they drank alone, reflectively calm and quiet, using alcohol in carefully measured applications to the raw edges of their many spiritual wounds. For the Bogart character, especially, life was serious and the kicks were hard. A man suffered, and he surely *deserved* his honest indulgences. He need not apologize. He drank like a man who had earned it; he smoked like a man who had found in the smoke some critical expression of his manhood. When the ultimate moral question before many people in the new society was what kind of person they should be, the Bogart model of a *drinking and smoking person* was enormously attractive to serious people kicked around by life—of whom there were many. Movies of the 1930s were, of course, profuse and diverse, and there were many other models—few of them, however, with the stamp of serious artistic conception. Hopalong Cassidy, the western hero, did not drink; nor did Judge Hardy. And when actor Lewis Stone played this part in the Andy Hardy movies he found that his characterization as a stern and sober WASP knight was so fixed in the popular mind that he could not in comfort drink in public, even while dining out as a private citizen. . . .

Remaining Restraints on Liquor After Prohibition

With repeal, the federal government gave up most of its prohibitions, though there was surely a strong element of control in heavy federal taxation. Some states abandoned all their liquor laws in 1933 and accepted liquor "wildcatting" and the consequent drink storms, at least for a while. Others restricted the hours of sale and through other codes attempted to prevent the new drinking establishments from assuming the character of the old-time saloon. Still others authorized state dispensaries to separate the liquor traffic from the profit motive and from competition. Some let in beer and wine but not hard booze. Some reverted to the earlier patterns of local option. In most cases the idea was that in preventing the resuscitation of the saloon, states could prevent public drunkenness, and thus society would have solved its problem. Of course, *individuals* might thereafter have problems, but these were surely a matter for the concern of social agencies, not state legislatures. Even when the frequency and the nature of drunken accidents on the highways took an increasingly bloody toll, most states were extremely relectant to impose liquor laws which might encourage the bootlegging that would then suggest that they had not "learned" from Prohibition.

The dominant view then was that Prohibition had been simply foolish from beginning to end. Problems of morbid drinking, in this view, were like problems of gambling and prostitution—the "moral by-products," not the root causes, of poverty and social inequity. Thus, by concentrating a scientific attack upon poverty and social inequity, reformers assumed they could cure crime and drunkenness without having to contaminate themselves in the moralism of the older generation. The results were not convincing.

Chapter 3

A New American Culture

Turning|Points
IN WORLD HISTORY

The Changing Values of a New Generation

Gilman M. Ostrander

Before World War I many American intellectuals had begun to feel at odds with their society. Finding America provincial and philistine (anti-intellectual), they looked to Europe for their inspiration. Charles Darwin's theory of evolution and Sigmund Freud's theories of human psychology deeply affected their thinking. Some of the most influential American writers, including the novelist Ernest Hemingway and the poets Ezra Pound and T.S. Eliot, lived abroad for most of the 1920s. The avant-garde writer Gertrude Stein, another American expatriate, called these young writers in exile the "lost generation."

At the same time, as later observers were to notice, back at home in America a revolution in everyday life was taking place. Millions of ordinary young Americans were taking it as their right to behave with a personal freedom that would have been unthinkable only a few years earlier. The sexual double standard, which had prevailed prior to World War I, was ignored. In this article historian Gilman M. Ostrander shows how the new leisure, new tools (automobiles and telephones), and new toys (movies and radio) available to the average American brought urban values to small-town America.

By the outset of the twenties the revolution in morals was already virtually complete so far as many American intellectuals were concerned. . . .

Though it was the "lost generation" of intellectuals who made articulate the repudiation of the old moral order, it was

Gilman M. Ostrander, "The Revolution in Morals," *Change and Continuity in Twentieth-Century America: The 1920's*, edited by John Braeman, Robert H. Bremner, and David Brody. Columbus: Ohio State University Press, 1968. Copyright © 1968 by the Ohio State University Press. All rights reserved. Reproduced by permission.

their despised Philistine America that gave body to the new concepts in the age of the flapper. The younger generation had already started on its way to freedom before the war, although it was by no means as far along in revolt as were the intellectuals. The most evident symptom was the much-discussed "dance craze," for ragtime was in vogue in the northern cities even before the wartime closing of the New Orleans brothels sent jazz musicians on their way to Chicago and New York. In 1911 Irving Berlin had written "Alexander's Ragtime Band," the waltz had suddenly faded in popularity, and the dance craze was on. There were the Fox Trot, the Horse Trot, the Grizzly Bear, and many others. One girl, according to a popular song of 1912, declared that "mother said I shouldn't dare/To try and do the grizzly bear," but girls nevertheless did try to do it. Of these new dances, the Bunny Hug was singled out by critics for special censure.

Young women were already divesting themselves of some of the clothing their parents had worn. Skirts rose from the ground to the ankle, and some undergarments were shucked off altogether. The president of the New York Cotton Exchange announced in 1912 that these changes in dress had "reduced consumption of cotton fabrics by at least twelve yards of finished goods for each adult female inhabitant." By 1915 the evolution of the new American woman had advanced sufficiently for [American commentator and writer] H.L. Mencken to herald her arrival and bestow upon her the name of flapper.

> Observe, then, this nameless one, this American Flapper. Her skirts have just reached her very trim and pretty ankles; her hair, newly coiled upon her skull, has just exposed the ravishing whiteness of her neck. . . .

> Life, indeed, is almost empty of surprises, mysteries, horrors to this Flapper of 1915. . . . She knows exactly what the Wassermann reaction [a blood test used to diagnose syphilis] is, and has made up her mind that she will never marry a man who can't show an unmistakable negative . . . is inclined to think that there must be something in this new doctrine of free motherhood. She is opposed to the double standard of morality, and favors a law prohibiting it. . . .

Then the war came for America, with its excitement, confusion, social disorientation, and call for service. Several million American men and a good many women went overseas to England and France. Mademoiselle from Armentièrs may not have made a lasting impression on most of them, but the whole violent disruption of their lives had an enduring effect. On the home front, bands played, lovers said good-bye, women went into war work, and everybody knew that everything was different and that life must be led according to new rules. Then, just as all was started, it all stopped. Armistice was declared, the boys came home, and a great deal of adrenalin, which was to have been used up on the enemy, was expended during the next few years domestically.

The Flapper Becomes a Symbol of Postwar Disillusionment

There followed a postwar period of disillusionment that remained a matter for puzzled comment by foreign observers, especially as it was reflected in American literature of the 1920's. Compared to Europe, America had been lightly touched by the war; yet the cynicism arising out of the war and its conclusion seemed to be more deeply felt in America than in the European nations that the war had ravaged. Americans loudly and rudely repudiated the moralistic idealism of the Wilsonian war aims along with the moralistic idealism of Wilsonian progressivism. The fighting war had directly touched relatively few Americans, but the mood that received its classic expression in Hemingway's *A Farewell to Arms* and *The Sun Also Rises* was widely shared. After the war the flapper almost at once made herself the flaming symbol of this cynical spirit.

Within the space of a half-dozen years, women's skirts rose from the ankle to the knee. The number of inches between the hemline and the ankle was rightly taken as the index of the revolutionary change in morals and manners that accompanied and followed the war, and responsible elements in the nation moved to check the revolution by putting women back into their old clothes. Fashion writers warned that the American woman had "lifted her skirts beyond any modest limitation," and they decreed that she should drop them the next year. The YWCA issued a national "Modesty Appeal" and reported that it was getting good results. Bills were introduced in the Utah legislature fixing skirts at three inches above the ankle and in the Virginia legislature fixing necklines to within three inches of the upper part of the throat, but the girls went right ahead with what they were wearing.

Some of them took to smoking publicly and conspicuously, and proprietors of public places, who would have ejected them five years earlier, retreated. Then they were overrunning the speak-easies. The pre-Prohibition saloons had been male sanctuaries where primarily beer had been dispensed. In the speak-easies mixed drinking of mixed drinks was the rule, the women bellying up to the bar with the men, skirts short, stockings rolled below the knees, and corsets sometimes checked at the cloak room. Many young women who did not frequent the speak-easies nevertheless felt obliged to school themselves in social drinking in their own homes and in those of their friends. Drinking, formerly proscribed for middle- and upper-middle-class women, became, under the pressure of Prohibition, socially mandatory in many of those circles.

The girls were petting also, and the "petting question" was anxiously discussed on and on in the ladies' magazines and elsewhere. The rule earlier had been that a nice girl did not allow a man to kiss her unless they were engaged to be married. By the early 1920's the polling of coeds showed that fairly indiscriminate petting was the rule. When it came to the question of extramarital sexual intercourse, fewer of these coeds were inclined to give their unqualified approval, but that question also was much mooted and in a spirit of open-mindedness that was frightening to fathers and mothers.

In sex as in other matters the girls were determined to demolish the double standard. They did not approve of a society in which men were free to wander back and forth across the tracks while women had to choose their side and stay there. In this wish they had been abetted by progressive reformers and later, during the war, by the Navy and War departments, which had fought against the red-light districts. The wartime antivice campaign had been highly successful, and thereafter the era of the roaring red-light district was substantially at an end except in some larger cities and some industrial and mining towns.

The war opened up unprecedented career opportunities to American women, and these opportunities were eagerly taken advantage of. In 1900 about one out of five American women was gainfully employed, but most of these were miserably victimized in sweatshops. Among the better people at that time it had been a matter for sorrow and concern that a girl one knew was reduced in circumstances to the point where she was obliged to take employment as a schoolmistress. The war turned the working girl into a patriot and opened up many opportunities to her, the single most important field being secretarial work. At the war's end women fought with some success to retain these positions and to enter new lines of activity formerly closed to them.

The American housewife was freed for outside activities as never before. The tendency in the twenties was to move to smaller houses or to apartments, and at the time when immigration restriction laws reduced the supply of servants, the much more manageable electrical household appliances took their place. Throughout American history the number-one killer of women had been childbearing. Advocates of birth control, led by Margaret Sanger, had long fought their cause against bitter official and unofficial opposition. Opposition continued throughout the 1920's, but the average size of families declined rapidly during the same period.

That the emancipated women in the 1920's did not know quite where to go with their new freedom was indicated in the styles, which combined short skirts and make-up with bobbed hair and boyish figures. Nevertheless, the flapper was the symbol of the Jazz Age. So far as men were concerned, alterations in morals and manners were in large measure forced upon them by the new relationship they found themselves in with respect to the new American woman.

The flapper as a type was on the way out even before the coming of the depression, giving way to the siren. Mothers had followed the fashions set by their daughters early in the decade. Then in the late 1920's both mother and daughter let their hair grow a little longer and dropped the hemline of their skirts five or six inches below the knee. They did not do this under social pressure, however; by the end of the decade the issues aroused by petting and short skirts had ceased to burn brightly, which is to say that the women had won that battle. . . .

Increased Leisure Time

The American majority was also given the leisure time to enjoy its new opportunities. In the nineteenth century the working day had commonly been from dawn to dusk, six days a week, the seventh day presumably being reserved for rest and prayer. The ten-hour day had been the best that the worker could hope for. In 1890 the average work week was estimated at 60 hours. In 1926 it was estimated at 49.8, and Americans at last had time on their hands. Real wages had risen substantially in the meantime, so Americans had more money in their pockets than ever before.

What would this do to their morals? Employers had long followed the pious practice of keeping wages down for the reason that the added money would simply go down the rum hole. Employers had also always defended long working hours as the only means of keeping the lower classes out of trouble. The 1920's was, among other things, the first experiment in the history of modern civilization, except during periods of depression, in mass leisure.

Perhaps surprisingly, the increased time and money, instead of debauching the working classes, proved an elevating influence, at least by the rum-hole standard. Where the old saloon had been known as the poor man's club, the speakeasy's clientele was drawn to a greater extent from the middle and upper-middle classes; and intoxication, so far as it manifested itself in public, was afflicting "a better class than formerly and a much younger class," according to the chief supervisor of dance halls in San Francisco.

What appears to have been the case is that blue-collar workers, untrained in the art of leisure, spent most of their free time working around the house and yard and listening to the radio with their families. Beyond that, sports provided them with their chief recreation. Fishing and hunting were the two sports in which they themselves participated to any great extent. Otherwise they remained spectators of baseball, football, boxing, and horse racing. They memorized baseball statistics and followed the exploits of Red Grange and Babe Ruth. . . .

The Effect of Technology on Morals

Happily, the new technology created new forms of popular entertainment at the same time that it created the new leisure class. Chief among these were the radio, the phonograph, motion pictures, and the automobile. In 1890 theatergoers in Muncie [Indiana] were limited to the Opera House, where performances were irregular. The theater would be dark for as much as a month at a time. In 1924 Muncie supported nine motion-picture houses, operating daily the year around. The western was the staple at five of the theaters, but movies with sex appeal drew the largest crowds. Patrons were attracted in large numbers to "*Alimony*—Brilliant men, beautiful jazz babies, champagne baths, midnight revels, petting parties in the purple dawn, all ending in one terrific smashing climax that makes you gasp." Others such as *Sinners in Silk*, *Women Who Give*, and *Rouged Lips* similarly tried for gasps. Opinions varied widely as to the influence these movies exerted on their audiences, composed mainly of children and women; but to the extent that they were influential, the direction is evident.

The impact of the automobile upon morals in America was undoubtedly greater than that of the movies and is easier to determine. By the end of 1923 there were two cars for every three families in Muncie, a good many of the car-owners being without bathtubs in their homes. The automobile had replaced the house as the chief status symbol in the community, and car-owners declared themselves willing to go without food or decent clothing rather than give up their automobiles. . . .

There were those who argued that the automobile served

to keep the family together by providing a diversion the whole family could share together. The opposite opinion, however, was the one more frequently expressed. Methods of courtship changed. In the days before the automobile, courtship might very likely consist of a boy and a girl attending a church social and then walking back to the girl's house to sit on the sofa and talk to her parents. What the automobile did, as [the journalist and historian] Frederick Lewis Allen pointed out, was to take that sofa out of the parlor and put it on wheels and move it off into the woods. A judge in Muncie declared that of thirty girls brought before his court during a year for "sex crimes," nineteen had committed their acts in automobiles. And whether it was used for sex purposes or for more conventionally acceptable diversions, the car, and who was going to get to use it, became a major source of family conflict.

[Roman orator] Cicero in the first century B.C. was worried that the younger generation was going to the dogs, and spokesmen for the older generation have frequently been of this opinion since then. A lot was said to that point by members of the older generation in the twenties, and during that decade there was much in what they said. It is no doubt true that every generation rebels to some extent against its elders, and it is also of course true that many young people in the twenties did not. The decade of the 1920's, nevertheless, remains the watershed. . . . The twenties was the decade when there occurred, to some extent in the country as well as the city, the urbanization of American morals.

The "New Feminism" of the 1920s

Lois W. Banner

The 1920s began with the triumphal conclusion of a century of agitation for women's rights: The United States ratified the Nineteenth Amendment to the Constitution, giving women the right to vote. Feminists of the time were dismayed by what happened next: Most of the country declared that women had won all the rights they needed. The younger generation of women—the "flappers" of the 1920s—seemed to agree, using their newfound freedom mainly to remake themselves into pleasant companions to men. Historians have argued ever since about whether the 1920s was a time of progress or regression for women in America. The following selection by Lois W. Banner describes the conflicts between the pre–World War I feminism and the "new feminism" that developed in the 1920s. Feminist historian Banner was one of the first academic historians to focus on women's history. Her books, *Women in Modern America: A Brief History* and *Elizabeth Cady Stanton: A Radical for Women's Rights*, are used in many college classes. Her other books include *American Beauty* and *Finding Fran: History and Memory in the Lives of Two Women*. She is a professor of history and gender studies at the University of Southern California.

Americans in the 1920s were tired of reform causes and dazzled by seeming prosperity and mass-produced consumer goods: automobiles, radios, and, for women in particular, washing machines, vacuum cleaners, and electric kitchens. What need was there for social service when industry was apparently fulfilling its promise of providing material prosperity to all Americans? What concerned Americans—at least of the middle class—were their cars, the availability of illicit liquor, the opportunities for stock-market and land speculation, the radio serials and the latest movies, the exploits of sports stars and cultural heroes, and the pursuit of beauty and youth. The women's clubs, which turned from social service to bridge, were indicative of the general mood of the middle class. Vida Scudder, a Wellesley College professor active in Boston settlements and in the Women's Trade Union League, concluded that "those ten exhausted years [the 1920s] were the worst I have ever known."

Antifeminism Disguised as New Feminism

By the mid-1920s, it had become a matter of belief—proclaimed by press and radio, businessmen, and politicians—that women had in fact achieved liberation. Suffrage had been won. The number of women's organizations had not diminished. Women had been employed in large numbers during the First World War in positions of responsibility; they had become men's comrades in the office and factory, or so it seemed. Legions of Vasser and Smith graduates descended on New York City every year to become secretaries, copy editors, and management trainees in department stores. Women were smoking in public, wearing short skirts, and demanding and gaining entry into saloons, speakeasies, men's clubs, and golf courses. Female sports stars, like Helen Wills in tennis and Gertrude Ederle in swimming, were challenging any remaining notions that women could not excel in athletics. And sports promoters were promoting them as vigorously as male athletes. Even Suzanne LaFollette, author of one of the few militant feminist treatises of the decade [*Concerning Women*], wrote in 1926 that the woman's struggle "is very largely won."

The premise that women had achieved liberation gave rise to a new antifeminism, although it was never stated as such. In essence, it involved the creation of a new female image—certainly a more modern one than before, but no less a stereotype and still based on traditional female functions. It was subtle in argument and compelling to a generation tired of reform causes and intent on enjoying itself. By the late 1920s, numerous articles appeared in popular journals contending that in gaining their "rights," women had given up their "privileges." What these privileges amounted to in this literature were self-indulgence, leisure, and freedom from working. The new antifeminists did not openly question women's right to work. They simply made it clear that they did not think women were capable of combining marriage and career. Women's world in the home was pictured as exotic and self-gratifying. One representative writer [Elizabeth Onatavia] contended that working women simply did not have the strange and delightful experience of taking "an hour to dress," of "spending the day strictly feminine pursuits," of "actually making the kind of cake that [now] comes from the bakery."

The proponents of this new antifeminism not only borrowed the rhetoric of the prewar feminists but claimed that they were the real feminists of the 1920s. [As Onatavia wrote] "It [the return to the home] is going to be almost as long and hard a struggle . . . as the struggle for women's rights." Prewar feminists were attacked as unfeminine and asexual. In 1927, writer Dorothy Dunbar Bromley defined a "new-style feminist" who bore no relationship to "the old school of fighting feminists who wore flat heels and had very little feminine charm, or the current species who antagonize men with their constant clamor about maiden names, equal rights, women's place in the world." The new-style feminist was well-dressed, admitted that she liked men, did not care for women in groups, and [according to Bromley] was convinced that "a full life calls for marriage and children as well as a career," with the stress on the former.

Other molders of public opinion spread the message far and wide. Advertising, which doubled in volume in the 1920s, found its major market in women, who spent the bulk of the family income. To sell dishwashers, refrigerators, and cleaning products, advertisers pictured the woman as the model consumer, whose existence was devoted to the improvement of family life through the purchase of new products. As the clothing and cosmetic industries began their phenomenal growth in the 1920s (a growth that was largely a product of advertising), women were shown as beings for whom fashion, beauty, and sex appeal were the most important concerns in life.

Influence of the New Psychology

New writings on the nature of women's sexuality drove the message home. Before the First World War, a few bold feminists and doctors had suggested that women could enjoy sex; now marriage manuals advocating sexual pleasure for women and spelling out erotic techniques were readily available. Their message was underlined by the scientific theories of Sigmund Freud, who had argued as early as the 1890s that unconscious drives, and especially sex, were central forces in human behavior. A small numbers of doctors and Greenwich Village intellectuals had known of Freud's work before the war, but it was not until the 1920s—an age preoccupied with the notion of pleasure—the Freudian theories became popular. Yet Freud's ideas were as confining for women as they were liberating. Although Freud gave the final scientific refutation to the old belief that sex was an unpleasant duty for women, he also argued that the crucial factor in female personality formation was the female child's envy for the male sex organ—an envy that produced a lifelong dissatisfaction with being a woman. The only way to overcome this discontent, according to Freud, was through motherhood.

However, the influence of Freudian theories in the 1920s must not be overemphasized. In the later years of the decade, the behaviorist ideas of John B. Watson were in vogue. Watson played down the importance of suppressed drives as factors controlling human actions and stressed that the individual could control his or her behavior through will power. His message to women was nonetheless ambiguous. In his *Psychological Care of Infant and Child* (1928), the standard reference on childrearing for a decade or more, Watson argued that most women were failures as mothers and that they should decide either not to have children or to realize that childrearing was such a complex skill that it required extensive training and complete dedication. Unlike Freud, Watson did not view motherhood as the natural role for all women, but his prescriptions for childrearing, which centered around the conscious withholding of parental affection and the establishment of fixed schedules of activity for the child in order to nurture self-reliance, placed heavy demands on mothers who wanted to work outside the home.

Yet the theories of Freud and Watson were secondary to the fact that the notion of the pleasures of sexuality permeated the culture. Women's magazines were full of it. The films and the radio made it a stock device. Sex-story magazines like *True Confessions* exploited it and quadrupled their sales. Mabel Dodge Luhan, whose psychoanalysis in 1915 set the example for many of her wealthy and intellectual friends, laid clear the ultimate meaning of the new ideas about sexuality. "The sex act," she wrote, is "the cornerstone of any life, and its chief reality," especially for women. "It is indeed the happy woman who has no history," because she has lived for erotic gratification, for her husband or lover, and for her children. . . .

New Liberties, Old Attitudes

Feminism also failed to take root in the 1920s largely because it did not appeal to the young women of that generation. No movement can prosper long without attracting younger members to its rank. In 1910, the suffrage campaign had been reactivated by a group of younger women, including Alice Paul and Rheta Childe Dorr. However, this was not true of the feminist cause in the 1920s—indeed, not until the 1960s.

Rarely before or since the 1920s has a generation of youths been so conscious of its own identity or of its perceived difference from an older generation. Their attitude was cavalier to the concerns and achievements of their elders, including the hard-won gains in women's rights. Lillian Hellman, playwright and member of this generation, has described their feelings:

> By the time I grew up the fight for the emancipation of women, their rights under the law, in the office, in bed, was

stale stuff. My generation didn't think much about the place or the problems of women, were not conscious that the designs we saw around us had so recently been formed or that we were still part of that formation.

Young people had other preoccupations. Foremost was their rebellion against the mores of Victorian culture, especially its sex taboos. They set the tone of the 1920s. They were the leaders in fashion, in dance, in the introduction of the freer morality. Young women were "flappers," and they lived for fun and freedom, which they defined in terms of short skirts, cigarettes, automobiles, dancing, sports, and speakeasies. Young, middle-class women began to adopt behavior already observable among the working class before the war as their percentage of the college population and the general attendance in high school rose rapidly.

In the 1920s, artist John Held, Jr., captured the "flapper" for *The New Yorker* magazine in a series of drawings that were widely reprinted. Like the Gibson girl of the 1890s, Held's flapper became the symbol of her generation. With her short, straight skirt, her lean torso and her cropped hair, the rouge on her cheeks and the cigarette in her mouth, she was the epitome of youth, adventure, and healthy sex.

To what extent such behavior constituted a true sexual revolution is debatable. Some rudimentary surveys of sex attitudes were attempted during the 1920s, but what they pointed to was a limited, rather than an extensive, change in behavior. Among her sample of about 2,000 older, middle-class women, Katherine B. Davis found that 7 percent of the married women and 14 percent of the unmarried women had had sexual relations before marriage. Among the latter group, 80 percent saw no justification for pre-marital sex. In Denver, Judge Ben Lindsey, whose work among teen-agers through the Juvenile Court there gained him a national reputation, judged that before the war, young men in sizable numbers commonly had had sexual relations with prostitutes; after the war, however, their schoolmates were their sexual partners—a change produced by the vice commission's success in breaking up the red-light districts, by the war experience, and by the new permissiveness among young women. Yet Lindsey was reluctant to estimate that more than 10 percent of Denver's young women were permissive when it came to sex. Indeed, surveys of the incidence of premarital sex among college students in the 1930s indicated that no more than 25 percent of all women students engaged in sex before marriage. . . .

Women at Work: Progress and Setbacks

The popular evidence of women's emancipation in the 1920s—the number of women at work, the freer sexuality, the new clothing styles—masked the discrimination against women that still existed. At the height of women's employment during the First World War, for example, only 5 percent of all women workers had not been in the labor force before the war. What seemed to reflect new employment actually reflected the fact that women who were already members of the work force were promoted to higher-paying, higher-skilled jobs during the war. In some cases, this meant a permanent transfer into clerical work. In other cases, women who had replaced men were demoted or fired when the war ended. In Cleveland, Ohio, the women who became streetcar operators were cultural heroines for a time but were laid off when returning male operators went on strike against the women's continued employment. In some industries, like automobiles or iron and steel, women had registered permanent gains by 1920. But according to Women's Bureau analysts, the opening of some new industries to women and the advancement of a few women to skilled positions were offset by the wage discrimination that existed in every category of women's employment.

Similarly, the common assumption that the proportion of women who worked increased during the 1920s is fallacious. It is true that an additional 2 million women had jobs, but this was primarily a reflection of the general population growth. In fact, whereas 23 percent of American women were employed in 1920, 24 percent were employed in 1930—an increase of only 1 percent. This stability in employment figures was partly due to the fact that the immigration restriction acts of the early 1920s cut off the flow of Eastern European families into the nation.

Furthermore, with the exception of their movement into clerical work, women did not substantially improve their position in the labor force in the 1920s. Although the number of women increased in most professions, women still held jobs that were less prestigious and lower-paying than men did. For example, although women received about one-third of the graduate degrees awarded annually, only 4 percent of the full professors in American colleges were women. Few colleges would promote women beyond the lower ranks: Mary Ellen Chase, novelist and distinguished scholar of English literature, left the University of Minnesota in 1926 for Smith College, because it was clear that Minnesota would not promote a woman beyond assistant professor. Smith, however, preserved enough of its feminist origins to deal more fairly with its female faculty.

In medicine, the proportion of women to men actually declined. Dr. Alice Hamilton thought that it had been easier for a woman to become a doctor earlier in the century, when feminism was still a powerful force and [wrote that] "a woman doctor could count on the loyalty of a group of devoted feminists who would choose a woman [doctor] because she was a woman." Few medical or law schools refused admission to women, but most applied quotas on female admission. (Until 1945, the quota was about 5 percent.) Most women lawyers and doctors continued to perform the less lucrative and challenging services in their fields or to minister principally to women and children. The few women who were dentists were primarily children's orthodontists, but they predominated in that lucrative field only temporarily; by the 1950s, most children's orthodontists were men.

Even the expanding fields of business administration and advertising offered limited opportunities for women aside from clerical work. Female Horatio Algers [character in a story symbolizing the values of hard work in achieving success], it is true, could always be found to bolster the nation's success mythology and its belief that feminism had achieved its goals. Often, these businesswomen made their money by marketing products designed for women. Industries like fashion and retailing have always been open to determined career women. And during these years, shrewd female entrepreneurs recognized the immense potential of the market created by the new sex consciousness. Helena Rubinstein, who parlayed her mother's home beauty cream into a gigantic cosmetics empire, was only of a number of such women. Another was her competitor, Elizabeth Arden.

Making their way in the masculine world of business was not easy. M. Louise Luckinbill, a secretary at the Schultz-McGregor Advertising Agency in New York City, declined a promotion to a vice presidency. Businessmen, she wrote, "would throw up their hands in horror at the idea of a woman being . . . vice-president of an [advertising] agency which served them." Edith Mae Cummings, who built her job as an insurance saleswoman into a firm of her own, contended that any woman could succeed in business through self-reliance and perseverance. Yet, she admitted, businessmen were hostile to businesswomen because they were afraid that women so employed would lose their "feminine daintiness." Helena Rubinstein recalled, "It was not easy being a hard-working woman in a man's world." To survive in the business world, she became a tyrant. Her rages were legendary. She married a count, lived in lavish style, and was known as "madame." For "added courage," she wore elaborate and expensive jewelry. To Rubinstein, the quest for beauty, which was central to her business and her life, did not represent enslavement, but was a "force . . . to make you feel greater than you are."

Writers and Artists

In keeping with women's continuing professional participation in the 1920s, women writers and artists appeared in greater numbers and received more and more critical acclaim. In the late nineteenth century, Emily Dickinson and Edith Wharton developed complex personal styles, initiating a trend away from the sentimentalism that characterized the writings of Harriet Beecher Stowe and the scores of best-selling women authors who dominated popular fiction in that century. In the 1920s, poet Edna St. Vincent Millay, with her candle burning "at both ends," became the symbol of the nihilism and emancipated life style that characterized writers in those years. Willa Cather continued her distinguished career as a writer of frontier fiction and a critic of the technological society. Dorothy Parker dominated the New York intellectuals and wits who gathered at the famed "round table" at the Algonquin Hotel. Gertrude Stein's Parisian salon was a center for important American artists abroad. Jessie Fauset and Zora Neale Hurston were central figures within the Harlem Renaissance—the outpouring of black writings that established blacks' claim to a powerful literary imagination.

Yet for most women artists and authors, difficulties still existed. In the 1920s, for example, painter Georgia O'Keeffe began her distinguished career, which has spawned the last seven decades. But gaining recognition was not easy. Her friendship with Alfred Stieglitz, the famed photographer and promoter of new talent, was initially important in securing New York shows for her and in attracting the critics' attention. Even then, her work was judged more in terms of her sex than her artistic ability. Her huge canvases filled with enormous, surrealistic flowers confounded critics; the paintings violated the canons that women were expected to do small and fragile works of art and that flowers were particularly appropriate subjects for them. O'Keeffe's flowers were deemed expressions of a female "eroticism" and of woman's greater "emotionality."

O'Keeffe's work would eventually receive universal acclaim, but artists in other fields were not so fortunate. Major symphony orchestras contained virtually no women musicians (despite a lengthy tradition that identified amateur music with women), and the field of conducting was especially closed to them. When conductor Antonia Brico returned to the United States in the 1930s after an acclaimed European debut, few orchestras were willing to engage her; ultimately, she founded her own orchestra of women players. What woman, it was said, possessed either the authority or the musicianship to mold 80 or more instrumentalists into an effective ensemble?

The Impact of Black Migration on American Culture

Gerald Early

During the 1920s millions of African Americans fled discrimination and sought jobs in a great migration from rural to urban areas and from south to north. The change turned the typical African American from a southern sharecropper into a city dweller, exposed both to the city's problems and to its opportunities for collective action. By bringing blacks together in the cities, where political organization was easier, the migration set the stage for the great civil rights battles of the twentieth century. It also helped to create a distinct African American culture that exerted a powerful influence on the mainstream culture of the United States. During the 1920s the two most visible channels for this influence were the Harlem Renaissance—a flowering of African American arts and letters that attracted the attention of sympathetic whites—and jazz, the music that quickly spread across the world as the authentic sound of modern America. Gerald Early is the Merle King Professor of Modern Letters at Washington University in St. Louis, Missouri. He is the author and editor of many books on cultural history, including *The Culture of Bruising: Essays on Literature, Prizefighting and Modern American Culture* and *Lure and Loathing: Essays on Race, Identity, and Ambivalence of Assimilation.*

In his essay *The New Negro*, which appeared in the seminal anthology of the same name that he edited in 1925, Howard [University] philosophy professor Alain Locke wrote about the changing nature and attitude of African-Americans since the early days of the 20th century. "A main change has been, of course," explained Locke, "that shifting of the Negro population which has made the Negro problem no longer exclusively or even predominantly Southern." For Locke, this was the main difference between the "Old Negro" and the "New Negro." The Old Negro was southern, rural, agricultural, tied to the past and to a feudal order of white political control and racist stereotype. The "New Negro," totally a result of a migration that had been occurring for the last 10 or so years before Locke wrote his essay, was northern, urban, industrial, freed from his past, more militant and assertive. The Harlem Renaissance—a complex set of political, cultural, and artistic movements involving a variety of blacks from Marcus Garvey and A. Philip Randolph to Charles S. Johnson and Jessie Fauset, black organizations from the Universal Negro Improvement Association to the Urban League, from the National Association for the Advancement of Colored People to the African Blood Brotherhood that centered mostly in New York in the 1920s and early 1930s—was built not only on the fact, but the mythical significance, of black migration in the United States. So important had this migration become that it changed the way black people saw themselves and their future as Americans. The mythical significance of this migration had even penetrated white popular culture; in 1926, Freeman Gosden and Charles Correll, two white men, started a radio program called *Sam 'n Henry* about two black men who had left the rural South to seek a better life in a northern city. By 1929, the show became *Amos 'n Andy*, one of the most popular radio programs of all time.

The First World War Creates Job Opportunities

The most immediate cause of this migration from the South was the First World War, which shut off the flow of cheap European immigrant labor in 1914. By 1915, with war production in full swing in the United States, the need for industrial workers was acute. Two unexpected and heretofore unwanted sources were tapped—white women and black southerners. Recruiting agents representing various northern industrial concerns went south to lure African-Americans north. White southerners did not greet them with open arms, and some, if they were discovered, were run out of town. The *Chicago Defender*, the most widely read black newspaper in the South, urged southern blacks to come north by publishing letters from newly transplanted blacks saying that life was better in the North, and by writing editorials that praised the North and condemned the South. When the United States entered the war in 1916, the labor shortage became even more severe, and the demand for black workers escalated. Work in northern industry paid more than agricultural work. Men could earn up to $2.50 a day in a Chicago meat packinghouse, or as much as $5.00 a day on an assembly line in the auto factories of Detroit. These rates of pay far exceeded anything African-Americans could make in the South. Even black women could make $2.00 a day as domestics in a northern city—as much as twice or more as doing the same work in the South. Despite the fact that the cost of living in northern cities was higher than in the South, blacks felt that the higher salaries more than compensated for the difference. What intensified the economic pull of the North was the fact that the South had been enduring some terrible growing seasons in the early 1910s, with severe blights caused by boll weevils and major crop damage caused by flooding. Also, the price of cotton had dropped sharply on the world market in the 1910s.

Resurgence of the KKK Adds to Pressures to Leave the South

Seemingly, the North also offered greater opportunities and more freedom. The North offered fewer racial restrictions because Jim Crow [laws restricting the integration of the races] was less blatant, and legalized segregation not nearly so widely enforced. Moreover, in the North there were far fewer lynchings, a form of ritualized violence in the South that helped whites maintain social and political control through overt terrorism that reached its zenith in the 1890s, but was still practiced often enough in the 1910s for national black leadership to call for a federal anti-lynching bill. The resurgence of the Ku Klux Klan after the release of D.W.

Griffith's immensely popular and artistically acclaimed *The Birth of a Nation* in 1915—an epic Civil War film that portrayed the Klan as heroic, and particularly after World War I—surely had to intensify the miasma of fear, loathing, and impending violence that permeated the South, and gave blacks more reason to leave. (During this period of resurgence, the Klan was enjoying its greatest growth in the Middle West.) Blacks were commonly run off their land in the South through both legal and extra-legal means called "white-capping." They were often robbed of their wages, in debt to the plantation store, denied equal access to a decent public education despite the fact that they paid taxes, ac-

---

The Threat of Jazz

The new music called jazz became popular with young people in the 1920s. However, many older people in the mainstream culture felt threatened by jazz's African American roots.

Jazz was greeted with disdain and dark suspicion by the guardians of culture, who objected especially to its connection with the racial "other." "Mezz" Mezzrow, an early Chicago jazzman, put it bluntly, "Our music was called 'nigger music' and 'whorehouse music' and 'nice' people turned up their noses at it." As early as 1917, the *Literary Digest* condensed a report from the New York *Sun* by vaudeville writer Walter Kingley, on this "strange" new word that had entered the American vocabulary:

> In the old plantation days, when the slaves were having one of their rare holidays and the fun languished, some West-Coast African would cry out, "Jaz her up," and this would be the cue for fast and furious fun. No doubt the witch-doctors and medicine-men on the Kongo used the same term at those jungle "parties" when the tomtoms throbbed and the sturdy warriors gave their pep an added kick with rich brew of Yohimbin bark. . . . Jazz music is the delerium tremens of syncopation.

Michele Hilmes, *Radio Voices: American Broadcasting, 1922–1952*. Minneapolis: University of Minnesota Press, 1997.

cording to their income, at the same rate as whites. They were also more likely to be imprisoned for petty crimes than whites, where, through the convict-lease system, they could be used as an uncompensated labor force.

But all of this, by itself, may not have been sufficient to induce the level of migration that occurred between 1915 and 1930. It must be remembered, after all, that there was also terrible racial violence in the North. Indeed, some of the worst racial violence in America occurred in places like East St. Louis in 1917 and Chicago in 1919, industrial cities that African-Americans had migrated to. Indeed, the summer of 1919 saw some of the worst racial violence in American history, and most of it was not in the South. Blacks were largely confined to certain sections of these cities where they lived in chronic poverty, overcrowded, unhealthy conditions, and with less access to public services. Although blacks received better health care in the North than in the South, they sustained mortality rates that were far higher than for any other group. So the North was not as much of a lure, after first blush, for many blacks as some might think, although in some respects it was clearly an improvement. Locke, in his essay, argued, "The wash and rush of this human tide on the beach line of the Northern city centers is to be explained primarily in terms of a new vision of opportunity, of social and economic freedom, of a spirit to seize, even in the face of an extortionate and heavy toll, a chance for the improvement of conditions. With each successive wave of it, the movement of the Negro becomes more and more a mass movement toward the larger and the more democratic chance—in the Negro's case a deliberate flight not only from countryside to city, but from medieval America to modern."

Whatever the welter of reasons, blacks left the South in large numbers. Between a half-million and a million southern blacks came north between 1914 and 1919, and another million between 1920 and 1930. New York's black population grew from 91,709 in 1910 to 152,467 by 1920, and to 328,000 by 1930. Chicago's jumped from 44,103 to 109,458 by 1920 and to 234,000 by 1930. St. Louis's black population increased from 45,000 in 1910 to 94,000 in 1930. Cleveland's went from 8,500 in 1910 to 72,000 in 1930. Detroit's skyrocketed over 600 percent during the war years and another 200 percent during the 1920s. Philadelphia's went from 84,500 in 1910 to 220,600 in 1930.

A Complex Movement

But black migration must be understood as a more complex move than simply blacks going from the South to the North. The majority of black people still lived in the South in the 1930s. The predominant pattern was for blacks to move from rural to urban, and so many, during these years, left the countryside for the southern cities. Some, like author Richard Wright, went on from places like Memphis, where he had migrated from Mississippi, to Chicago; others did not. This pattern of moving from rural to urban fit the general pattern of population shift for the United States as a whole, as whites, from the Progressive Era onward, were leaving the country and agriculture for more urban settings.

It must also be remembered that this migration of 1915 to 1930 was not the first important migration of African-Americans since the end of the Civil War. When Reconstruction [the period after the Civil War] ended, many southern blacks—thousands of them, called Exodusters—left the South and migrated to all-black towns in the Middle West, particularly Kansas and Oklahoma. This was a rural-to-rural shift, and did not involve nearly as many people but significant in many ways nonetheless, revealing that blacks were, even then, looking for the main chance and were in a constant quest to improve their situation, as many people were, by moving somewhere else. Clearly, a concern about black migration from the South was present in the 1890s, several years before the migration started. Otherwise, Booker T. Washington, founder of Tuskegee Institute in 1881, and the most powerful black leader of the 1890s and early 1900s, would not have found it necessary to reassure his white audience in his famous Atlanta Exposition speech of 1895 that blacks were southerners, that they wished to remain in the South, and that they saw the South as the place that gave them the best chance for group success.

The Great Migration in Literature

Migration of all sorts has been a major theme in black literature. The slave narratives, written by fugitive slaves between 1830 and 1860, were all about the movement South to North, or from slavery to freedom. Among other things, they could all be considered migration narratives. This is because American geography had such obvious political implications for blacks since the early 1800s when the North abandoned slavery.

In the years after the Civil War, migration is an important theme in a range of literature, from James Weldon Johnson's *The Autobiography of an Ex-Colored Man* to Ralph Ellison's *Invisible Man*, from Richard Wright's *Black Boy*, and to a lesser extent, *Native Son*, to William Attaway's *Blood on the Forge*, from James Baldwin's *Go Tell It on the Mountain* to Toni Morrison's *Paradise*. The geographical movement of black characters and its sociological, psychological, and political implications is probably one of the most persistent themes in all of black literature, and is hardly surprising for a group of people for whom a major form of their persecution for a good deal of their history was their inability to move freely in a country that valued mobility almost as an inalienable right.

The Impact on Jazz

The shift in black population between 1915 and 1930 certainly had a major impact on the development of jazz. First, jazz was largely an urban music to begin with. It required access to machine-made instruments, some network of organization for musical instruction, and places where people could go and hear this music. The spread of blacks to other cities simply intensified the spread of the music. The increase in black income as blacks became more urban meant that blacks could afford to buy records and phonographs. It should come as no surprise that race records—that is, records made by blacks for a black audience—came into their own as an industry category in the 1920s, when the migration was at its height.

The urbanization of blacks also meant a greater level of

sophistication and cultural exposure that would further expand not only the audience for jazz, but the development of
jazz itself as black musicians became more knowledgeable
about music, about art in general, and more self-aware about
what they were doing as musicians. Cultural trends and innovations in the United States are started in the major
cities—not, generally, in small towns or rural areas. Cities,
after all, among other things, exist to produce culture. In this
sense, when Louis Armstrong, jazz's first genius, migrated to
Chicago in 1922, it might be said that jazz as a modern
music, jazz as a modernist art, was born. It is almost impossible to think that jazz would have become the rage (or
scourge, depending on one's point of view at the time) of the
nation had this black migration, within the larger population
shift of the United States itself, not taken place.

Greenwich Village Challenged Old Ideas

Malcolm Cowley

Due to its cheap rents and central location, the New York City neighborhood of Greenwich Village had been a magnet for hopeful artists since the late 1800s. By the 1920s it was already widely regarded, with a mixture of envy and resentment, as the place where writers, radicals, painters, and poets defied the standards of middle-class society. The villagers were the nation's "bohemians" (as American journalists liked to call nonconformist artists, referring to the down-and-out painters, poets, and musicians described in the nineteenth-century French novel by Henri Murger *Scènes de la vie de Bohème*). American writers and artists, for their part, felt embattled as they struggled to find a voice in a country whose heroes were business leaders and sports figures. Many of them sought exile, first in Greenwich Village, and later in Europe. In this excerpt from *Exile's Return*, a memoir of the 1920s literary scene, literary critic Malcolm Cowley makes the point that despite the "war" between Greenwich Village and middle-class America (symbolized by the leading magazine the *Saturday Evening Post*) many of Greenwich Village's values were well suited to the new consumer society, and many trends begun in Greenwich Village were ultimately adopted by the country at large. In the course of a long and varied literary career, Cowley was an editor of the *New Republic*, the chancellor of the American Academy of Arts and Letters, and the author and editor of numerous books of criticism, essays, and poetry.

In those days when division after division was landing in Hoboken and marching up Fifth Avenue in full battle equipment [references to World War I], when Americans were fighting the Bolshies [Bolsheviks] in Siberia and guarding the Rhine—in those still belligerent days that followed the Armistice there was a private war between Greenwich Village and the *Saturday Evening Post.*

Other magazines fought in the same cause, but the *Post* was persistent and powerful enough to be regarded as chief of the aggressor nations. It published stories about the Villagers, editorials and articles against them, grave or flippant serials dealing with their customs in a mood of disparagement or alarm, humorous pieces done to order by its staff writers, cartoons in which the Villagers were depicted as long-haired men and short-haired women with ridiculous bone-rimmed spectacles—in all, a long campaign of invective beginning before the steel strike or the Palmer Raids and continuing through the jazz era, the boom and the depression. The burden of it was always the same: that the Village was the haunt of affectation; that it was inhabited by fools and fakers; that the fakers hid Moscow heresies under the disguise of cubism and free verse; that the fools would eventually be cured of their folly: they would forget this funny business about art and return to domesticity in South Bend, Indiana, and sell motorcars, and in the evenings sit with slippered feet while their children romped about them in paper caps made from the advertising pages of the *Saturday Evening Post.* The Village was dying, had died already, smelled to high heaven and Philadelphia. . . .

The Villagers did not answer this attack directly: instead they carried on a campaign of their own against the culture of which the *Post* seemed to be the final expression. They performed autopsies, they wrote obituaries of civilization in the United States, they shook the standardized dust of the country from their feet. Here, apparently, was a symbolic struggle: on the one side, the great megaphone of middle-class America; on the other, the American disciples of art and artistic living. Here, in its latest incarnation, was the eternal warfare of bohemian against bourgeois, poet against propriety. . . .

The Doctrine of Greenwich Village

Greenwich Village was not only a place, a mood, a way of life: like all bohemias, it was also a doctrine. Since the days of [nineteenth-century French poet and novelist Theophile] Gautier and [nineteenth-century French novelist Henry] Murger, this doctrine had remained the same in spirit, but it had changed in several details. By 1920, it had become a system of ideas that could roughly be summarized as follows:

1. The idea of salvation by the child.—Each of us at birth has special potentialities which are slowly crushed and destroyed by a standardized society and mechanical methods of teaching. If a new educational system can be introduced, one by which children are encouraged to develop their own personalities, to blossom freely like flowers, then the world will be saved by this new, free generation.

2. The idea of self-expression.—Each man's, each woman's, purpose in life is to express himself, to realize his full individuality through creative work and beautiful living in beautiful surroundings.

3. The idea of paganism.—The body is a temple in which there is nothing unclean, a shrine to be adorned for the ritual of love.

4. The idea of living for the moment.—It is stupid to pile up treasures that we can enjoy only in old age, when we have lost the capacity for enjoyment. Better to seize the moment as it comes, to dwell in it intensely, even at the cost of future suffering. Better to live extravagantly, gather June rosebuds, "burn my candle at both ends. . . . It gives a lovely light."

5. The idea of liberty.—Every law, convention or rule of art that prevents self-expression or the full enjoyment of the moment should be shattered and abolished. Puritanism is the great enemy. The crusade against puritanism is the only crusade with which free individuals are justified in allying themselves.

6. The idea of female equality.—Women should be the economic and moral equals of men. They should have the same pay, the same working conditions, the same opportunity for drinking, smoking, taking or dismissing lovers.

7. The idea of psychological adjustment.—We are un-

happy because we are maladjusted, and maladjusted because we are repressed. If our individual repressions can be removed—by confessing them to a Freudian psychologist—then we can adjust ourselves to any situation, and be happy in it. (But Freudianism is only one method of adjustment. What is wrong with us may be our glands, and by a slight operation, or merely by taking a daily dose of thyroid, we may alter our whole personalities. Again, we may adjust ourselves by some such psycho-physical discipline as was taught by Gurdjieff. The implication of all these methods is the same—that the environment itself need not be altered. That explains why most radicals who became converted to psychoanalysis or glands or [the teachings of Russian mystic] Gurdjieff gradually abandoned their political radicalism.)

8. The idea of changing place.—"They do things better in Europe." England and Germany have the wisdom of old cultures; the Latin peoples have admirably preserved their pagan heritage. By expatriating himself, by living in Paris, Capri or the South of France, the artist can break the puritan shackles, drink, live freely and be wholly creative.

All these, from the standpoint of the business-Christian ethic then represented by the *Saturday Evening Post*, were corrupt ideas. This older ethic is familiar to most people, but one feature of it has not been sufficiently emphasized. Substantially, it was a *production* ethic. The great virtues it taught were industry, foresight, thrift and personal initiative. The workman should be industrious in order to produce more for his employer; he should look ahead to the future; he should save money in order to become a capitalist himself; then he should exercise personal initiative and found new factories where other workmen would toil industriously, and save, and become capitalists in their turn.

During the process many people would suffer privations: most workers would live meagerly and wrack their bodies with labor; even the employers would deny themselves luxuries that they could easily purchase, choosing instead to put back the money into their business; but after all, our bodies were not to be pampered; they were temporary dwelling places, and we should be rewarded in Heaven for our self-denial. On earth, our duty was to accumulate more wealth and produce more goods, the ultimate use of which was no subject for worry. They would somehow be absorbed, by new markets opened in the West, or overseas in new countries, or by the increased purchasing power of workmen who had saved and bettered their position.

Greenwich Village and the Consumption Ethic

That was the ethic of a young capitalism, and it worked admirably, so long as the territory and population of the country were expanding faster than its industrial plant. But after the war the situation changed. Our industries had grown enormously to satisfy a demand that suddenly ceased. To keep the factory wheels turning, a new domestic market had to be created. Industry and thrift were no longer adequate. There must be a new ethic that encouraged people to buy, a *consumption* ethic.

It happened that many of the Greenwich Village ideas proved useful in the altered situation. Thus, *self-expression* and *paganism* encouraged a demand for all sorts of products—modern furniture, beach pajamas, cosmetics, colored bathrooms with toilet paper to match. *Living for the moment* meant buying an automobile, radio or house, using it now and paying for it tomorrow. *Female equality* was capable of doubling the consumption of products—cigarettes, for example—that had formerly been used by men alone. Even *changing place* would help to stimulate business in the country from which the artist was being expatriated. The exiles of art were also trade missionaries: involuntarily they increased the foreign demand for fountain pens, silk stockings, grapefruit and portable typewriters. They drew after them an invading army of tourists, thus swelling the profits of steamship lines and travel agencies. Everything fitted into the business picture.

I don't mean to say that Greenwich Village was the source of the revolution in morals that affected all our lives in the decade after the war, and neither do I mean that big business deliberately plotted to render the nation extravagant, pleasure worshiping and reckless of tomorrow.

The new moral standards arose from conditions that had nothing to do with the Village. They were, as a matter of fact, not really new. Always, even in the great age of the Puritans, there had been currents of licentiousness that were favored by the immoderate American climate and held in check only by hellfire preaching and the hardships of settling a new country. Old Boston, Providence, rural Connecticut, all had their underworlds. The reason puritanism became so strong in America was perhaps that it had to be strong in order to checkmate its enemies. But it was already weakening as the country grew richer in the twenty years before the war; and the war itself was the puritan crisis and defeat.

All standards were relaxed in the stormy-sultry wartime atmosphere. It wasn't only the boys of my age, those serving in the army, who were transformed by events: their sisters and younger brothers were affected in a different fashion. With their fathers away, perhaps, and their mothers making bandages or tea-dancing with lonely officers, it was possible for boys and girls to do what they pleased. For the first time they could go to dances unchaperoned, drive the family car and park it by the roadside while they made love, and come home after midnight, a little tipsy, with nobody to reproach them in the hallway. They took advantage of these stolen liberties—indeed, one might say that the revolution in morals began as a middle-class children's revolt.

But everything conspired to further it. Prohibition came and surrounded the new customs with illicit glamour; prosperity made it possible to practice them; Freudian psychology provided a philosophical justification and made it unfashionable to be repressed; still later the sex magazines and the movies, even the pulpit, would advertise a revolution that had taken place silently and triumphed without a struggle. In all this Greenwich Village had no part. The revolution would have occured if the Village had never existed, but—the point is important—it would not have followed the same course. The Village, older in revolt, gave form to the movement, created its fashions, and supplied the writers and illustrators who would render them popular. As for American business, though it laid no plots in advance, it was quick enough to use the situation, to exploit the new markets for cigarettes and cosmetics, and to realize that, in advertising pages and movie palaces, sex appeal was now the surest appeal.

The Greenwich Village standards, with the help of business, had spread through the country. Young women east and west had bobbed their hair, let it grow and bobbed it again; they had passed through the period when corsets were checked in the cloakroom at dances and the period when corsets were not worn. They were not very self-conscious when they talked about taking a lover; and the conversations ran from mother fixations to birth control while they smoked cigarettes between the courses of luncheons eaten in black-and-orange tea shops just like those in the Village. People of forty had been affected by the younger generation: they spent too much money, drank too much gin, made love to one another's wives and talked about their neuroses. Houses were furnished to look like studios. Stenographers went on parties, following the example of the boss and his girl friend and her husband. The "party," conceived as a gathering together of men and women to drink gin cocktails, flirt, dance to the phonograph or radio and gossip about their absent friends, had in fact become one of the most popular American institutions; nobody stopped to think how short its history had been in this country. It developed out of the "orgies" celebrated by the French 1830 Romantics, but it was introduced into this country by Greenwich Villagers—before being adopted by salesmen from Kokomo and the younger country-club set in Kansas City.

Wherever one turned the Greenwich Village ideas were making their way: even the *Saturday Evening Post* was feeling their influence. Long before Repeal, it began to wobble on Prohibition. It allowed drinking, petting and unfaithfulness to be mentioned in the stories it published; its illustrations showed women smoking. Its advertising columns admitted one after another of the strictly pagan products—cosmetics, toilet tissues, cigarettes—yet still it continued to thunder against Greenwich Village and bohemian immorality. It even nourished the illusion that its long campaign had been successful. On more than one occasion it announced that the

Village was dead and buried: "The sad truth is," it said in the autumn of 1931, "that the Village was a flop." Perhaps it was true that the Village was moribund—of that we can't be sure, for creeds and ways of life among artists are hard to kill. If, however, the Village was really dying, it was dying of success. It was dying because it became so popular that too many people insisted on living there. It was dying because women smoked cigarettes on the streets of the Bronx, drank gin cocktails in Omaha and had perfectly swell parties in Seattle and Middletown—in other words, because American business and the whole of middle-class America had been going Greenwich Village.

Machine-Made Goods Become Fashionable

Gary Dean Best

One of the reasons the 1920s seems familiar to contemporary Americans was that it was the decade during which things began to look "modern." As historian Gary Dean Best explains in this excerpt from *The Dollar Decade: Mammon and the Machine in 1920s America*, the 1920s revolution in design was based on a new aesthetic. In the period before World War I, designers of every product from living room sofas to steel suspension bridges had gone out of their way to hide the fact that their products were machine made. The new aesthetic embraced the evidence of mass production, implicitly glorifying the might and efficiency of the machine. Best is a professor emeritus of history at the University of Hawaii. Best's other works include *The Politics of American Individualism: Herbert Hoover in Transition, 1918–1929* and *The Retreat from Liberalism: Collectivists Versus Progressives in the New Deal Years.*

In their initial quest for novelty after World War I, clothing and fabric manufacturers found inspiration in the museums, borrowing, as one writer described it, from the costumes of "Arab chieftains, Chinese mandarins, guildsmen of medieval Japan, the tribes of the frozen Siberian tundras, the graves of ancient Peru, the ceramics of Mexico, and the Indians of our own plains and woodlands," in the process searching "the art history of the universe in an effort to add distinction to the home furnishings and costumes of America." Symbolic of the new trend in design was a major exhibit in the American Museum of Natural History in late 1919. [According to scholar M.D.C. Crawford] at the exhibition:

A number of the leading representatives of decorative industries and artists combined . . . to show what actually had been accomplished in America. The idea back of the exhibit was twofold: in the first place, to show the general advance in American decorative arts, and secondly the more important . . . concern was to show how these arts had benefited through museum contacts. . . . All these materials were presented in such a manner as to show the correlation between modern production and ancient source of inspiration. . . .

Embracing the Machine

By contrast with this preoccupation with past and distant cultures for inspiration, the machine was already exerting its influence on design, as some had begun to recognize. Among the many great debates of the 1920s was that over the aesthetic value of the machine and its products. The battle raged at all levels, from architecture to commonplace decorative household items. Detractors of the machine, and they were legion, deprecated its products as ugly and tasteless, as must invariably be the case, they said, when the emphasis was on quantity through mass production. As one critic put it, "The extinction of craftsmanship and its replacement by machine production" exerted a very appreciable influence on general culture, as the "habitual contemplation of ugliness produces, first tolerance and finally complete acceptance." It produced "a machine mind," which found "satisfaction in purely mechanical qualities, in geometrically regular form, in smooth finish, in perfective repetition." This "atrophy of the aesthetic faculty," he wrote, was not confined to the masses, but was also found "among the governing class and even among scholars and men of learning."

New York City's Metropolitan Museum of Art, however, weighed in on the side of the machine's defenders with a 1924 exhibition devoted to industrial art. A defender of the machine's influence wrote:

There have been those who have seen in the machine just another tool inviting mastery at the hands of the craftsman, the creative designer, the artist—a tool infinitely complex and recalcitrant, but yet only an extension of the human brain and hand not essentially different from the ax, the adze, the awl, the plane, the gage, the amazing variety of tools in the guildsman's kit as those are viewed in historical retrospect against the flints of paleolithic and neolithic man. For them, "cheap and nasty" has not been an inherent characteristic either of democracy or machine production, but an incident in the slow struggle of the soul of man to reassert the dominion of beauty and excellence over this strange new extension of the human brain.

The "vindication of this faith," he wrote, "is forecast in an exhibition of industrial art at the Metropolitan Museum, New York."

By contrast with those who decried the impact of mass production on their surroundings, a few had begun to see in it the early stages of a modern style. [Urban planning critic] Lewis Mumford was one of these, writing of the early 1920s lunchroom that:

> its excellence is due to the fact that it has been made by a machine, and that it exhibits the accuracy, the fine finish, and the unerring fidelity to design which makes machine work delightful to everyone who knows how to take pleasure in geometrical perfection.

Admittedly, the new style was in its infancy, but it showed a capacity for growth and change now that had been absent earlier in the Machine Age. Of the opportunities and challenges Mumford wrote:

> To create designs which will respect the logic of the machine and at the same time have regard for the vagaries of human psychology is the problem whose solution will give us a satisfactory, genuine modern style.

Walter Pach [another contemporary writer] agreed that the "steel bridges, the steel buildings, the newly designed machines and utensils of all kinds, show an adaptation to function that is recognized as one of the great elements of art," even though it had not yet been fully appreciated by the public.

Advertising Affects Design

Easily one of the greatest and most observable of influences on design in the 1920s was advertising. From a relatively minor industry at the beginning of the decade, the corps of designers swelled by the end of the 1920s to the point where no American could avoid their influence in countless ways daily. It was largely under the impetus of advertising that the new style came on with such a rush in the 1920s. Late in the decade, [the critic] Gilbert Seldes wrote:

> Six years ago some of the finest industrial designers were unable to find work to do; in 1928 a single central agency placed fifty-three designers of textiles in contact with manufacturers in one month; a year later the same agency had calls for 200 . . . and was unable to fill the demand. . . . Within eighteen months of the first exploitation of radical departures in furniture, glassware, silver, and so on, all these things were being produced by large-scale factory methods. You cannot be sure you are touching wood when you rap on the table; it is just as likely to have legs of chromium-plated steel and a metal top. In ten months one designer worked on some thirty-five different objects, ranging from trucks to table glass, from refrigerators to fountain pens, for each of which he created a new design, a new form; at the least, a new color scheme.

Much of the stimulus for the new designs came from The Art Center in New York City, what Seldes described as "a central institution . . . with the single object of creating a new level of taste and a new, entirely native style in the arts," to whom manufacturers came for advice on design.

The result was, Seldes wrote, "that everything we touch and see and use in our daily lives is being changed in shape and color, that the visual aspect of America is being transformed." One of the principal agents in the change was advertising, which insisted that it could not sell products unless they were pleasing to the eye of the consumer. The result was that the influence of advertising was involved from the inception of the designing process, rather than only being felt when it was time for the product to be marketed. As Seldes put it, the advertising artist "began to operate inside the factory instead of outside it in a studio." For the most part, such painters tended to be illustrators like Rockwell Kent, or the designers of theater sets, like Joseph Urban.

Modernist Furniture

Seldes was particularly struck by "modernist" furniture, not only its angles and "efforts to be striking and smart," but also the use of "new woods, of cork and insulating material, of new kinds of glass, of steel and copper—all the things which come from the experts and engineers." It was not an age in which houses were being built for the display of works of art, but instead, as Assistant Secretary of Commerce Julius Klein put it:

> Art has come to the dish pan, to the washstand, to dust mops and to the garage. . . . Even for commodities such as electric washing machines, the manufacturers declare that artistic design is getting to be a more important factor every year. . . . Art is on our floors and art is on our roofs.

Lewis Mumford observed in 1929 that, despite resistance, "attempts at modern design have been made in almost every department of furnishing and decoration," with much of the initiative coming from the nation's largest department stores. Noting that furniture manufacturers planned to sell "a new suite of furniture to every family in America *every six years*," Mumford pointed out that the goal could be attained only by producing shoddy goods or by continually changing styles. These new styles, like *art moderne*, were, Mumford sneered, only serving "the purposes of salesmanship."

An exhibition at Macy's department store was showing how modern decorative art could be applied to the home. Lee Simonson, designer for Theater Guild Productions, was responsible for the exhibition, and said he had "attacked the problem just as I would the staging of a play." "The setting, as well as the 5,000 exhibits, is made to tell the story of modern industrial design." The exhibition consisted of fifteen furnished rooms, in which, he said:

> We have avoided the use of wood wherever possible. . . . I believe that wood is not a modern building material. It has out-

lived its usefulness. The important thing is to develop materials that will eliminate the great labor that has gone into the finishing of woods. This is essential if beautiful objects are to become inexpensive and prevalent enough for general use. The high finishes traditional in furniture are a relic of the old days when craft labor was abundant and cheap. Why continue this practise in a day when all the emphasis is placed on labor-saving devices for the home? I predict that metal will be increasingly used in modern ornament and furniture. Its beauty is in itself. Its finish is inherent in the nature of the material. What remains to be done is to work into it color and texture, and this some chemical process will eventually solve. I believe the exposition will demonstrate the effectiveness of this theory: it is illustrated by the metal, asbestos and cork which are used in its construction. . . . In other words, the art of to-day is capturing the discoveries of the scientist in his laboratory for the purpose of combining utility, beauty, and economy to meet the needs of present-day life.

President Coolidge agreed:

We need to put more effort into translating art into the daily life of the people. If we could surround ourselves with forms of beauty, the evil things of life would tend to disappear and our moral standards would be raised. . . . Our country has reached a position where this is no longer a visionary desire, but is becoming an actual reality. With general prosperity, with high wages, with reasonable hours of labor, has come both the means and the time to cultivate the artistic spirit.

With similar ebullience, the head of a New York advertising agency declared that "open plumbing has become one of the fine arts in America."

John Cotton Dana, creator and director of the Newark Museum, said: "Study the beautiful lines of American bathtubs, plumbing fixtures, and modern electrical refrigerators if you want to see beauty wedded to utility." His museum was devoted "primarily to the bringing of beauty into the machine-made things that we use in our every-day life, especially in the home." A pioneer in this kind of enterprise for over a decade, he now saw decorative art being exhibited all over the country, and he regarded department stores as "the museums of today."

Dana wrote:

> We hear a good deal about this "new spirit" in the arts these days. What is this new spirit? Briefly, it is the spirit of the machine. We are a machine civilization. Our things are made by machines, and because of that, some years ago, we had settled down to believe that we must either have ugly things or do away with machine production. We see now how wrong that idea was, and that the machine is leading us to new vistas of design in the objectives of every-day life. The machine is freeing us from the cast-off art clothing of the past.

> The modern movement in the decorative arts is really a movement toward machine art. The severe simplicity which is characteristic of modern design is a search for technical form, which is fundamentally a form of simple lines with a minimum of surface decoration. This technical form to meet the demands of machine production must be of a geometric simplicity, and the beauty of that kind of form depends upon mathematics and upon the fact that we can apprehend and appreciate it clearly. The art is industry which produced the modern American bathroom and kitchen is an art of to-day. It derives from the life we are living, a life in which machine production, highly organized industry and commerce, science and invention play the dominant roles. Ours is not a period of revery and reminiscence. It is pointed toward the future. And so we do not want art in industry which is reminiscent of the art of the past. A new epoch is here.

Late in the decade Lewis Mumford wrote:

> By transforming technology, the physical sciences have created new forms and patterns, in instruments of precision, in machines and grain elevators and warehouses and bridges; and the artist has seized upon these forms as fresh materials for his art. A subway station, for instance, with its regular piers, its monotonous surfaces, its sudden crystallization of color in red and green signal lights, presents an aesthetic ex-

perience. The hardness, the abstraction, the absence of surface variations, which characterize machine work, the intricate relation of parts, the lack of subtle modulations in color, the uniform illumination of electricity—all these things belong particularly to the modern world and have not, in the precise form, existed before. To these new products of exact technology the modern artist has become sensitive. Dismissed as mere utilitarian ugliness in one generation, they come back to use through the purer experience of the artist, as things of beauty. . . .

Mumford added:

During the last thirty years we have become more conscious of the aesthetic possibilities of the exact arts; and it is no accident that our new instruments, the automobile and the aeroplane, are not the weakest but the best of our machined products, a distinction which they share with American kitchen equipment and bathroom fixtures. Under our very eyes, an improvement of design has taken place, transforming the awkward mass and the broken lines of the primitive auto into the unified mass and the slick streamlines of the modern car; or, by an even greater revolution in design, turning the imperfectly related planes of the push-power aeroplane into the more buoying, gull-like tract plane of today, with body and wing both gaining in beauty as they were adapted more carefully to the mechanical requirements of flight.

It was a decade of fads, in large part cultivated and spread by advertising. As [the writer] Charles Merz described it:

The stage was set in this America for a rapid flux in fads and interests, and a rapid flux in fads and interests was the inevitable goal of the great machine of modern industry itself. For with competition keen, with overproduction a constant menace, with a relentless demand for reducing costs and with cost-reduction usually dependent upon quantity output, the great machine had to cultivate new fashions in order to unload its goods.

This it did to the tune of a billion dollars' worth of advertising launched at the American public every year in an effort to create new styles, shorten the period between them as they came along, make people who were behind-times feel uncomfortable and out of date, train the public to want new things before it had used up old ones and develop the average man's desires until they far outreached his needs. . . . So rapidly were fashions changing, so regularly were new fads arriving, and so distracted was the modern merchant, trying to keep pace with his supply on one end and his market on the other, that trade conventions spent hours deliberating what was now in style. . . . Radio sets went Florentine one year, only to go Louis Quinze the next and Jacobean twelve months later. Styles in furniture, styles in diets, styles in wall paper and styles in floor coverings varied with the seasons. New cigarettes, new shaving creams, and new laundry soaps appeared from nowhere, covered the billboards with their claims, and wrote their virtues in airplane smoke against the heavens. Zipper galoshes, lizard-skin shoes, Russian boots, and Helen Wills eyeshades scored new triumphs in the market. Colour made its appearance as the handmaid of industry. Linoleum dropped its prim triangles for the rich lustre of a Turkish rug. Bed linens went all colours of the rainbow. Scorning the colour-blind conservative who had been satisfied all these years with what it described as "hospital white," the Lady Pepperell Company began advertising sheets in orchid, maize and nile.

Chapter 4

The Angry Twenties

Turning Points

IN WORLD HISTORY

Red Scare Leads to Political Repression

Stanley Coben

The years immediately after World War I were times of uncertainty and disorder in the United States. The war had worked small-town America into such a fever pitch of patriotism that a man in Hammond, Indiana, was shot for saying "To hell with the United States," and a jury acquitted the murderer. Most Americans were in no mood to tolerate dissent. At the same time, expressions of discontent and social unrest were widespread as Socialists, anarchists, and over a million striking workers responded to employers' attempts to lower wages in the immediate aftermath of the war. Against this turbulent background, an unknown anarchist managed to explode a bomb on the doorstep of U.S. attorney general A. Mitchell Palmer on June 2, 1919. In response, the outraged attorney general launched a series of illegal roundups of suspected "reds" (a term which included both Communists and anarchists). The following selection by historian Stanley Coben describes the time of the "red scare" and its repercussions. Coben is the author of *A. Mitchell Palmer, Politician; The Development of American Culture;* and *Rebellion Against Victorianism: The Impetus for Cultural Change in 1920s America.*

At a victory loan pageant in the District of Columbia on May 6, 1919, a man refused to rise for the playing of "The Star-Spangled Banner." As soon as the national anthem was completed an enraged sailor fired three shots into the unpatriotic spectator's back. When the man fell, the *Washington*

Stanley Coben, "A Study in Nativism: The American Red Scare of 1919–1920," *Political Science Quarterly*, vol. 79, March 1964, pp. 52–57. Copyright © 1964 by The Academy of Political Science. Reproduced by permission.

Post reported, "the crowd burst into cheering and ha
ping." In February of the same year, a jury in Hammc
diana, took two minutes to acquit the assassin of an alien
who yelled, "To Hell with the United States." Early in 1920,
a clothing store salesman in Waterbury, Connecticut, was
sentenced to six months in jail for having remarked to a customer that [Russian revolutionary Vladimir Ilyich] Lenin
was "the brainiest," or "one of the brainiest" of the world's
political leaders. Dramatic episodes like these, or the better
known Centralia Massacre, Palmer Raids, or May Day riots,
were not everyday occurrences, even at the height of the Red
Scare [a nativist movement based on fear of Communists
and anarchists]. But the fanatical one hundred percent
Americanism reflected by the Washington crowd, the Hammond jury, and the Waterbury judge pervaded a large part of
our society between early 1919 and mid-1920. . . .

The ferocious outbreak of nativism in the United States
after World War I was not consciously planned or provoked
by any individual or group, although some Americans took
advantage of the movement once it started. Rather, the Red
Scare . . . was brought on largely by a number of severe social and economic dislocations which threatened the national equilibrium. The full extent and the shocking effects
of these disturbances of 1919 have not yet been adequately
described. Runaway prices, a brief but sharp stock market
crash and business depression, revolutions throughout Europe, widespread fear of domestic revolt, bomb explosions,
and an outpouring of radical literature were distressing
enough. These sudden difficulties, moreover, served to ex-
aggerate the disruptive effects already produced by the social
and intellectual ravages of the World War and the preceding
reform era, and by the arrival, before the war, of millions of
new immigrants. This added stress intensified the hostility
of Americans strongly antagonistic to minority groups, and
brought new converts to blatant nativism from among those
who ordinarily were not overtly hostile toward radicals or
recent immigrants.

Citizens who joined the crusade for one hundred percent
Americanism sought, primarily, a unifying force which would

halt the apparent disintegration of their culture. The movement, they felt, would eliminate those foreign influences which the one hundred percenters believed were the major cause of their anxiety.

War Leaves Behind a Climate of Crisis

Many of the postwar sources of stress were also present during World War I, and the Red Scare, as [historian] John Higham has observed, was partly an exaggeration of wartime passions. In 1917–1918 German-Americans served as the object of almost all our nativistic fervor; they were the threatening intruders who refused to become good citizens. "They used America," a patriotic author declared in 1918 of two million German-Americans, "they never loved her. They clung to their old language, their old customs, and cared nothing for ours. . . . As a class they were clannish beyond all other races coming here." Fear of subversion by German agents was almost as extravagant in 1917–1918 as anxiety about "reds" in the postwar period. Attorney General Thomas Watt Gregory reported to a friend in May 1918 that "we not infrequently receive as many as fifteen hundred letters in a single day suggesting disloyalty and the making of investigations."

Opposition to the war by radical groups helped smooth the transition among American nativists from hatred of everything German to fear of radical revolution. The two groups of enemies were associated also for other reasons. High government officials declared after the war that German leaders planned and subsidized the Bolshevik Revolution. When bombs blasted homes and public buildings in nine cities in June 1919, the director of the Justice Department's Bureau of Investigation asserted that the bombers were "connected with Russian bolshevism, aided by Hun [German] money." In November 1919, a year after the armistice, a popular magazine warned of "the Russo-German movement that is now trying to dominate America.". . .

Soldiers Return to a Changed America

Americans were jolted by new blows to their equilibrium after entering the war. Four million men were drafted away from familiar surroundings and some of them experienced the terrible carnage of trench warfare. Great numbers of women left home to work in war industries or to replace men in other jobs. Negroes flocked to northern industrial areas by the hundreds of thousands, and their first mass migration from the South created violent racial antagonism in northern cities.

During the war, also, Americans sanctioned a degree of government control over the economy which deviated sharply from traditional economic individualism. Again, fears aroused before the war were aggravated, for the reform legislation of the Progressive era had tended to increase government intervention, and many citizens were further perturbed by demands that the federal government enforce even higher standards of economic and social morality. By 1919, therefore, some prewar progressives as well as conservatives feared the gradual disappearance of highly valued individual opportunity and responsibility. Their fears were fed by strong postwar calls for continued large-scale government controls—extension of federal operation of railroads and of the Food Administration for example.

Effects of the Russian Revolution

The prime threat to these long-held individualistic values, however, and the most powerful immediate stimulus to the revitalistic response, came from Russia. There the Bolshevik conquerors proclaimed their intention of exporting Marxist ideology. If millions of Americans were disturbed in 1919 by the specter of communism, the underlying reason was not fear of foreign invasion—Russia, after all, was still a backward nation recently badly defeated by German armies. The real threat was the potential spread of communist ideas. These, the one hundred percenters realized with horror, possessed a genuine appeal for reformers and for the economically underprivileged, and if accepted they would complete the transformation of America.

A clear picture of the Bolshevik tyranny was not yet available; therefore, as after the French Revolution, those who feared the newly successful ideology turned to fight the revolutionary ideals. So the *Saturday Evening Post* declared editorially in November 1919 that "History will see our present state of mind as one with that preceding the burning of witches, the children's crusade, the great tulip craze, and other examples of softening of the world brain." The *Post* referred not to the Red Scare or the impending Palmer Raids, but to the spread of communist ideology. Its editorial concluded: "The need of the country is not more idealism, but more pragmatism; not communism, but common sense." One of the most powerful patriotic groups, the National Security League, called upon members early in 1919 to "teach 'Americanism.' This means the fighting of Bolshevism . . . by the creation of well-defined National Ideals." Members "must preach Americanism and instill the idealism of America's Wars, and that American spirit of service which believes in giving as well as getting." New York attorney, author, and educator Henry Waters Taft warned a Carnegie Hall audience late in 1919 that Americans must battle "a propaganda which is tending to undermine our most cherished social and political institutions and is having the effect of producing widespread unrest among the poor and the ignorant, especially those of foreign birth."

When the war ended Americans also confronted the disturbing possibility, pointed up in 1919 by the struggle over the League of Nations, that Europe's struggles would continue to be their own. These factors combined to make World War I a traumatic experience for millions of citizens. As Senator James Reed of Missouri observed in August 1919, "This country is still suffering from shell shock. Hardly anyone is in a normal state of mind. . . . A great storm has swept over the intellectual world and its ravages and disturbances still exist."

The wartime "shell shock" left many Americans extraordinarily susceptible to psychological stress caused by postwar social and economic turbulence. Most important for the course of the Red Scare, many of these disturbances had their greatest effect on individuals already antagonistic toward minorities. First of all, there was some real evidence of danger to the nation in 1919, and the nation provided the chief emotional support for many Americans who responded easily to charges of an alien radical menace. Violence flared throughout Europe after the war and revolt lifted radicals to power in several Eastern and Central European nations. Combined with the earlier Bolshevik triumph in Russia these revolutions made Americans look more anxiously at radicals here. Domestic radicals encouraged these fears; they became unduly optimistic about their own chances of success and boasted openly of their coming triumph. Scores of new foreign language anarchist and communist journals, most of them written by and for Southern and Eastern European immigrants, commenced publication, and the established radical press became more exuberant. These periodicals never tired of assuring readers in 1919 that "the United States seems to be on the verge of a revolutionary crisis." American newspapers and magazines reprinted selections from radical speeches, pamphlets, and periodicals so their readers could see what dangerous ideas were abroad in the land. Several mysterious bomb explosions and bombing attempts, reported in bold front page headlines in newspapers across the country, frightened the public in 1919. To many citizens these seemed part of an organized campaign of terror carried on by alien radicals intending to bring down the federal government. The great strikes of 1919 and early 1920 aroused similar fears.

Actually American radical organizations in 1919 were disorganized and poverty-stricken. The Communists were inept, almost without contact with American workers and not yet dominated or subsidized by Moscow. The IWW [Industrial Workers of the World, a union with a strong anarchist history] was shorn of its effective leaders, distrusted by labor, and generally declining in influence and power. Violent anarchists were isolated in a handful of tiny, unconnected local organizations. One or two of these anarchist groups probably carried out the "bomb conspiracy" of 1919; but the extent of the "conspiracy" can be judged from the fact that the bombs killed a total of two men during the year, a night watchman and one of the bomb throwers, and seriously wounded one person, a maid in the home of a Georgia senator.

Nevertheless, prophesies of national disaster abounded in 1919, even among high government officials. Secretary of State Robert Lansing confided to his diary that we were in real peril of social revolution. Attorney General A. Mitchell Palmer advised the House Appropriations Committee that "on a certain day, which we have been advised of," radicals would attempt "to rise up and destroy the Government at one fell swoop." Senator Charles Thomas of Colorado warned that "the country is on the verge of a volcanic upheaval." And Senator Miles Poindexter of Washington declared, "There is real danger that the government will fall.". . .

The slight evidence of danger from radical organizations aroused such wild fear only because Americans had already encountered other threats to cultural stability. However, the dislocations caused by the war and the menace of communism alone would not have produced such a vehement nativistic response. Other postwar challenges to the social and economic order made the crucial difference.

Economic Disorder Adds to Fear

Of considerable importance was the skyrocketing cost of living. Retail prices more than doubled between 1915 and 1920, and the price rise began gathering momentum in the spring of 1919. . . .

Then the wave of postwar strikes—there were 3,600 of them in 1919 involving over 4,000,000 workers—reached a climax in the fall of 1919. A national steel strike began in September and nationwide coal and rail walkouts were scheduled for November 1. Unions gained in membership and power during the war, and in 1919 labor leaders were under strong pressure to help workers catch up to or go ahead of mounting living costs. Nevertheless, influential government officials attributed the walkouts to radical activities. Early in 1919, Secretary of Labor William B. Wilson declared in a public speech that recent major strikes in Seattle, Butte, Montana, and Lawrence, Massachusetts, had been instituted by the Bolsheviks and the IWW for the sole purpose of bringing about a nationwide revolution in the United States. During the steel strike of early fall, 1919, a Senate investigating committee reported that "behind this strike there is massed a considerable element of IWW's, anarchists, revolutionists, and Russian soviets.". . . In April 1920 the head of the Justice Department's General Intelligence Division, J. Edgar Hoover, declared in a public hearing that at least fifty percent of the influence behind the recent series of strikes was traceable directly to communist agents.

Furthermore, the nation suffered a sharp economic depression in late 1918 and early 1919, caused largely by sudden cancellations of war orders. Returning servicemen found it difficult to obtain jobs during this period, which coincided with the beginning of the Red Scare. The former soldiers had been uprooted from their homes and told that they were engaged in a patriotic crusade. Now they came back to find "reds" criticizing their country and threatening the government with violence, Negroes holding good jobs in the big cities, prices terribly high, and workers who had not served in the armed forces striking for higher wages. A delegate won prolonged applause from the 1919 American Legion Convention when he denounced radical aliens, exclaiming, "Now that the war is over and they are in lucrative positions while our boys haven't a job, we've got to send those scamps to hell." The major part of the mobs which invaded meeting halls of immigrant organizations and broke up radical parades, especially during the first half of 1919, was comprised of men in uniform.

Fear of "Reds" Meets Fear of Aliens

A variety of other circumstances combined to add even more force to the postwar nativistic movement. Long before the new immigrants were seen as potential revolutionists they became the objects of widespread hostility. The peak of immigration from Southern and Eastern Europe occurred in the fifteen years before the war; during that period almost ten million immigrants from those areas entered the country. Before the anxious eyes of members of all classes of Americans, the newcomers crowded the cities and began to disturb the economic and social order. Even without other postwar disturbances a nativistic movement of some strength could have been predicted when the wartime solidarity against the German enemy began to wear off in 1919.

In addition, not only were the European revolutions most successful in Eastern and to a lesser extent in Southern Europe, but aliens from these areas predominated in American radical organizations. At least ninety percent of the members of the two American Communist parties formed in 1919 were born in Eastern Europe. The anarchist groups whose literature and bombs captured the imagination of the American public in 1919 were composed almost entirely of Italian, Spanish, and Slavic aliens. Justice Department announcements and statements by politicians and the press stressed the predominance of recent immigrants in radical organizations. Smoldering prejudice against new immigrants and identification of these immigrants with European as well as American radical movements, combined with other sources of postwar stress to create one of the most frenzied and one of the most widespread nativistic movements in the nation's history. . . .

Hysteria Disguised as Patriotism

Panegyrics celebrating our history and institutions were delivered regularly in almost every American school, church, and public hall in 1919 and 1920. Many of these fervent addresses went far beyond the usual patriotic declarations. Audiences were usually urged to join a crusade to protect our hallowed institutions. Typical of the more moderate statements was Columbia University President Nicholas Murray Butler's insistence in April 1919 that "America will be saved, not by those who have only contempt and despite for her founders and her history, but by those who look with respect and reverence upon the great series of happenings extending from the voyage of the Mayflower.". . .

The American flag became a sacred symbol. Legionaires demanded that citizens "Run the Reds out from the land whose flag they sully." Men suspected of radical leanings were forced to kiss the stars and stripes. . . .

Recent immigrants, especially, were called upon to show evidence of real conversion. Great pressure was brought to bear upon the foreign-born to learn English and to forget their native tongues. As Senator William S. Kenyon of Iowa declared in October 1919, "The time has come to make this a one-language nation." An editorial in the *American Legion Weekly* took a further step and insisted that the one language must be called "American. Why even in Mexico they do not stand for calling the language the Spanish language."

Immigrants were also expected to adopt our customs and to snuff out remnants of Old World cultures. Genteel prewar and wartime movements to speed up assimilation took on a "frightened and feverish aspect." Welcoming members of an Americanization conference called by his department, Secretary of the Interior Franklin K. Lane exclaimed in May 1919, "You have been gathered together as crusaders in a great cause. . . . There is no other question of such importance before the American people as the solidifying and strengthening of true American sentiment." A Harvard University official told the conference that "The Americanization movement . . . gives men a new and holy religion. . . . It challenges each one of us to a renewed consecration and devotion to the welfare of the nation." The National Security League boasted, in 1919, of establishing one thousand study groups to teach teachers how to inculcate "Americanism" in their foreign-born students. A critic of the prevailing mood protested against "one of our best advertised American mottoes, 'One country, one language, one flag,'" which, he complained, had become the basis for a fervent nationwide program.

Deportation of Aliens

As the postwar movement for one hundred percent Americanism gathered momentum, the deportation of alien nonconformists became increasingly its most compelling objective. Asked to suggest a remedy for the nationwide upsurge in radical activity, the Mayor of Gary, Indiana, replied, "Deportation is the answer, deportation of these leaders who talk treason in America and deportation of those who agree with them and work with them." "We must remake America," a popular author averred, "We must purify the source of America's population and keep it pure. . . . We must insist

that there shall be an American loyalty, brooking no amendment or qualification.". . .

Politicians quickly sensed the possibilities of the popular
frenzy for Americanism. Mayor Ole Hanson of Seattle,
Governor Calvin Coolidge of Massachusetts, and General
Leonard Wood became the early heroes of the movement.
The man in the best political position to take advantage of
the popular feeling, however, was Attorney General A.
Mitchell Palmer. In 1919, especially after the President's
physical collapse, only Palmer had the authority, staff, and
money necessary to arrest and deport huge numbers of radical aliens. The virulent phase of the movement for one hundred percent Americanism came early in 1920, when
Palmer's agents rounded up for deportation over six thousand aliens and prepared to arrest thousands more suspected
of membership in radical organizations. Most of these aliens
were taken without warrants, many were detained for unjus-
tifiably long periods of time, and some suffered incredible
hardships. Almost all, however, were eventually released.

After Palmer decided that he could ride the postwar fears
into the presidency, he set out calculatingly to become the
symbol of one hundred percent Americanism. The Palmer
raids, his antilabor activities, and his frequent pious professions of patriotism during the campaign were all part of this
effort. Palmer was introduced by a political associate to the
Democratic party's annual Jackson Day dinner in January
1920 as "an American whose Americanism cannot be misunderstood." In a speech delivered in Georgia shortly before
the primary election (in which Palmer won control of the
state's delegation to the Democratic National Convention),
the Attorney General asserted: "I am myself an American and
I love to preach my doctrine before undiluted one hundred
percent Americans, because my platform is, in a word, undiluted Americanism and undying loyalty to the republic.". . .

Unfortunately for political candidates like Palmer and
Wood, most of the social and economic disturbances which
had activated the movement they sought to lead gradually
disappeared during the first half of 1920. The European revolutions were put down; by 1920 communism seemed to

have been isolated in Russia. Bombings ceased abruptly after June 1919, and fear of new outrages gradually abated. Prices of food and clothing began to recede during the spring. Labor strife almost vanished from our major industries after a brief railroad walkout in April. Prosperity returned after mid-1919 and by early 1920 business activity and employment levels exceeded their wartime peaks. At the same time, it became clear that the Senate would not pass Wilson's peace treaty and that America was free to turn its back on the responsibilities of world leadership. The problems associated with the new immigrants remained; so did the disillusionment with Europe and with many old intellectual ideals. Nativism did not disappear from the American scene; but the frenzied attempt to revitalize the culture did peter out in 1920. The handful of unintimidated men, especially Assistant Secretary of Labor Louis F. Post, who had used the safeguards provided by American law to protect many victims of the Red Scare, found increasing public support. On the other hand, politicians like Palmer, Wood, and Hanson were left high and dry, proclaiming the need for one hundred percent Americanism to an audience which no longer urgently cared.

It is ironic that in 1920 the Russian leaders of the Comintern finally took charge of the American Communist movement, provided funds and leadership, and ordered the Communist factions to unite and participate actively in labor organizations and strikes. These facts were reported in the American press. Thus a potentially serious foreign threat to national security appeared just as the Red Scare evaporated, providing a final illustration of the fact that the frenzied one hundred percenters of 1919–1920 were affected less by the "red menace" than by a series of social and economic dislocations.

The Red Scare Left Behind a Spirit of Conformity

Although the Red Scare died out in 1920, its effects lingered. Hostility toward immigrants, mobilized in 1919–1920, remained strong enough to force congressional passage of restrictive immigration laws. Some of the die-hard one hundred percenters found a temporary home in the Ku Klux

Klan until that organization withered away during the mid-twenties. As its most lasting accomplishments, the movement for one hundred percent Americanism fostered a spirit of conformity in the country, a satisfaction with the status quo, and the equation of reform ideologies with foreign enemies. Revitalization movements have helped many societies adapt successfully to new conditions. The movement associated with the American Red Scare, however, had no such effect. True, it unified the culture against the threats faced in 1919–1920; but the basic problems—a damaged value system, an unrestrained business cycle, a hostile Russia, and communism—were left for future generations of Americans to deal with in their own fashion.

The Reemergence and Fall of the Ku Klux Klan

David J. Goldberg

Originally formed as a terrorist organization during the reconstruction of the South following the Civil War, the Ku Klux Klan was revived in 1915. In the early 1920s it grew quickly with the help of modern sales and promotional techniques, feeding on a host of new hatreds. The revived Ku Klux Klan found its version of Americanism threatened not only by African Americans but also by Jews, Catholics, immigrants, "immodest" urban women, and the patrons of speakeasies. It appealed to people who sensed that traditional values were being eroded by a new order emerging all around them. David J. Goldberg, a professor of history at Cleveland State University, describes the rise and decline of the Ku Klux Klan in this excerpt from his study of grassroots politics in the 1920s. As Goldberg demonstrates, the Klan was far from unopposed. Organized and sometimes violent action by politicians and workers hostile to the Klan played an important role in its ultimate decline.

During the early 1920s, the Ku Klux Klan rose to a position of influence in many areas of the country. Appealing to Protestants' anti-Catholicism, emphasizing the need to enforce Prohibition, and capitalizing on the sour, antiforeign mood, the Klan became a lightning rod for many of the postwar fears and resentments. By 1923, it had become a force to reckon with in states such as Texas, Indiana, Colorado, and Oregon, and the source of great national controversy. But the Klan also provoked widespread opposition and

David J. Goldberg, "The Rapid Rise and the Swift Decline of the Ku Klux Klan," *Discontented America: The United States in the 1920s.* Baltimore: Johns Hopkins University Press, 1999. Copyright © 1999 by Johns Hopkins University Press. All rights reserved. Reproduced by permission.

faced a number of internal difficulties; amid the mid-decade prosperity, it fell into insignificance.

The Reborn Klan

The original Ku Klux Klan was a terrorist organization that used violence in an effort to overthrow the Reconstruction governments that had been established in the South following the Civil War. Disguised in long flowing robes, hooded Klansmen had assassinated a number of African Americans and their white supporters, and targeted schoolteachers and African-American officeholders. Klansmen included some of the South's leading citizens. In 1871, the federal government suppressed the Klan, although a number of similar organizations continued its work until the final overthrow of Reconstruction in 1877.

Interest in the Klan revived with the appearance of *The Birth of a Nation* in 1915. A movie based on a 1905 novel, *The Clansman* by Thomas Dixon, it has been described by historian Fred Silva as "the most controversial American film ever made." The first half of the motion picture depicted Civil War battle scenes so graphic that they might have convinced many Americans not to participate in the slaughter then taking place in Europe. The second half of the film, however, which portrayed the heroic Ku Klux Klan rescuing southern white women from brutal and bestial blacks and their northern allies, captured the most attention and helped account for the record-breaking audiences that saw the movie.

Hoping to capitalize on the film's popularity, an obscure circuit-riding Methodist Episcopal minister and Spanish-American War veteran by the name of William J. Simmons decided that the time had come to revive the Klan. On Thanksgiving Eve in 1915, Simmons and about fifteen of his friends climbed to the peak of Stone Mountain near Atlanta and set fire to a cross, signaling the rebirth of the Klan. Although this second Klan had no direct connection to the first, it claimed to be its successor and adopted its rituals, language, and costumes.

The new Klan limited membership to native-born, white Protestants; it excluded Catholics and Jews as well as African

Americans. Between 1915 and 1920, despite the use of *The Birth of a Nation* as a recruiting tool, it attracted only a few supporters. But in 1920, Colonel Simmons (the title had been conferred by a fraternal organization, the Woodmen of the World) hired two publicists, Edward Clarke and Elizabeth Tyler, who had raised money for groups such as the Red Cross, the YMCA, and the Anti-Saloon League. During the war, Clarke and Tyler had been impressed by the power of propaganda and advertising. They typified the opportunists that the Klan attracted in that these two "salesmen of hate" viewed the hooded order mainly as a moneymaking scheme. Clarke and Tyler convinced Simmons that the Klan needed to adopt modern sales techniques, and they instituted a system by which each local recruiter received four dollars of the ten-dollar initiation fee. Appealing to the heightened sense of nationalism engendered by the war, the Red Scare, and the League of Nations debate, they began to advertise the Klan as a 100 percent American organization that would clamp down on African Americans, foreigners, Catholics, Jews, law violators, immoral men and women, and a host of other evil forces.

Making use of Clarke's and Tyler's marketing techniques, during the depression years of 1920 and 1921 the Klan began to gain members throughout Georgia and in Alabama, Louisiana, Oklahoma, and Texas. Even in the Deep South states, the Klan did not focus on African Americans; its rise coincided with the decline in lynchings. It primarily aimed its fire at Prohibition violators and at those who transgressed its own moral standards. Portraying itself as the defender of "pure womanhood" and expressing the belief that the war had led to a loosening of morals, the Klan voiced concern with evils such as "loose dancing," "petting parties," and "roadside parking." Particularly in Texas and Oklahoma, the Klan began to mete out its own version of rough justice to those it accused of being adulterers, joyriders, wife-beaters, and abortionists. Violators of the Victorian moral code might be kidnapped, whipped, flogged, branded, mutilated, tarred and feathered, or simply warned by signs with messages such as "Wife-beaters, family-deserters, home-wreckers, we have no room for you," "Go joy riding with your own wife," or "Fooling around the other fellow's home is not wise." Most of the victims were white men and women, although the Klan also used violence against African Americans whom it viewed as stepping out of line or accused of cohabiting with whites.

Reports of Klan activities alarmed many liberal-minded Americans already concerned by the extent to which wartime hatreds had been perpetuated in the postwar period. In September 1921, the *New York World* published a series of articles exposing the Klan that a number of other leading newspapers reprinted. Partly because of the publicity that the *New York World* series received, the House of Representatives initiated an investigation of the Klan. To the disappointment of the Klan's opponents, this inquiry backfired, and according to John Moffatt Mecklin, a critic of the KKK, it provided the Klan with "a vast amount of gratuitous and invaluable advertising." William J. Simmons, appearing before a congressional committee, gave a masterful performance. Fighting to restrain his tears, he disavowed all acts of violence committed in the Klan's name. Faced with a counterthreat to investigate the Knights of Columbus, an embarrassed House of Representatives dropped the investigation on 17 October 1921.

Reform of the Klan

The congressional hearings brought the Klan helpful publicity, and during 1922 the Klan began to expand into the North. But many Klansmen were disturbed by the negative publicity that Clarke and Tyler brought to the organization. The *New York World* had reported that a partially clad Clarke and Tyler had been arrested by Atlanta police in 1919 and charged with disorderly conduct, and that Clarke had deserted his wife. In September 1922, shortly after having delivered a speech calling for the enforcement of Prohibition, Clarke was arrested and charged with possession of alcohol. Colonel Simmons, who also had a fondness for the bottle, stood by his comrades, but other Klansmen demanded that the organization be cleaned up.

In November 1922, a Dallas dentist, Hiram Wesley Evans,

seized control of the Klan, expelled Simmons, Clarke, and Tyler, and proclaimed himself the new imperial wizard of the KKK. (The takeover occurred soon after Clarke's much-publicized meeting with Marcus Garvey [leader of an influential "back to Africa" movement in the 1920s], but this was not an issue in the Klan infighting.) Evans set out to reform the Klan. He tried to make the Klan more respectable by stressing its belief in "education, temperance, the flag, Protestantism and charity." A strong advocate of Nordic superiority and fearful of those he labeled the mongrel races, he stressed the danger that immigrants posed to the nation. The Klan made great use of local recruiters and expanded into many areas of the country. According to some estimates, it gained more than two million new members. It attracted many of those who belonged to the Masons and other fraternal groups. The Klan won its greatest support in heavily Protestant areas of Michigan, Ohio, Indiana, Illinois, Colorado, and Oregon, but it also developed pockets of support in areas as diverse as Worcester, Massachusetts, southern New Jersey, and Anaheim, California.

The Klan's burst of growth surprised many people. A number of observers at the time blamed it on the aftereffects of the war. According to this interpretation, the war had unleashed hatreds that needed a new focus. Some columnists suggested that the military conflict had ended so abruptly that the extreme anti-German feeling that the government had stimulated needed new targets. Other pundits pointed out that the war had accustomed people to propaganda and exaggeration and to spying on their neighbors. In addition, many Americans had been frustrated by events since the armistice. The Senate's rejection of the treaty made it appear that the war had been fought for nothing. The request of the European nations for debt relief made the beneficiaries of American aid appear ungrateful. Despite the passage of the 1921 quota bill, immigrants continued to arrive in large numbers. Conflicts between labor and capital tore at the country, and the depression led to large-scale unemployment. Prohibition had been enacted but it had been openly violated. And perhaps the cruelest blow of all fell when the American public, in the autumn of 1920, learned that the 1919 World Series had been fixed. To some disillusioned Americans, the Klan appeared to provide a cure for the postwar malaise. That it continued to grow in 1923 indicated that it also spoke to some deeper concerns of native-born, white, Protestant Americans.

The Klan's Appeals

Wherever it appeared, the Klan made use of local prejudices and concerns. This could mean focusing on the supposed menace posed by Japanese, Mexicans, Italians, Greeks, or some other immigrant group, or exposing the peccadilloes of a corrupt political machine. But all Klansmen shared certain core concerns. The two causes that received the most attention from them were the alleged power and subversive intentions of the Roman Catholic church and the failure of authorities to enforce Prohibition. . . .

Klan newspapers, speakers, and publications aired all the standard anti-Catholic themes and added a number of twists of their own. They voiced contempt for Catholic practices such as celibacy and the refusal to eat meat on Fridays. . . . Making frequent use of the slogan "One flag, one school, one Bible," they criticized Catholics for sending their children to parochial schools and for launching campaigns to remove the Protestant Bible from the public schools. They accused Catholics of engaging in bloc voting and of marching voters to the polls to select handpicked candidates. They charged that Catholics did not properly respect the Sabbath and that they defied the blue laws [local ordinances prohibiting commercial activity on Sunday].

The Klan also claimed that Catholics could never be good citizens because they owed their primary loyalty to the pope. During the war, immigrants had been accused of having dual loyalties, and this charge still resonated during the postwar period. . . .

The Klan Carries Out Raids to Enforce Prohibition

Wherever it appeared, the Klan referred to itself as a law-and-order organization. Although it called for the enforcement of laws against gambling and prostitution, it focused most of all on the need for Prohibition to be enforced. Widespread violations of Prohibition had begun as soon as the constitutional amendment and the Volstead Act had been passed. In the early 1920s, many Americans were concerned about a crime wave, a condition they were at first prone to blame on the unsettling effects of the war. But by 1922 and 1923, it had become quite clear that Prohibition, rather than the war, had been the cause of the growth in crime.

Prohibition violations were common in some heavily Protestant areas such as Appalachia, where moonshiners and home stills had been part of the social landscape since the first white settlers crossed the Blue Ridge. But in much of the country, immigrants from Catholic and Jewish backgrounds were the most visible offenders. Some immigrants had gotten involved in crime on their arrival in the United States. Prohibition gave them an opportunity to expand their criminal activities beyond their own ethnic communities. Chicago gained the most notoriety, but during the 1920s, organized criminal networks and syndicates expanded their operations in almost all large and medium-sized cities.

The Klan aimed to halt the activities of the rumrunners. Viewing itself as an agent of moral reform, the KKK gained members in the same Protestant areas where there had been substantial support for the Prohibition amendment. The KKK, often working hand in hand with agents of the Anti-Saloon League, gathered information on "dance halls," "road houses," and "pool rooms" selling "white mule," "rot gut," and other illegal beverages. Bristling with anger at the complacence of local officials, the Klan conducted its own "clean up your town" campaigns. The KKK felt this was necessary because there were hundreds of towns and cities where local police, city officials, and mayors took bribes from mobsters. Where corruption flourished, the Klan argued that it had no choice but to carry out its own vice raids to enforce Prohibition. This earned it the support of local dry forces who appreciated the Klan's exposure of Prohibition violators. But the Klan's antivice campaigns also led to some extremely violent confrontations with those who did not take kindly to being described in the Indiana Klan organ, the *Fiery Cross*, as "dregs from putrefied vomit" or as "thugs, degenerates and social parasites" and who did not appreciate having their operations exposed by the KKK. . . .

Preserving "Racial Purity"

Jews came in for their share of abuse from the Klan, although anti-Semitism was secondary to anti-Catholicism. Following the lead of Henry Ford, the KKK aimed its fire at "money grasping Jews" and suggested that Jewish financiers had been responsible for World War I. Klan newspapers frequently carried reprints from the *Dearborn Independent* and reported favorably about the Detroit automobile manufacturer's crusade against the "International Jew." Jewish organizations showed far more concern about Henry Ford than they did about the Klan; they did not view the Klan as a serious threat, despite reports of scattered physical attacks on Jews.

The Klan billed itself as a white supremacist organization that believed in the need to preserve racial purity. In cities such as Indianapolis, Indiana, Springfield, Ohio, and Coffeyville, Kansas, the Klan joined campaigns for segregated schools while claiming to be "the friend of the Negro." As proof of its good intentions, the Klan made financial contributions to black churches. In response, incredulous African-American newspaper editors heaped scorn on ministers who "betrayed" their congregations for "paltry" dollars. Blacks living in the heart of Klan country openly defied the hooded order. In Columbus, Ohio, black leaders sought a court injunction against Klan activities and organized a boycott of Klan stores; in Dayton, Ohio, black residents organized a countermarch over the same route that a Klan parade had taken the day before; in Indianapolis, African Americans held numerous meetings protesting the activities of the KKK. Klansmen in the South put far more emphasis on the dangers that African Americans' new aspirations resulting from the war posed to the status quo, and the KKK's racist appeals carried more of a threat of violence in Dixie than in the North. There were instances in the South where Klansmen whipped African Americans for voting, for refusing to enter Jim Crow railroad cars, for being "too free" with hotel guests, and for demanding more pay for picking cotton.

Uneasy with manifestations of female sexuality such as open necking and petting, "suggestive dances," and "immodest dress," the Klan also called for the protection of "pure womanhood." Many of the Klan's concerns dealt with changes in female behavior that had begun to be apparent in the prewar era, although contemporaries blamed the war for the "unloosening" of morals. During the 1920s, these new forms of conduct became associated with the flapper, whom the Klan viewed as little more than a vamp. Klansmen, like other Americans, were made uncomfortable by young women bobbing their hair, smoking, drinking, wearing less-constrictive clothing, enjoying leisure-time pursuits with male companions, and using the automobile to escape the watchful eyes of their parents.

In searching for the cause of the decline in morals, the Klan targeted the film industry, and it blamed "aliens" (Jews) for the "stream of pollution" it saw emanating from the new Hol-

Members of the Ku Klux Klan march down Pennsylvania Avenue in 1925.
The Klan both rose to prominence and fell from grace during the 1920s.

lywood studios. By the early 1920s, movies had become a highly affordable and popular form of entertainment. Catholic church leaders and many other Americans had begun, like the Klan, to express concern about brazen displays of female sexuality on the screen (and perhaps about what happened in the theaters when the lights went out). A number of cities and states had formed their own censorship boards; in an effort to head off further government intervention, the Motion Picture Producers and Distributors of America hired Will Hays to police the motion-picture industry.

In the year after Hays assumed his new position (at the munificent salary of one hundred thousand dollars a year), the Klan responded with indignation when Charlie Chaplin played a Protestant minister in a film entitled *The Pilgrim*, a movie that ridiculed small-town life. Films in which "the wife" was "always shown as inferior" and "the mistress as a heroine" continued to raise their ire. The *Fiery Cross*, fed up with Hays's alleged kowtowing to Hollywood producers, called upon the Hollywood film czar to resign. Merging with the Klan's call for "pure womanhood," the demand for cleaner films had less success in the 1920s than it would in the 1930s, when the Catholic Legion of Decency began to exercise influence.

Bitter, humorless, and fearful of all things foreign, the Klan seized on an astonishing array of issues as it extended its reach across much of the United States. Klan supporters knew something was wrong but they were not sure what it was. In addition to lashing out at "thugs," "home wreckers," "shyster lawyers," and a host of other enemies, the Klan campaigned for cleaner government, improved schools, and freedom of speech and the press. The Klan said little about Communism, because the Red Scare fears had receded by the early 1920s and the Klan's enemy across the seas resided in Rome rather than in Moscow. The Klan's creed called for "a closer relationship between capital and labor" and for "the prevention of unwanted strikes by foreign labor agitators," but the KKK said little about the labor question; a few Klaverns (local Klan organizations) even supported the 1922 railroad strike.

Although it took some positions that could be considered progressive, the Klan appeals indicate that it was an intensely nationalistic, xenophobic Protestant reform organization that captured the resentments and grievances of Americans upset by the changes brought about by the war, disturbed by the government's failure to enforce Prohibition, and fearful of an increasingly urban and racially mixed society. . . .

Opposing the Klan

Roman Catholics took the lead in organizing opposition to the Klan. Some Catholic leaders had initially believed that the KKK would quickly pass from the scene, but the passage of the 1922 Oregon initiative [a state ballot initiative requiring all children ages 8 to 16 to attend only public schools] jolted them into action. If the Oregon measure had gone into effect, the parochial school, the bedrock of Catholic education, would have been outlawed. This was of special importance because the meeting of the church's Third Plenary Council in Baltimore in 1884 had held that Catholic parents were "duty bound" to send their children to parochial schools. In any case, Catholic parents wanted their children to learn a fourth R, religion. . . .

Irish-Catholic officials did not hesitate to ban Klan gatherings and to outlaw Klan activities. Chicago chief of police Charles Fitzmorris barred the Klan from parading, and New York City mayor John Hylan ordered the police to run the Klan out of town. Cleveland mayor W.S. Fitzgerald supported a city council ordinance providing a five-hundred-dollar fine and six months' imprisonment for anyone belonging to a society "tending to promote racial hatred and religious bigotry," and told the council: "This is a city of many different nationalities, many different creeds and colors. . . . There is no place here for such an order." Boston mayor James Michael Curley exaggerated the Klan's presence for his own purposes. Curley had earlier barred birth-control advocate Margaret Sanger from speaking, and he jumped at the opportunity to issue a similar ban on the Klan. While running for governor of Massachusetts in 1924, he pledged to run the Klan out of the state and arranged for his campaign workers to burn crosses when he spoke so he could appear brave in condemning the KKK.

Some state legislatures passed laws making it a crime for anyone to appear in public wearing a mask, hood, robe, or other disguise. New York passed the nation's most drastic anti-Klan law, which was named the Walker Bill after New York City assemblyman (soon to be mayor) Jimmy Walker. Al Smith signed the measure in May 1923, which ensured the Klan's hostility to Smith when he sought the Democratic presidential nomination in 1924. Specifically exempting labor unions, the law required each unincorporated oath-bound organization to file a list of its members, constitution, oaths, bylaws, and rules with the secretary of state. It attached penalties for the sending of anonymous documents or letters. The bill did not specifically mention the Klan, but everyone knew that it was aimed at the KKK, which vociferously protested its passage and attempted to evade its provisions by incorporating as a fraternity, Alpha Pi Sigma. . . .

Having gained considerable strength in the overwhelmingly Protestant areas of central Ohio and Indiana, the Klan faced a major dilemma. If it was to expand beyond the Protestant core, it would have to recruit new members in areas where many Catholics also lived. Once it attempted to move into industrial districts where workers had often engaged in violent strikes, the Klan found that it could not operate so freely as it had in its secure bastions. The Klan quickly discovered that, particularly in the tristate area of the West Virginia panhandle, eastern Ohio, and western Pennsylvania, the opponents of the Klan, often with the connivance of the local police, were prepared to use considerable violence against the KKK. In 1923 and 1924, anti-Klan forces used far more violence than the Klan had ever employed in the North.

The string of incidents began in April 1923, when a bomb destroyed the office of *Dawn*, the chief organ of the Chicago-area Klan. The next month, an angry crowd forced five hundred frightened Klansmen to take refuge in a church in Bound Brook, New Jersey, before they could be rescued by state police. Then in August and September 1923, a series of extremely violent attacks on the Klan took place in quick succession in Steubenville, Ohio, Carnegie, Pennsylvania, Perth Amboy, New Jersey, and New Castle, Delaware. The attacks continued in 1924, when mobs assaulted Klansmen in Waukesha, Wisconsin, and Niles, Ohio; forced Klansmen to flee South Bend, Indiana; ran the Klan out of the coal-mining town of Lilly, Pennsylvania (killing two Klan members); and skirmished with the Klan in Herrin, Illinois, a town in which violence appeared to be endemic.

In all of these incidents, the Klan got the worst of the encounters. It demonstrated a curious lack of will to engage in battle with its enemies on city streets. In Steubenville, the mob severely beat Klansmen, forcing them to call off a planned march. Thousands of local citizens in Carnegie disrupted a "Karnegie Day celebration," killing one Klansman, destroying a ten-foot-high electric cross, and forcing Klan members to retreat under a hail of bricks. In Perth Amboy, six thousand counterdemonstrators forced Klan members to seek refuge in an Odd Fellows hall. A New Castle crowd pelted Klansmen after an initiation ceremony. In Waukesha, a crowd shouting "The meeting is off" stormed a hotel where the Klan had gathered. Crowds administered a terrible beating to Klan members in Niles. In El Paso, fear of facing an armed mob caused the Klan to call off a planned parade. Retreating Klansmen in South Bend fled a crowd composed primarily of college students. . . .

The Klan's timid response is revealing. The organization attracted its share of hatemongers, but for the most part, its rank and file consisted of ordinary, naive, fearful, gullible citizens. These were not the American equivalent of Blackshirts; [paramilitary Italian Fascists] or Brownshirts [paramilitary German Nazis]; these were not Fascists or even proto-Fascists anxious to spill blood in the streets. The United States during the 1920s bore little resemblance to European societies in which a weak commitment to liberal democracy and fears of the left spawned Fascist movements. Intimidated by the violence and unprepared to respond in kind, the Klan discovered that it could not hope to organize in any community where a significant number of those ineligible to join the KKK had decided to take the law into their own hands.

The incidents did not merely block the Klan's advance; they played a role in its decline. Although the Klan did not want to be viewed as violent, the string of confrontations associated the Klan with violence and made it easier for enemies of the KKK to attack it as disruptive and as an enemy of law and order.

The Decline of the Klan

By mid-1923, the Klan appeared to be on the rise, but by early 1925, many members who had rushed to join were rushing to get out. Even by the time of the great Democratic Party debate of 1924, the KKK was beginning to lose strength. What happened?

None of the Klan's leaders was prepared for its sudden growth. Hiram Evans was a small-town dentist, devoid of charisma, incapable of providing direction to an organization with some three to five million members. By 1923 and 1924, local Klansmen essentially made their own decisions, and the Dallas central office had little control over them.

Even if Evans and his associates had exercised leadership, they were not sure themselves what they wanted the Klan to be. It was not strictly a fraternal organization, although it had the trappings of one. The KKK backed political candidates but it did not claim to be a political organization, and hooded Klansmen were certainly in no position to act as lobbyists. It worked with local officials in enforcing Prohibition, but it was not prepared to take over their responsibilities. In the North, it could not be considered a terrorist group, and even in the South, the use of violence lessened after Evans's takeover. A strange hybrid, the Klan never fully understood what direction it wanted to take. Journalist Robert Duffus's 1923 description of it in *World's Work* as a "cumbersome monster of an organization, ill-planned in every way except as a means of raising money" proved correct.

Money could be made in the Klan. Even after the ouster of Simmons, Clarke, and Tyler, the KKK continued to attract a steady stream of opportunists who had no particular belief in the Klan's principles, and who often engaged in precisely the type of conduct the Klan condemned. As a series of messy scandals hit the Klan in 1924 and 1925, those who had joined the KKK thinking it genuinely intended to combat vice quickly left the organization.

The Klan attracted some peculiar characters, but none caused the organization more embarrassment than D.C. Stephenson. A pathological liar, a drifter, a heavy drinker who had abandoned his wife, Stephenson was also a master hustler. In 1923, he had become the grand dragon of the Indiana Klan; he used that position to acquire a small fortune and an ornate Indianapolis mansion. He was known to fellow Klansmen by the code name "Old Man." The *Fiery Cross* had hailed his "unselfish devotion, sterling integrity, honor and loving personality," but his behind-the-scenes activity conflicted with this benign image. In 1923 and 1924, he was involved in a number of sexual attacks and was arrested for public intoxication. Stephenson managed to cover up these incidents until March 1925, when he kidnapped and raped an Indiana government employee named Madge Oberholzer, leaving human bite marks all over her body. Shortly thereafter, Oberholzer committed suicide. During the summer and fall of 1925, just as a Klan-backed governor took office, these facts became public. Stephenson was soon convicted of second-degree murder and the Indiana Klan never recovered from its disgrace. . . .

Even without the scandals, the Klan had trouble maintaining its membership. By 1925, the postwar tensions had largely faded as the United States truly entered a new era in which automobiles, radio, and films filled people's leisure time and fraternal organizations began to appear old-fashioned. As Americans relaxed, the Klan's stridency seemed out of place. The enactment of the 1924 quota bill fulfilled one of the Klan's most sought-after goals and eased the fear of immigrants. Many Americans had come to accept that Prohibition could never be fully enforced. Frustrated by its inability to gain complete implementation, the leadership of the Anti-Saloon League became increasingly sour during the decade of its greatest triumph. Anti-Catholicism persisted, but anti-Catholic movements had never been able to sustain themselves.

The Klan's rapid demise fulfilled the predictions of those who had warned against taking the hooded order seriously. When thousands of unmasked Klansmen marched down Pennsylvania Avenue in August 1925, the event marked the Klan's last hurrah rather than a revival. By that time, even President Coolidge, who had refused to denounce the Klan during the 1924 presidential campaign, had decided it was time to speak out against the KKK. The Klan could still cause mischief (the "radio priest," Father Charles Coughlin, first took to the airwaves in 1926 after a cross-burning outside his church), but even the huge outcry over Al Smith's 1928 nomination could not revive the dormant Klan. For communities whose normal life had been disrupted, the damage had already been done, and some people never forgot the sight of a burning cross, or who among their neighbors had been a "Kluxer."

Deep-seated and powerful social movements do not generally fall apart overnight. The Klan's rapid demise suggests how shallow much of the support for this sometimes ridiculous, sometimes scary organization had been. In retrospect, [historian and social commentator] André Siegfried appears to have been quite correct in his observation that the Klan was more significant for "the atmosphere it expresse[d]" than for the power it possessed. A catchall for postwar disappointments and frustrations, the Klan expressed the hatreds of many people confused by a world that appeared so different from the Victorian America they fondly remembered.

The Battle over the Right to Teach Evolution

Page Smith

On January 28, 1925, the Tennessee legislature passed a law that forbade the teaching of Charles Darwin's theory of evolution in the state public schools. Intending to set a legal precedent for academic freedom, the American Civil Liberties Union (ACLU) persuaded a Dayton, Tennessee, schoolteacher named John Thomas Scopes to help challenge the law. The beloved populist hero William Jennings Bryan served as the lawyer for the prosecution while the celebrated freethinking lawyer Clarence Darrow served on the defense. Darrow was the country's most famous trial lawyer. Bryan, a former secretary of state, was adored by farmers and small-town Americans as the man who had delivered the famous "Cross-of-Gold" speech in the defense of the silver standard at the 1896 Democratic National Convention. The presence of Darrow and Bryan attracted national news coverage and made the trial a heavily symbolic drama that was widely seen as pitting everything old-fashioned against everything modern: fundamentalism against science, rural values against urban values, even Prohibition (in the person of Bryan, who was a well-known Prohibitionist) against those who drank in defiance of the law (in the person of Darrow). The historian Page Smith is best known for his works on the American Revolution and for his multivolume *A People's History of the United States*. In this excerpt Smith depicts the high points of the trial and analyzes the outcome. Although the ACLU did not get the precedent it wanted, the embarrassment of the Scopes trial probably prevented other states from passing antievolutionist legislation.

Page Smith, *Redeeming the Time: A People's History of the 1920s and the New Deal.* New York: McGraw-Hill, 1987. Copyright © 1987 by McGraw Hill Book Company. All rights reserved. Reproduced by permission.

The legislation was sponsored by John Washington Butler, a former teacher, a farmer, and a man renowned for his kindness and public spirit. The bill he presented to his fellow legislators read in part: "An Act prohibiting the teaching of Evolution Theory in all the Universities, Normals, and all other public schools of the State." It would be unlawful for any teacher "to teach any theory that denies the story of the Divine Creation of man as taught in the Bible, and to teach instead that man has descended from a lower order of animals." He introduced his bill, as he explained, because he believed that "The evolutionist who denies the Biblical story of creation, as well as other Biblical accounts, cannot be a Christian. . . . It goes hand in hand with Modernism, makes Jesus Christ a fakir, robs the Christian of his hope and undermines the foundation of our Government. . . ."

There was only token opposition to the bill in Tennessee. The faculty of the University of Tennessee had little say on the subject. The Tennessee Academy of Science was silent. On January 28, 1925, the lower house passed the bill by a vote of 71 to 5. The next day William Jennings Bryan appeared in Nashville to speak on the topic "Is the Bible True?" His answer, which surprised none of his auditors, was that every word was literally true.

The liberal and reform-minded governor of Tennessee, Austin Peay, signed the bill reluctantly while expressing the hope that it would never be enforced. "Nobody," he wrote, "believes that it is going to be an active statute." In other words, it was intended as nothing more than a pious gesture.

The ACLU Steps In

When the Butler Law came to the attention of Roger Baldwin, one of the founders and head of the American Civil Liberties Union, Baldwin decided to have the ACLU challenge its constitutionality. He appealed to John W. Davis, Democratic presidential candidate recently defeated by Calvin Coolidge, to take the case. When Davis refused, Baldwin advertised in the Tennessee papers for an attorney willing to take the case. He received a reply from George W. Rappelyea, a mining engineer, in Dayton, Tennessee, who had grown up in New York City and was in charge of six coal and iron mines owned by the Cumberland Coal Company. Rappelyea enlisted two young lawyers, and the three men then prevailed on John Thomas Scopes, a recent graduate of the University of Kentucky who had come to Dayton to coach football and teach science, to defy the law. Scopes's arrest would then be arranged. "That will make a big sensation," Rappelyea said. "Why not bring a lot of doctors and preachers here? Let's get H.G. Wells and a lot of big fellows." Scopes was reluctant. He believed that "evolution is easily reconciled with the Bible." Finally the young teacher agreed. "It was just a drugstore discussion that got past control," he said later.

Roger Baldwin agreed to the plan. Scopes was arrested, and Baldwin announced to the papers: "We shall take the Scopes case to the supreme court if necessary to establish that a teacher may tell the truth without being thrown in jail." The World Christian Fundamentalist Association promptly enlisted the most famous fundamentalist of them all, William Jennings Bryan, who announced, "For the first time in my life I'm on the side of the majority." Bryan had shouted in challenge to the evolutionists: "You believe in the age of rocks. I believe in the Rock of Ages." He declared: "I would rather begin with God and reason down than begin with a piece of dirt and reason up." And again: "A teacher receiving pay in dollars on which are stamped 'In God We Trust,' should not be permitted to teach the children there is no God."

John Randolph Neal was appointed chief counsel for Scopes. Dean of the law school at the University of Tennessee, Neal had been fired for assigning James Harvey Robinson's *The Mind in the Making* to his students. Encouraged by, among others, [journalist and magazine editor] Henry Mencken, Clarence Darrow volunteered to assist Neal. The judge was John T. Raulston, a native of Gizzards Cove, Tennessee, and a lay preacher in the Methodist Episcopal Church. Judge Raulston announced that God "the Author of all truth and justice shall direct every official act of mine," a statement that the defense did not find reassuring. . . .

The Bible Crusaders of America joined forces with the Supreme Kingdom—an organization founded by Edward

Young Clarke, former head of the Ku Klux Klan—the World Christian Fundamentalist Association of Minneapolis, and the Bryan Leaguers to support the Tennessee law. Millions of words were thus written and uttered on the subject before the trial itself ever began. Politicians and preachers rivaled, if they did not outstrip, professors and other secular prophets. Both sides of the controversy were free to predict disaster if the opposition prevailed. The ideological differences of the two Americas were thrown into sharp relief. Eleven scientists were recruited by the ACLU, with advice from the American Association for the Advancement of Science, to testify in Dayton. . . .

Spotlight on Dayton

Reporters, scientists, fundamentalists, and the merely curious descended on Dayton. For most of the citizens of that rural town, the trial seemed heaven-sent. A Dayton merchant named Darwin hung out a sign that proclaimed: "Darwin is right." In much smaller letters was written: "inside." The front of the Aqua Hotel was painted a garish yellow, and cots were placed in the halls to accommodate the flood of visiting dignitaries. A reporter asked a grizzled old-timer what he thought of the evolution case, and he replied, alarmed, "Land's sake! Who's got it?"

When the orator of the Platte [William Jennings Bryan] arrived, to much fanfare, he was dressed in striped trousers, a black coat, and a white pith helmet to guard against the dangerous rays of Tennessee's July sun. Bryan and John Washington Butler [the Tennessee legislator who had sponsored the law against teaching evolution] were photographed together with their hands on a Bible. At a testimonial dinner for Bryan he was introduced as "the greatest man in the world and its leading citizen."

H.L. Mencken, enraptured by the whole affair, arrived, trailing admiring reporters; two movie crews recorded everything even mildly noteworthy. Local wits greeted out-of-towners with such gibes as "Brother, thy tail hangs down behind." A blind man went about with a sign proclaiming him the world's greatest authority on the Bible. The journalist Joseph Wood Krutch was pleased by the willingness of Daytonians to give their views on theology, cosmology, and astrology. They were in sharp contrast with the state's intelligentsia. Bigotry, Krutch noted, was "militant and sincere," while "intelligence is timid and hypocritical."

Mencken, in his articles for the *Baltimore Sun*, used such terms as "morons" and "peasants" to describe the residents of Rhea County. Of Bryan, he wrote: "Once he had one leg in the White House and the nation trembled under his roars. Now he is a tinpot pope in the Coca-Cola belt and a brother to the forlorn pastors who belabor halfwits in galvanized iron tabernacles behind the railroad yards."

When Clarence Darrow arrived, his reputation as a great lawyer, however heretical, was recognized by the prefixing of "Colonel" to his name. His opinions were respectfully solicited by the more enlightened spirits of the town. . . .

Of the jurors chosen on July 10 [1925], nine were farmers; six were Baptists, four were Methodists; two unrecorded; one was illiterate, and three declared that they read only the Bible. While the judge was cooled by a small electric fan, the jurors beat the air futilely with fans bearing a toothpaste advertisement that read: "Do your gums bleed?" It was all Henry Mencken could have wished.

The Dual Between Darrow and Bryan

Darrow began his case for the defense by declaring that Scopes was on trial "because the fundamentalists are after everybody who thinks . . . [and] he is here because ignorance and bigotry are rampant. . . ." With a style that evoked memories of his defense of Big Bill Haywood in the bombing trial of the Western Federation of Miners in Caldwell, Idaho, in 1906, Darrow treated the aficionados of court trials to a classic performance. He was sixty-eight, and his adversary, Bryan, was sixty-five. What they were doing was reenacting a drama as old as the Republic: faith versus skepticism; science versus religion; the South and Midwest against the Northeast; rural townfolk against big-city slickers (Darrow had, to be sure, been born in Kinsman, Ohio, but he had long since shed any trace of provincialism).

Darrow described the consequences of attempting to restrain the free circulation of ideas: "Today it is the public
school teachers, tomorrow the private. The next day the
preachers and lecturers, the magazines, the books, the newspapers. After a while, Your Honor, it is the setting of man
against man and creed against creed until . . . we are marching backward to the glorious age of the sixteenth century
when bigots lighted faggots to burn the men who dared
bring any intelligence and enlightenment and culture to the
human mind."

Ben McKenzie was a lawyer for the prosecution whose
courtesy title of General indicated his standing in the community. He pulled out all the stops on the Yankee invader
theme. "They had better go back to their homes," he declared, "the seats of thugs, thieves, and Haymarket rioters,
and educate their criminals than to try to proselyte here in
the South. . . ." The defense was trying "to put words into
God's mouth, and have Him say that he issued some sort of
protoplasm, or soft dish rag, and put it in the ocean and said,
'Old boy, if you wait around about 6,000 years, I will make
something out of you.'"

When Bryan finally spoke in the latter days of the trial
(which lasted eight days), he denounced the evolutionists for
classifying man with the mammals, "with lions and tigers and
everything that is bad!" Children taught such notions would
"scoff at the religion of their parents! And the parents have a
right to say that no teacher paid by their money shall rob
their children of faith in God and send them back to their
homes, skeptical, infidels or agnostics or atheists. . . . The
Bible, the record of the Son of God, Savior of the world,
born of the Virgin Mary, crucified and risen again—that
Bible is not going to be driven out of this court by experts
who come hundreds of miles to testify that they can reconcile evolution, with its ancestors in the jungle, with man
made by God in His image, and put here for His purposes as
part of a divine plan." People in the courtroom cheered
Bryan's words, and there were periodic shouts of "Amen."

Much time was taken up with legal technicalities that had
little to do with evolution, and the court audience dwindled.

The judge refused to hear testimony from the scientific experts who had been assembled, a serious blow to the defense that was vigorously protested. Darrow began to bait Judge Raulston, hoping to provoke him into some reaction that would provide the basis for an appeal. He failed. The judge indeed bade fair to outmaneuver Darrow, but Darrow had a final strategy in reserve. He was determined to get Bryan himself on the witness stand and grill him about the literal truth of the Book of Genesis. . . .

Bryan Is Called to the Stand

After the reading of the testimony of the eminent scientists and theologians into the record, the defense called a startled Bryan to the stand, and Clarence Darrow began his work of destruction. It was one of the strangest and most revealing confrontations in our history, loaded or overloaded with symbolic connotations. Did Bryan indeed take every word of the Bible to be literally true? Bryan affirmed that he did. Did Jonah remain three days in the belly of a whale? God could perform any miracle he wished, Bryan replied. Did Joshua make the sun stand still? On many questions Bryan skillfully evaded a direct answer, and Darrow grew increasingly hectoring in his manner. When did the Flood occur? Was the Bible dating calculated at 4004 B.C. accurate? When one of Bryan's answers brought cheers from the audience, Darrow said caustically, "Great applause from the bleachers."

"From those whom you call 'yokels,'" Bryan replied.

Stung, Darrow denied he had used the word.

"Those are people you insult."

"You insult every man of science and learning in the world because he does not believe in your fool religion."

That was too much. The judge cautioned Darrow. But the remorseless questioning went on. When Bryan protested that the questions had "no other purpose than ridiculing every Christian who believes in the Bible," Darrow replied: "We have the purpose of preventing bigots and ignoramuses from controlling the education of the United States and you know it—and that is all."

The questioning of Bryan by Darrow, a matter strictly

speaking, extraneous to the trial itself and improperly allowed by a rattled Judge Raulston, polarized public sentiment more severely than any other event of the trial or the events attendant upon it. Many people who admired and indeed loved Bryan as the embodiment of the democratic faith, the ancient enemy of the capitalists, the champion of rural America were deeply offended by Darrow's treatment of the ancient hero. One Southern editor described it not inaccurately as "a thing of immense cruelty." It was also a serious error on Darrow's part. The judge, after a night's reflection, ordered the exchange stricken from the record, but the damage had been done. Opinion hardened against the defense. Bryan was ravaged by the experience.

The next day the case went to the jury, which took nine minutes to return a verdict of guilty. The judge imposed a fine of $100 on Scopes, who replied with considerable dignity: "Your Honor, I feel that I have been convicted under an unjust statute. I will continue in the future as I have in the past to oppose this law in any way I can. Any other action would be a violation of my ideal of academic freedom—that is, to teach the truth—as guaranteed by our constitution, of personal and religious freedom. I think the fine is unjust." He would refuse to pay the fine and appeal the verdict. The judge set a bond of $500, which Mencken posted. Soon after the trial Scopes confessed to a reporter that he was innocent. He had missed his class on the days when the theory of evolution would normally have been discussed.

The reporters who had swarmed over the town for a fortnight or more hired a band from Chattanooga and put on a dance for the townspeople. Clarence Darrow danced with some of the high school girls. He was clearly the hero. Bryan, tired and ill, slipped away quietly. Five days after the end of the trial he died in his sleep. . . .

Outcomes

The State Supreme Court threw out the *Scopes* case entirely, stating, "We see nothing to be gained by prolonging the life of this bizarre case." The indictment was ordered dropped, and the possibility of an appeal to the U.S. Supreme Court blocked. Nothing in a legal or constitutional way resulted from the whole affair. At the same time it could be said that the case had served some purpose. It had provided the kind of spectacle that the American public doted on; it had given a vast amount of publicity to the doctrines of evolution and helped at the same time to make the point that, at least in the opinion of a substantial number of liberal ministers and theologians, there was no necessary conflict between Christianity and evolution. While the fundamentalists pressed their campaign to ban the teaching of evolution in public schools and colleges with renewed vigor for a time, the tide definitely turned against them. Few states followed the example of Tennessee, and some that had passed similar legislation repealed it. From the time of the Scopes trial the fundamentalists perceived themselves as increasingly beleaguered. . . .

There were, of course, buried or suppressed issues below the surface. There was something, after all, to Bryan's impassioned cry that Christianity itself was on trial. It was religion that came to science, hat in hand, anxious to resolve ancient quarrels and clearly ready to do so primarily on science's terms. The "real experts" were the scientists; the theologians were there to salvage what they could from the debacle. . . .

The issues, practical and symbolic, in the Scopes trial have proved remarkably enduring. The fundamentalists, left for dead, have revived and recently resumed their attack on "secular humanism," on "liberals" and "professors" and the doctrine of evolution. The arguments are much the same as those paraded by the various factions at the time of the Scopes trial. The scientists and liberal theologians have checked in. Once more the fundamentalists perceive their mission as "saving the Bible" (and Americans in general) from infidelism and skepticism. It does little good to assert that there need be no conflict. The tension will be there as long as the aims of life remain shrouded in mystery.

Racism Leads to New Immigration Restrictions

Thomas F. Gossett

Racism in the United States during the 1920s was not re-stricted to any one region of the country, nor to one class of disgruntled people left behind by progress. Rather, it was a widespread point of view. Its adherents could point to prominent scientists who held that the races of human beings were as distinct as different breeds of dogs and that racial mixing would have dire consequences. With the blessings of the government and of universities, scientists pursued programs of psychological testing designed to measure differences in intelligence and personality among the races. Beyond lending support to Jim Crow (segrega-tionist) laws in the South, the scientific racism of the 1920s fed paranoia about the immigrant hordes threaten-ing to overwhelm America's "superior Nordic stock" and helped lead to new restrictions on immigration. Thomas F. Gossett is professor emeritus of English at Wake Forest University and the author of *Race: The History of an Idea in America* and *"Uncle Tom's Cabin" and American Culture*.

During the [First World] War, the energies of the American people were mainly channeled into immediate practical ob-jectives. When the victory had been won, however, the pas-sions and resentments which usually had been restrained for the sake of national unity were freer to indulge themselves. The factory and industrial workers—many of whom were im-migrants or the children of immigrants from southern and eastern Europe—were determined to improve their economic position, through strikes if necessary. The Negro, aware from his experience in Europe that ideas of racial caste were by no means universal, was determined to better his position in this country. And the Americans of the older ethnic groups were more and more intent upon holding the line against the rise in status of ethnic groups they believed to be inferior.

The unrest showed itself in the wave of strikes which began in 1919. Many Americans who participated in the postwar strikes were unquestionably of the older ethnic stocks. Among the 60,000 union members in Seattle and on the West Coast who struck in February 1919, were many native-born American workers of north European stock. Other important strikes, however, were carried on largely by immigrants of more recent origin. In January, a strike of 35,000 New York garment workers began and spread through New England and the middle Atlantic states. In Lawrence, Massachusetts, the English-speaking employees mainly stayed at work while the "foreigners" went out. Many of the 376,000 workers who took part in the great steel strike of 1919 were representatives of the more recent immigrant stock. In addition to these disturbances, there was a relatively small—but at the time immensely significant—number of bombings by anarchists of the homes of judges, police superintendents, and other men in public life, and these bombings led to much comment on the innate character of the racial stocks which had come in recent years from Europe. . . .

Racism and Discrimination Increased in the 1920s

It was about this time that anti-Semitism became a really significant phenomenon in this country. In addition to the fulminations of the [Ku Klux] Klan, the *Dearborn Independent*, a magazine owned by Henry Ford and distributed to thousands of his dealers, began in May 1920, to expose the "International Jew" who encouraged nations to go to war in order to batten on the profits of the munitions industry. "The Founding fathers were men of Anglo-Saxon-Celtic race," said the *Independent*. "Into the camp of this race comes a people that has no civilization to point to, no aspiring religion, no universal speech, no great achievement in any realm but the realm of 'get,' cast out of every land that gave them hospitality, and these people endeavor to tell the sons of the Saxons what is needed to make the world what it ought to be." As evidence of the conspiracy of the Jews, the magazine utilized the "Protocols of the Learned Elders of Zion," documents which purport to show widespread conspiracy to subvert governments but which are recognized by most authorities as forgeries.

Less spectacularly, both Jews and Negroes suffered discrimination from sources which had traditionally been more tolerant of them. One sign of the change was the decision of a number of colleges and universities, particularly in the East, to institute quota systems for Jews. Columbia University, for example, suffered from the taunts of the alumni of schools where few of the students were Jews. A writer in 1921 mentions that those institutions which had sizable numbers of Jews were "made the butt of sly jokes by after-dinner speeches in rival universities, to the effect that such and such a college is safe from fire and flood, since He that keepeth Israel neither slumbers nor sleeps." A campus song put the matter more crudely:

> Oh, Harvard's run by millionaires,
>   And Yale is run by booze,
> Cornell is run by farmers' sons,
>   Columbia's run by Jews.

Columbia acted to remove the basis of the charge by instituting a Jewish quota. New York University, Princeton, and Williams College also instituted a quota. President A. Lawrence Lowell of Harvard strongly supported a quota for Jews at Harvard and instituted a ban on Negroes' living in freshman dormitories—where residence was compulsory—but he was overruled on both scores by a faculty committee and the Harvard Board of Overseers after widespread public protest.

All these incidents suggest that racism was increasing in the United States in terms not merely of violence and open hatred but of subtle and insidious forms of discrimination. Our concern here is not to describe in detail the manifestations of American prejudice and nativism, but primarily to examine the debate over race within the academic disciplines. At first glance, these disciplines may seem somewhat remote from overt manifestations of violence. A man did not need to read an article or book on the biological, anthropological, psychological, or sociological aspects of race in order to participate in a race riot. Still, ideas have a way of trickling down. The academic disciplines would eventually provide a real defense against the ideas of the racists. At the time, however, they were in a state of confusion and unable effectively to combat the onrush of prejudice.

Racism and Intelligence Testing

There were plenty of zealots in the 1920's who frantically proclaimed a gospel of racism. We misinterpret the strength of the racism of the period, however, if we imagine that its most formidable proponents were emotional bigots like the Ku Kluxers. It is essential to understand that quite a large number of people eminent in the sciences and the social sciences were then genuinely convinced that races vary greatly in innate intelligence and temperament. It is futile to condemn these people as villains or hypocrites or fools. They were reflecting very powerful ideas of their time and drawing conclusions from them according to their lights. . . .

The most powerful weapon of the racism of the period continued to be the intelligence test. Because mental tests were thought to be an objective measurement of innate ability and because they showed wide divergences in scores among races and nationality groups, they inevitably entered into the rising debate on the importance of race as a factor in national life. Then too, the tests seemed to make irrelevant all the arguments which had been developed over the past 150 years as to what race actually *is*. What did it matter now that anthropologists had been unable to find any scale by which races could be measured and distinguished from one another? The fact that the median scores for all races and ethnic groups in the country were lower than the scores of the native white Americans of English or north European stock was widely interpreted to mean one thing: all the non-Nordic races were inferior. One observer in 1922 said that everybody in America, even in the remotest villages, was learning the word *moron* and it "showed signs of running 'damn fool' out of the language. . . ." The menace of the "under-man" was widely discussed, and he often turned out to be a member of an "inferior" race.

The psychologists followed the initial success of the army mental tests with a veritable avalanche of testing. In many of these studies, the racist implications were not far below the surface. E.L. Thorndike declared that "race directly and indirectly produces differences so great that government, business, industry, marriage, friendship, and almost every other feature of human instinctive and civilized life have to take account of a man's race." The original uncertainties about the effect of environment upon test scores all but disappeared. As late as 1940, Thorndike was willing to express the relative importance of heredity and environment in terms of percentages. Intelligence could be allocated "roughly" 80 per cent to the genes, 17 per cent to training, and 3 per cent to "accident."

Dr. Carl C. Brigham, an assistant professor of psychology at Princeton, wrote one of the most bizarre of the studies of mental tests as applied to race. In *A Study of American Intelligence*, he accepted the division of Europeans into the three races of Nordic, Alpine, and Mediterranean and interpreted the army intelligence tests of 1917 and 1918 in such a way as to prove the superiority of the Nordic. The army had not attempted this sort of classification of the soldiers taking the test, but it had listed the national origin or descent of the soldiers. Brigham attempted to estimate the amount of Nordic, Alpine, and Mediterranean in each of the European nations. Sweden had 100 per cent Nordic blood, Norway had 90 per cent; Denmark, Holland, and Scotland followed with 85 per cent; England 80 per cent; Wales and Germany, 40 per cent; France and Ireland, 30 per cent; Poland and Spain, 10 per cent; Italy, Russia, and Portugal, 5 per cent. The nations with the highest Nordic blood contributed the largest number of soldiers with "A" and "B" ratings, so Brigham concluded the Nordics must be the most intelligent. "In a very definite way, the results which we obtain by interpreting the army data by means of the race hypothesis support Mr. Madison Grant's thesis of the superiority of the Nordic type." [Grant is the author of *The Passing of the Great Race*, which suggested that people of northern European descent might be overwhelmed by "inferior" races.]

Looking back upon this test, one hardly knows which is its more curious aspect—Brigham's conviction that it was possible to express Nordic, Alpine, and Mediterranean "races" in terms of percentages for whole nations, or his conviction that intelligence was almost wholly unrelated to the quality of the education which different ethnic groups had received. How far he was willing to carry the argument that environmental differences were negligible in determining mental ability may be judged by the conclusion he drew from the fact that more recent immigrants from a given country did not do as well on these tests as those who had been here a considerable time. He discovered that immigrants who had been here twenty years did better on the tests than those who had been here fifteen; those who had been here ten years did better than those who had been here five. These facts did not lead him to conclude that perhaps environment might be a considerable factor; instead, he interpreted the figures as conclusive proof that the innate quality of the more recent immigrants was lower and was steadily declining. From the point of view of the racists among the advocates of immigration restriction, Brigham's study was a real triumph. Even Jewish immigrants did badly on the tests. "Our figures, then," Brigham concluded, "would rather tend to disprove the popular belief that the Jew is highly intelligent."

A critic of Brigham's pointed out that not merely did northern Negroes do better than southern Negroes on the army tests, but the Negroes of some northern states did better than the whites of some southern states. The literate Negroes from Illinois had higher median scores than the literate whites from nine southern states; the literate Negroes from New York surpassed the literate whites from five southern states; the literate Negroes from Pennsylvania surpassed the literate whites from two southern states. None of this convinced Dr. Brigham that education and environment might radically change the intelligence scores. . . .

It was probably inevitable that the psychologists should devise scales for testing the "personalities" of race, now that the matter of racial intelligence medians had apparently been established. A study of the "will-temperament" of Negroes appeared in 1922. An elaborate racial personality study was made on Japanese schoolchildren and another on Chinese, Japanese, and Hawaiians; there was a study of the personalities of Indian children with the implication that the innate character of the race was thus disclosed. Psychologists attempted to measure such "racial" characters as "integrity," "kindliness," "courage," "unselfishness," "reasonableness," "refinement," "cheerfulness and optimism," "motor inhibition," "noncompliance," and "finality of judgment." As one might have predicted, the tests generally showed that Negroes, Indians, Mexicans, and other nonwhite races were ordinarily inferior in their personality traits to the whites. The difficulty common to all the studies was that the researchers had discovered no means of determining the differences between traits caused by heredity and those caused by environment. . . .

Biologists Opposing Race Mixture

The racists could take comfort from many prominent biologists as well as from the psychologists. Some of the biologists regarded it as axiomatic that race mixture, at least among peoples widely different from one another, would lead to "disharmonies." These disharmonies were not necessarily produced by any defects of either race, but simply resulted from the fact that each of them was so unlike the other that to mix them led to physical, mental, and emotional deformities. Even biologists who recognized that the proof for this contention was lacking often thought that race mixture was bad because certain races were poor biological material, and therefore intermarriage with them would have "dysgenic" effects.

Dr. Charles B. Davenport, director of the Eugenics Record Office, a private organization at Cold Spring Harbor, New York, was probably the most positive advocate of the theory that race intermixture led to biological abnormalities. Although warning his readers that the subject had not been sufficiently investigated, Davenport proceeded to issue a series of disturbing conclusions. The Scotch, for example, were "long-lived" and had "internal organs . . . well adapted to care for the large frames." South Italians, on the other hand, had small, short bodies. The hybrids of these two "races" could be expected to yield "children with large frames and inadequate viscera—children of whom it is said every inch over 5'10" is an inch of danger; children of insufficient circulation.". . .

The debates over the dangers of race intermixture were not, of course, merely academic. They took place against the background of a powerful movement drastically to reduce immigration from foreign countries. This movement might have been carried on without becoming involved in race theories, but with the mood of the times this was most unlikely. E.A. Ross, though in former years one of the most vociferous advocates among the sociologists of the idea of race superiority and inferiority, had by 1924 come to see clearly that the blatant racism used in the anti-immigration arguments could have only evil consequences for the nation. An opponent of large-scale immigration, he nonetheless attempted to combat the racist arguments and to argue immigration restriction wholly on its social and economic consequences. He declared:

> The injury suffered by America has not come from an essential inferiority of the immigrants in respect to race fibre, but from their being unfamiliar with our language and institutions and ignorant of how to keep from being exploited economically and politically. It is particularly "the newer immigration," coming from southern and southeastern Europe, which has lacked the background of culture and experience needed for working our institutions.

The census of 1920 had shown that there were nearly 14,000,000 people in the United States who had been born in some other country. The proponents of immigration restriction might have developed an argument which did not imply the innate inferiority of any race. They might have contended that it was not possible to keep immigrants from being exploited as cheap labor if great numbers of them were allowed to come in. It might further have been argued that a readily available cheap labor force would, in turn, serve to depress the wages of workmen already here.

Not all the proponents of immigration were members of ethnic minorities, nor were they all moved chiefly by humanitarian considerations. Judge Elbert H. Gary, for example, had not had a reputation for racial tolerance. As head of the United States Steel Corporation he had defeated the strike of 1919 against a twelve-hour day and a seven-day week largely by pinning the Red label on the strikers and by exploiting race cleavages among the employees. But after an immigration restriction law was passed in 1920, Gary denounced it bitterly as "one of the worst things that this country has ever done for itself economically." This opposition, like the opposition of the National Association of Manufacturers to legislation restricting immigration, was probably due to a desire for cheap labor.

This situation merely emphasizes strange alliances which had been developing for a long time on both sides of the immigration controversy. In favor of large-scale immigration were both high-minded defenders of the immigrants as real or potential good Americans and employers who wanted an uninterrupted supply of cheap labor. Opposed to large-scale immigration were conservative social thinkers who thought socialism and radicalism would flourish if immigration were not curtailed, and liberal thinkers who feared the effects of a continuing source of cheap labor upon the efforts of the unions to improve their status and power. . . . To cement this uneasy alliance, large amounts of racism were apparently necessary. The alliance continued into the 1920's, although the names of the leaders on both sides changed. Now upper-class conservatives like Madison Grant opposed immigration and a group of liberal thinkers—men who would have opposed Grant on every other conceivable issue—agreed with him that immigration must be stopped or at least radically curtailed. . . . It was a reliance upon racism which brought these two points of view, so different from one another, into a powerful alliance. . . .

In the translation of these new "truths" of race to the area of legislation, naturally some caution had to be employed. There were large groups of immigrants from southern and eastern European countries in a number of states, and they could have done considerable harm to any political leader who spoke openly in the manner of Madison Grant, Lothrop Stoddard [writer who wrote widely on the "dangers" of race mixing], or even Alfred E. Wiggam [a racist thinker who tried to reconcile racism with the ideas of religion]. Thus we find that the political leaders who favored immigration restriction spoke with more circumspection. Warren G. Harding, in one of his campaign speeches for the Presidency in 1920, cautiously enunciated the doctrine of racial "differences" in advocating an immigration restriction law. "There is abundant evidence of the dangers which lurk in racial differences," he declared. "I do not say racial inequalities, I say racial differences." No one could "tranquilly contemplate the future of this Republic without anxiety for abundant provision for admission to our shores of only the immigrant who can be assimilated and thoroughly imbued with the American spirit.". . .

Calvin Coolidge expressed the racist implications of immigration restriction more bluntly. In a popular article written in 1922, when he was Vice-President, he argued that biological laws show us that Nordics deteriorate when mixed with other races. But neither Harding nor Coolidge was as forthright as James J. Davis, Secretary of Labor under both administrations, who said that the older immigrants to America were the beaver type that built up America, whereas the newer immigrants were rat-men trying to tear it down; and obviously rat-men could never become beavers. . . .

The campaign for restriction of immigration gained steadily in power. Although the race argument was probably in most peoples' minds, politics demanded that restriction should not seem to be directly aimed at any particular race or nationality. Accordingly, the Immigration Act of 1921 was set up under a "national origins quota," which limited the number of immigrants from any given country in Europe to 3 per cent of the immigrants from that country who were living here in the year 1910. This law was criticized as too liberal and in 1924 a more stringent immigration act was passed, one which reduced the annual quota of each nationality group from 3 to 2 per cent and by using the census of 1890 instead of that of 1910 favored the older immigrant stocks—the English, Irish, German, and Scandinavian immigrants—over the newer immigrant stocks, those from Italy, Austria, Russia, Poland, and other southern and eastern European countries. In addition, the law excluded Japanese immigrants altogether, extending the ban which had previously existed against other Orientals. Even so, the bill was not as stringent as many advocates of restriction would have liked, since both Canada and Latin American countries were exempted from the quota. Because difficulties of determining national origins quotas, the figure of 150,000 annual immigrants set by the bill did not go into effect until 1929. Until the late twenties, a yearly average of 287,000 immigrants were permitted to enter.

Even with its "defects," the immigration restrictionists hailed the Act of 1924 as a great victory. In signing the bill, President Coolidge tersely commented, "America must be kept American," apparently implying that the basis of unity of the country was racial. In a statement to the press, Senator David A. Reed—who had introduced the Senate version of the act—explained that "the races of men who have been coming to us in recent years are wholly dissimilar to the native-born Americans," that "they are untrained in self-government—a faculty that it has taken the Northwestern Europeans many centuries to acquire," and that it was best for America "that our incoming immigrants should hereafter be of the same races as those of us who are already here, so that each year's immigration should so far as possible be a miniature America, resembling in national origins the persons who are already settled in our country." Secretary of Labor Davis described American immigration policy as having passed through three phases: (1) the ideal of "asylum"; (2) the economic attitude; (3) the biological ideal. The *Chicago Tribune* said that the act was "a Declaration of Independence, not less significant and epoch-making for America and the world than the Declaration of 1776."

The act was also significant in ways which were not immediately obvious. The heavy reliance upon racism, the perpetual appeals to the truths of biology, anthropology, sociology, and psychology, could hardly fail to arouse in reflective people—especially those who were working in the disciplines concerned—the question of whether such conclusions were in fact justifiable. The racists, particularly the advocates of Nordic superiority, might seem at the time to have had things much their own way, but a revolt against their ideas was beginning to gain momentum. Although race problems would continue to bedevil the nation for a long time to come, it would be progressively more difficult to call upon the names of eminent men in the sciences and social sciences who were convinced of innate racial inequalities and of the necessity for keeping the inferior races in a subordinate position in society. The idea that races have innate characteristics of mentality and temperament would suffer a crushing series of defeats at the hands of the biological and social scientists of the next generation.

Chapter 5

The Twenties End with a Crash

Turning | Points
IN WORLD HISTORY

Speculation and Government Mismanagement Led to the Crash of 1929

William E. Leuchtenburg

"Never was a decade snuffed out so quickly as the 1920s," writes noted historian William E. Leuchtenburg, referring to the effects of the 1929 stock market crash. Of all the events of the 1920s, none is so distinctly a turning point as the crash that signaled the end of prosperity and the beginning of the Great Depression. With the advantage of hindsight, many economists would decide that the disaster had been brewing ever since the end of World War I—in the suffering of American farmers who had never shared in the decade's prosperity, in the uncertain economies of Europe, and in the bad fiscal policies of both the U.S. government and its European counterparts.

Leuchtenburg is a professor of history at the University of North Carolina at Chapel Hill. In this excerpt from his book *The Perils of Prosperity* he explores the background and the causes of the crash, finding them in unbalanced government policies that led to "maldistribution of income, a weak banking structure, and an overdependence on consumer durable goods."

The prosperity of the 1920s encouraged the contagious feeling that everyone was meant to get rich. The decade witnessed a series of speculative orgies, from "get-rich-quick" schemes to the Florida real estate boom, climaxed in 1928 and 1929 by the Great Bull Market. Before the war, stock market investment had been almost wholly a preserve of the wealthy; in the 1920s, clerks and bootblacks talked know-

merican Can or Cities Service and bought five
margin." In later years, it was frequently said that
by the end of the twenties "everyone was in the market,"
though there were actually fewer, probably far fewer, than a
million people involved. What is closer to the truth is that
millions of Americans followed the market with avid interest; it became, as [economist] J. Kenneth Galbraith remarks,
"central to the culture."

No one can explain what caused the Great Bull Market. It
is true that credit was easy, but credit had been easy before
without producing a speculative mania. Moreover, much of
the speculation was carried on at rates of interest that by any
reasonable standard were tight. More important was the
spirit of optimism that permeated the decade. "We grew up
founding our dreams on the infinite promises of American
advertising," [novelist] Scott Fitzgerald's wife Zelda once remarked. "I still believe that one can learn to play the piano
by mail and that mud will give you a perfect complexion."
The faith people had that they, too, could be rich was deliberately cultivated by people in positions of responsibility—
bankers and heads of investment trusts, who gave every indication of believing what they were saying. In an article
called "Everybody Ought to Be Rich," John J. Raskob argued in the *Ladies' Home Journal* that anyone who saved fifteen dollars a month and bought sound common stocks
would in twenty years be worth $80,000. Since commodity
prices were remarkably stable throughout the boom, economists were confident that, despite the speculative fever, the
economy was basically sound.

The volume of sales on the New York Stock Exchange
leaped from 236 million shares in 1923 to 1,125 million in
1928. That was a year when everything one touched seemed
to turn to gold: industrial stocks went up a then astonishing
86.5 points. Customers borrowed money, bought more
stock, watched the stock go up, and borrowed still more
money to buy still more stock. By 1928, the stock market
was carrying the whole economy. If it had not been for the
wave of speculation, the prosperity of the twenties might
have ended much earlier than it did. [President Calvin]

Coolidge's deflationary policies had withdrawn government funds from the economy, consumers had cut spending for durable goods in 1927, and the market for housing had been glutted as early as 1926. But with the economy sparked by fresh funds poured into speculation, a depression was avoided and the boom continued.

The stock market frenzy began in March 1928. On Saturday, March 3, Radio sold at 94½. By the next Friday, it had surged to 108. On the following day it bounded to 120½. It seemed impossible, but when the market closed on Monday morning, Radio had gained another 18 points and was selling at 138½. The next morning, Radio opened at 160, a gain of 21½ points overnight. And it did not stop. After a few days of relative quiet, Radio jumped 18 points on March 20. The Big Bull Market was under way. Not long before he left office, President Coolidge announced that stocks were "cheap at current prices." The summer of 1929 not only bore out his dictum but made the gains of 1928 look modest in comparison. In three months—from June to August—industrials climbed 110 points; in a single summer, the value of industrial stocks increased by almost a quarter.

Even by the summer of 1928, the market had drawn people who never dreamed they would be caught in the speculative delirium. How much longer could you hold out when your neighbor who bought General Motors at 99 in 1925 sold it at 212 in 1928? There were stories of a plunger who entered the market with a million dollars and ran it up to thirty millions in eight months, of a peddler who parlayed $4,000 into $250,000. The Bull Market was not simply a phenomenon of New York and Chicago; there were brokerage offices in towns such as Steubenville, Ohio, and Storm Lake, Iowa. In an era of prohibition, as Charles Merz points out, [in a 1929 *Harpers* magazine article on the bull market] the broker's office took the place of the barroom; it had "the same swinging doors, the same half-darkened windows." In midmorning, men would slump into the mahogany chairs of the smoke-filled room to search the blackboard or the hieroglyphics of the chattering ticker tape for news of the fate of Anaconda or Tel. and Tel. and remain until closing time.

The Crash

In early September 1929, the stock market broke, rallied, then broke again. By early October, Radio had tumbled 32 points, General Electric over 50 points, U.S. Steel almost 60 points. Still there was no panic. "Stock prices," announced Professor Irving Fisher of Yale, in what was to become a classic statement, "have reached what looks like a permanently high plateau." In the last week in October, the situation turned suddenly worse. On October 23, rails and industrials fell 18 points. On Thursday, October 24, prices broke violently, and a stampede set in. The gains of many months were wiped out in a few hours. Radio opened at 68¾, closed at 44½. After a brief respite, the downward plunge resumed with reckless fury. On Monday Steel lost 17½, Westinghouse 34½, General Electric 47½. The next day, Tuesday, October 29, was one of sickening disaster. The ticker closed two and a half hours behind; when the last sales had been listed, industrial stocks had zoomed down 43 points.

On November 13, the market reached the lowest point it was to hit that year, but this was only the beginning of the end. On that day, industrial stocks were 228 points lower than they had been in early September; their value had been cut in half. In September, industrials had stood at 452; in November 1929, they were 224. On July 8, 1932, at the bottom of the depression, they would sink to 58. In three years General Motors plummeted from 92 to 8, U.S. Steel from 262 to 22, Montgomery Ward from 138 to 4.

One can assign no single cause to the crash and the ensuing depression, but much of the blame for both falls on the foolhardy assumption that the special interests of business and the national interest were identical. Management had siphoned off gains in productivity in high profits, while the farmer got far less, and the worker, though better off, received wage increases disproportionately small compared to profits. As a result, the purchasing power of workers and farmers was not great enough to sustain prosperity. For a while this was partly obscured by the fact that consumers bought goods on installment at a rate faster than their income was expanding, but when the time came that they had to reduce purchases, the cutback in buying sapped the whole economy. With no counteraction from labor unions, which were weak, or from government, business increased profits at twice the rate of the growth in productivity. So huge were profits that many corporations no longer needed to borrow, and as a result Federal Reserve banks had only minimal control when profits were then plunged into the stock market, fueling a runaway speculation.

The policies of the federal government in the 1920s were disastrous. Its tax policies made the maldistribution of income and oversaving by the rich still more serious. Its oligopoly policies added to the rigidity of the market and left business corporations too insensitive to changes of price. Its farm policies sanctioned a dangerous imbalance in the economy. Its tariff policies made a difficult foreign-trade situation still worse. Its monetary policies were irresponsible, and at critical junctures the fiscal policy of the Coolidge administration moved in precisely the wrong direction.

The Depression Begins

The market crash played an important, but not the critical, role in precipitating the Great Depression. It shattered business confidence, ruined many investors, and wiped out holding company and investment trust structures. It destroyed an important source of long-term capital and sharply cut back consumer demand. Yet business would have been able to weather even the shock of the crash, if business had been fundamentally sound. The crash exposed the weaknesses that underlay the prosperous economy of the twenties—the overexpansion of major industries, the maldistribution of income, the weak banking structure, and the overdependence of the economy on consumer durable goods.

Developments in the construction and automobile industries foreshadowed what was to come. Residential building, which had stood at five billion dollars in 1925, was down to three billion by 1929. Auto manufacturing continued to grow, but after 1925 at a much slower rate, which meant cutting back purchases of steel and other materials; the cycle of events, whereby an increase in car production stimulated the steel, rubber, glass, and other industries, now operated in a reverse manner to speed the country toward a major depression. By 1929, the automobile industry—and satellites such as the rubber-tire business—were badly overbuilt. Since there was no new industry to take the place of automobiles and no policy of federal spending to provide new investment ([Secretary of the Treasury Andrew] Mellon, in fact, was working in the opposite direction), it was inevitable that as investment fell off and the rate of production slackened, there would be a serious slump.

Furthermore, no other industrial nation in the world had as unstable or as irresponsible a banking system. "The banks," noted one writer, "provided everything for their customers but a roulette wheel." During these years, wrote [economist] Joseph Schumpeter, "a new type of bank executive emerged who had little of the banker and looked much like a bond salesman"; these banker-promoters financed speculation and loaded the banks with dubious assets. By the time the banking crisis reached its height in [President Herbert] Hoover's last three weeks in office, nine million savings accounts would be wiped out. Nothing did more to turn the stock market crash of 1929 into a prolonged depression than the destruction of business and public morale by the collapse of the banks.

By 1932, manufacturing output had fallen to 54 percent of what it had been in 1929; it was a shade less than production in 1913. All the gains of the golden twenties were wiped out in a few months. By the last year of the Hoover administration, the automobile industry was operating at only one-fifth of its 1929 capacity. As the great auto plants in Detroit lay idle, fires were banked in the steel furnaces on the Allegheny and the Mahoning. By the summer of 1932, steel plants operated at 12 percent of capacity, and the output of pig iron was the lowest since 1896. Between 1929 and 1932, freight shipments were cut in half, and major railroad systems such as the Missouri Pacific, the Chicago and North Western, and the Wabash passed into receivership.

In heavily industrialized cities, the roll of the depression read, as one observer noted, like British casualty lists at the

Somme [a World War I battle resulting in an estimated 500,000 British casualties]—so awesome as to become in the end meaningless, for the sheer statistics numbed the mind. By 1932, there were 660,000 jobless in Chicago, a million in New York City. In Cleveland, 50 percent were unemployed; in Akron, 60 percent; in Toledo, 80 percent. In Donora, Pennsylvania, only 277 of 13,900 workers held regular jobs. In the three years after the crash, 100,000 people were fired on the average every week.

Like a chill bay fog, fear of the bread line drifted up into the middle class. Detroit counted 30 former bank tellers on its relief rolls. Universities graduated thousands of engineers, architects, and lawyers who had not the slightest prospect of a job. With no hope of employment, young people postponed marriage or, if they were married, did not have children. In 1932, there were 250,000 fewer weddings than in 1929, and the birth rate slipped from 18.8 to 17.4 per thousand. Hundreds of thousands of working women had to go back to their homes. Economy-minded school boards halted building projects and slashed teachers' salaries. Chicago teachers, unpaid for months, lost their savings, had to surrender their insurance policies, and were forced to borrow from loan sharks at 42 percent annual interest. By the middle of 1932, over 750 had lost their homes.

Farmers, who had not known the best of times in the 1920s, were devastated by the depression. The crash—and the ensuing financial debacle—destroyed much of what remained of their foreign markets. American trade abroad declined from $10 billion in 1929 to $3 billion in 1932. Foreign capital issues fell from $1500 million in 1928 to an abysmally small $88 million in 1932. As other nations erected additional barriers to U.S. products and unemployment cut heavily into the domestic market, crop prices skidded to new lows. Wheat dropped from $1.05 a bushel in 1929 to 39 cents in 1932, corn from 81 cents to 33 cents a bushel, cotton from 17 cents to 6 cents a pound, tobacco from 19 cents to 10 cents a pound. The result was catastrophic. Gross farm income fell from nearly $12 billion to the pitiful sum of $5 billion.

The depression touched every area of American life.

Bergdorf Goodman slashed sables 40 percent, Marcus and Company offered a $50,000 emerald ring for $37,500, and the Pullman Company reduced rates on upper berths 20 percent. The Yankees mailed Babe Ruth a contract for the 1932 season with a $10,000 salary cut, and the Giants offered their star first baseman, Bill Terry, 40 percent less. The United Hospital Fund reported that donors not only reneged on pledges but even asked that the previous year's contributions be returned to them. On Broadway, theater lights were darkened; on Fifth Avenue, strollers no longer heard the sound of riveters. The managers of the Empire State Building ended all pretext that its offices were rented; elevators stopped running from the 42d to the 67th floors.

Wall Street Crashes

Edward Robb Ellis

The 1929 Wall Street stock market crash tends to be remembered as a single event that occurred on a single day, but it actually lasted for about a week in October 1929. From Wednesday, October 23, through Tuesday, October 29, the country watched as panicked selling by frantic investors swamped the exchange. On Thursday leading bankers tried to restore confidence by pouring money into key stocks. On Friday bargain hunting by people who thought the crash might be over sent the market up slightly. Brokers promised their clients that a quick recovery was on the way. But on Monday morning a great backlog of selling orders awaited the brokers, sending the market spiraling down once more. On the legendary Black Tuesday, chaos reigned and the stock market led the world into a grim new era. Newspaper journalist Edward Robb Ellis experienced the consequences of the economic collapse firsthand when his hometown bank failed. In this excerpt from his history of the Great Depression, Ellis vividly depicts the atmosphere of the New York Stock Exchange during the worst days of the crash.

On Thursday, October 24, 1929, the New York *Times* reported the previous day's trading in a front-page two-column headline that said:

PRICES OF STOCKS CRASH

IN HEAVY LIQUIDATION;

TOTAL DROP OF BILLIONS

The *Times* and other morning papers published Washington dispatches quoting treasury officials as saying that the market break had been due to speculation and did not represent any basic weakness in American business. . . .

When the clock on the west wall of the trading room [of the New York Stock Exchange] struck ten, Superintendent William B. Crawford hit the gong to signal the opening of trading. Brokers rushed toward the posts clutching handfuls of customers' orders. Orders to sell. After holding firm for a few minutes, most stocks began declining. The securities were not sold in small lots but in huge blocks; they were being dumped into the market. Six thousand shares of Montgomery Ward sold at 83 points; earlier in the year this stock went for 156. Twenty thousand shares of Kennecott Copper were sold. So enormous was the volume of trading that by 10:30 A.M. the ticker was fifteen minutes behind. This lag was confusing, for spreads of up to 30 points developed between prices quoted on the floor and those recorded on the tardy tape.

By 11 A.M. all was panic. Prices were plunging 5, 10, even 15 points a minute. It seemed that everyone was scrambling to sell at whatever price he could get. On this spectacular day 1,100 brokers and 1,000 assistants thronged the trading floor and clustered about the trading posts, shouting and signaling. They were doing their best to handle the thousands upon thousands of selling orders that poured into Wall Street. Brokers feverishly made long-distance calls the length and breadth of America to demand margin, more margin, from their customers.

By this date the Marx Brothers had taken their show *Animal Crackers* to Baltimore, and during the morning a telephone call awakened Groucho Marx in his Baltimore hotel room. It was his broker.

"Sorry to disturb you," said the broker, "but there's been a little slump in the market and I'll have to ask you for more margin."

Groucho, who thought he was worth $240,000 in securities, asked in disbelief: "Margin? What kind of a slump *is* it? I thought I had everything covered so nothing could touch it."

"Well-ll-l," the broker replied, "it's sort of a . . . a crisis. . . . I don't know how much longer I can hold out.". . .

Leading Bankers Try to Restore Confidence

At 12 noon reporters saw three prominent bankers enter J.P. Morgan's private bank at 23 Wall Street, just across the street from the exchange. They were Charles E. Mitchell, chairman of the National City Bank; Albert H. Wiggin, chairman of the Chase National Bank; and William Potter, president of the Guaranty Trust Company. Sidewalk gawkers did not recognize these men, but reporters shouted their names and titles to one another.

Morgan's bank was a squat, five-story gray building worth nearly $6 million—double the cost of the main building of the New York Stock Exchange. With the great Morgan himself vacationing in Great Britain, the other bankers had been summoned by the senior Morgan partner, Thomas Lamont. Already present inside the bank was Seward Prosser, chairman of the Morgan firm, and the group was later joined by George F. Baker, Jr., chairman of the First National Bank of New York. . . .

Aware of the sickening crisis on the floor of the exchange, the six bankers decided to form a coalition to pump new life into the dying market. This they did by forming a pool, with each pledging $40 million for a total of $240 million. An additional $100 million was supplied by other financial firms, including the Guggenheim Brothers and James Speyer and Company. It was by far the largest concentration of pool buying power ever directed at the stock market. The bankers did not seek to establish any particular price level in the market. What they wanted to do was to indulge in a bold psychological gesture to end the panic—and protect themselves.

This strategy was agreed on in a mere twenty minutes. The bankers understood that to make a success of this pool, unlike other pools, they needed all the publicity they could get. As the other grim-faced financiers hurried back to their own offices, Lamont walked down one flight to the lobby of the Morgan bank, where he faced reporters. His expression serious, but his voice calm, Lamont announced to the press that "there has been a little distress selling on the Stock Exchange." This understatement has since become a Wall Street classic. Distress selling means a feverish wish to sell at any price. However, Lamont continued, this selling was "due to a technical condition of the market," rather than to any fundamental trouble. He was sure that things were "susceptible to betterment."

During the morning the frenetic action on the floor of the exchange drew 722 sightseers to the visitors' gallery, where their excited cries added to the deafening noise in the big room. At 12:30 P.M. these people were ushered out, and the gallery was closed. Among those who had been watching was a visiting Englishman, Winston Churchill, who recently had resigned as Great Britain's chancellor of the exchequer.

By 1 P.M., with the ticker now ninety-two minutes behind, stock values had shrunk a total of about $11 billion, and the newly formed bankers' pool was about to swing into action. E.H.H. Simmons, the president of the New York Stock Exchange, was far away in Hawaii on his honeymoon. In his absence, Lamont and the other bankers had chosen the vice-president [of the stock exchange], Richard Whitney, to make their move. Whitney was about to have his hour of glory.

At 1:15 P.M. he sauntered out onto the floor. Because Whitney was seldom seen there, because word of the bankers' emergency meeting had seeped into the exchange and because everyone could guess his mission, brokers gasped when they saw him. Debonair, almost jaunty, Whitney shouldered his way through the masses of men and up to trading post No. 2, where United States Steel was sold. When trading had begun in the morning, Steel had started at 205½, a point or two above the previous day's closing. During the day it sank to a low of 193½, and minutes before Whitney's appearance it had been hovering around 195.

In a loud and confident voice, Whitney now offered to buy 25,000 shares of Steel at 205—or 10 points *above* the asking price. This *beau geste*, this expression of confidence in the market, was so heartening to brokers that they burst into cheers. Order clerks shouted the electrifying news through direct-wire telephones to every brokerage house in New York, and within seconds it was relayed to every corner of the nation. The big bankers had made their move. They were protecting the market. The longed-for organized support had come to the rescue in the nick of time.

Then and there, Whitney bought 200 shares of United States Steel, leaving the balance of his order with a specialist—an exchange member who executes orders given him by other brokers. With all eyes following him, Whitney then moved on to other trading posts, purchasing other stocks in blocks of 10,000 and 20,000 shares. Inside half an hour he bought 200,000 shares of various securities at a cost to the bankers' pool of more than $20 million.

By 2 P.M. the market had taken a vigorous upward turn. Although some selling continued, Whitney's grandstand play seemed to have stemmed the panic. Stock prices rallied. General Electric, for example, bounced back 25 points. At the end of the day's trading, United States Steel closed at 206.

At 3 P.M., with the ringing of the gong, trading ended. Brokers leaned wearily against trading posts, their collars torn, their faces wet with sweat. A record-breaking total of 12,894,650 shares had been traded, and the industrial average was down a little more than 12 points. The ticker had fallen so far behind transactions that it did not stop chattering until 7:08½ P.M., more than four hours after the exchange closed for the day.

Only then could the magnitude of the disaster be calculated. All day long the exchange's telephone system had been clogged with calls from speculators eager to learn where they stood. Thousands of small investors now heard that they had been wiped out. In one small community in upper New York State 108 of 150 families had been playing the market on margin; now only 6 of these families had any securities left. Thousands of brokerage and bank accounts, prosperous a mere week earlier, had been wrecked. . . .

The Market Rallies

On Friday, October 25, the New York *Times* published a front-page story under this four-column headline:

WORST STOCK CRASH STEMMED BY BANKS;
12,894,650-SHARE DAY SWAMPS MARKET;
LEADERS CONFER, FIND CONDITIONS SOUND

The New York *World* published an eight-column streamer that said:

NATION'S FINANCIERS DECLARE
SECURITY PANIC HAS NO ECONOMIC BASIS

President Hoover, as requested, had issued a statement saying in part: "The fundamental business of the country—that is, the production and distribution of goods and services—is on a sound and prosperous basis." Years later, in his memoirs, Hoover explained his reasoning: "Obviously, as President, I had no business to make things worse in the middle of a crash. Loath to speak of the stock market, I offered as encouragement a short statement on our progress in the productive system and the long-view strength of the country.". . .

All day long on that Friday, October 25, the market was orderly and temperate, with a total of 5,923,220 shares being traded. Some foolhardy speculators bought wildly in the hope of getting stocks at bargain prices, touching off a mild upswing that continued throughout the day, with only a few declines. For the most part, however, trading proceeded at an even pace. Thirty-five of the largest brokerage houses on the exchange, which did 70 percent of all trading there, had wired clients all over the country predicting that the market would recover quickly.

On Saturday, October 26, eighty-five newspapers across the land published paid advertisements prepared by the house of Hornblower and Weeks recommending the purchase of "sound securities." Alfred P. Sloan, Jr., president of General Motors, called the decline in stock prices beneficial to the market. . . .

Rumors of Recovery

Monday, October 28, opened with rumors about a gigantic backlog of buying orders that had piled up over the weekend. The morning papers carried still more advertisements by brokers advising smart people to pick up stock bargains while they could. All these heartening words meant nothing, though, for the moment the Stock Exchange opened at 10 A.M. utter panic erupted.

Not buying orders but selling orders had accumulated. Country bankers had decided to liquidate their holdings, and individual speculators simply refused to believe the reassuring statements. Brokers soon learned that once again thousands of their customers wanted to sell at any price, however low, just to get out of the market. Margin accounts became exhausted as commission men sent out other frantic calls for more cash. . . .

Black Tuesday

Then came Tuesday, October 29, 1929.

The weather was on the chilly side, the sky partly cloudy and the temperature averaging 44 degrees. New Yorkers read in their morning papers that the great George M. Cohan could be seen at the Fulton Theater in his new play called *Gambling*. William Randolph Hearst's friend Marion Davies was appearing on the screen of the Capitol Theater in *Marianne*, billed as "M-G-M's greatest of all talking, musical pictures." Up in the Bronx movie star John Gilbert's latest film, *His Glorious Night*, was being shown at Loew's Paradise.

At 10 A.M., when trading opened on the New York Stock Exchange, it was hit by a tidal wave of selling. Never had the nation seen such a fury of liquidation. Obviously, the big speculators were now scrambling to get out of the market, for at first most of the trading consisted of huge blocks of 5,000 and even 50,000 shares. Regardless of price, these were unloaded like so many bales of hay.

By 10:20 A.M. the ticker was six minutes late. Corporations and out-of-town bankers wanted to convert their securities into cash amounting to billions of dollars. Housewives who had speculated with the grocery money wanted to liquidate before their husbands discovered what they had done. Bookkeepers who had embezzled company funds to play the market were frantic lest they lose all, be discovered, go to jail.

By 10:30 A.M. a total of 3,259,800 shares had been traded. This alone was almost a full day's work for the exchange. As the figure appeared on the ticker tape uncurling from inverted glass bowls in brokerage houses and newspaper offices, men involuntarily whistled in amazement. Bending over a ticker in the city room of the New York *World*, Franklin P. Adams reflected that it is more fascinating to be an observer of the news when things are going badly than when they are going well. Samuel Cahan, a staff artist for the *World*, grabbed pencils and pens and sped to the floor of the exchange to sketch the historic scene. Claude A. Jagger, filling in as financial editor of the New York *Times*, sent squads of reporters galloping to Wall Street.

Reactions Across the Country

It would be misleading to imply that *all* Americans were concerned with the crisis on Wall Street, for they were not. One eighteen-year-old college freshman, a self-proclaimed sheik in the parlance of that era, wrote that day in his diary: "I took Clyda to Workshop to see three plays presented, two of which had Kappa Sigs in the leading roles. It was drizzling a trifle when we got out, but we walked a few minutes and then took to our favorite bench. Here I grasped her to me to kiss her repeatedly. . . ." Twenty-five-year-old J. Robert Op-

A crowd gathers outside the New York Stock Exchange following the crash of October 29, 1929.

penheimer, a brilliant physicist, was so intent on his own theories that he read no newspapers, had no telephone and did not learn about the Crash until the spring of 1930.

Here and there across the nation ordinary folks, as well as unusual people, lived their daily lives as ever, unaware that prosperity was coming apart at the seams. The bull market was dying. A nation was trying to sell out. The country's financial structure was tumbling down. From the swamps of Louisiana to the timberland of Oregon, from New England hamlets to Miami Beach hotels, big and little speculators rushed to telephones and to Western Union offices to order their brokers to sell, sell, sell—sell at any price, however low! The New York Telephone Company recorded 11,000 more calls than on a normal Tuesday. Western Union reported that telegraphic traffic between the Far West and New York was up almost 300 percent. Transatlantic telephone messages more than doubled, as Americans vacationing in Europe and financiers living in Asian capitals tried to get out of the market before it was too late.

On the floor of the New York Stock Exchange frenzied brokers milled about, fought their way to trading posts, sought bids. There were almost no buyers. The visitors' gallery was still closed, empty. The volume of trading was immensely greater than on the previous Black Thursday. At noon a few clerks, sneaking out for a quick bite, yelled to people on the street that in the first two hours of business more than 8,000,000 shares had been exchanged. Police Commissioner Whalen had sent still more policemen to the financial district, where a few political speakers were now haranguing the crowds.

Although brokers had solicited business from women, they considered women poor losers. Elderly ladies now jammed uptown brokerage offices, and when they learned of the developing debacle, they turned on their brokers, blaming them for everything. One old woman wearing four rings on one hand and smoking gold-tipped cigarettes taken from a jewel-studded gold case stalked about announcing in a brassy voice that she had lost $10,000. She seemed almost proud of the fact.

Four other women left in a chauffeur-driven limousine to visit one commission house after another on upper Broadway, making a social occasion of a national disaster. At each office they would enter regally and parade to positions from which they could see the latest quotations and stare about haughtily. All wore the rimless helmet-shaped hats then in fashion. One of the proud ladies let it be known that she had dropped $15,000, raked the room with disdainful eyes and remarked: "This place is depressing." The quartet then departed to descend upon another office.

Trying to Stem the Tide

A businessman took to the radio to warn Congress against making any "ill-advised" moves against the nation's various stock exchanges. Members of the Federal Reserve Board sat in continuous session in Washington, not even breaking for lunch. Treasury Secretary Mellon, an ex officio member of the board, attended the early part of the meeting and then left for the White House to attend a Cabinet meeting. Washington correspondents were unable to learn whether the market situation was discussed by President Hoover and the Cabinet members.

On Wall Street one of the vital questions was whether to shut the Stock Exchange. This action had been considered and then rejected on Friday, October 25. Some brokers felt that the present day's frenzy was due to the fact that word had leaked out about closing the exchange. By now, however, hysteria was sweeping the country, the market had gone out of control, and order was dissolving into chaos. A decision to close the exchange could be made only by that institution's governing committee of about forty members.

Beginning at noon, committee members slipped away from the trading floor in twos and threes, hoping their absence would not be noted in the excitement. They did not go to their usual conference room, gathering instead in the office of the president of the Stock Clearing Corporation, directly below the big room. This office was too small to accommodate all of them easily, so some sat or stood on tables. They lit cigarettes with shaking hands, took a drag or two, ground them out, lit up again. Every few minutes they heard that certain stocks had dropped to new lows. Even so, they decided that to close the exchange would only aggravate an already critical situation.

Another noon meeting of grave importance was in progress elsewhere. Once again members of the bankers' coalition met in the House of Morgan. All were agitated by the fact that the exchange floor was rife with rumors that they were selling, rather than buying. Aware that these reports were being believed, the bankers feared for their reputations. They admitted to one another that their pool was falling apart. Very well, then, since they were unable to continue to prop up the prices of selected stocks, at least they could try to maintain some semblance of order, beat an orderly retreat. On into the day the bankers debated how to do this.

By 1:30 P.M. of this October 29 a total of 12,652,000 shares had been traded on the disintegrating exchange, and early editions of New York's afternoon papers reported the growing calamity. On the Bowery, a few blocks north of the financial district, some ragged bums got the idea that stocks were selling at a nickel a share, so they panhandled some money, pooled their coins as the bankers had pooled their millions, and descended upon Wall Street with the intention of investing in the future of America. This ragged individualism was thwarted by hard-faced cops, who turned them away.

The panhandlers were not too far off in their evaluation of the crisis. White Sewing Machine stock, which had hit a high of 48 in the previous months, had closed at 11 the night before and now sank to almost nothing. Nobody bid for White stock, except a bright messenger boy who worked for the exchange. He offered to pay $1 a share and immediately was given a chance to purchase 10,000 shares.

Various attempts were made to restore confidence. Jimmy Walker, the city's playboy mayor who always spent more than he earned, showed up in the Hotel Astor at a meeting of film exhibitors and begged them to "show pictures which will reinstate courage and hope in the hearts of people." John J. Raskob of General Motors declared that now was the time to buy stock at bargain prices. State Superintendent of

Insurance Albert Conway urged firms under his jurisdiction to buy common stocks. United States Steel and the American Can Company declared extra dividends of $1 per share. But all these gestures were as futile as King Canute's command to the tide to stay away from his royal feet.

Chaos

The floor of the Stock Exchange had become a bubbling caldron of confusion. Brokers frantically wigwagged hand signals to one another, sweat staining the armpits of their jackets. Afraid of losing collateral, they mauled one another to close in on the few buyers who appeared. They tore at one another's hair and coat lapels. They lost shoes and glasses and false teeth. They thronged the trading posts like college boys storming the goalposts at the end of a football game. They gathered in agitated knots, made frenzied deals, broke apart. They scurried to and from conferences. When ever another key stock sank to a new low, here and there a trader collapsed and fell to the floor. All was bedlam. The uproar sounded different to different people. Some said it reminded them of the roar of lions, others the yowling of tigers, still others the yelping of hyenas. One witness to the day's insanity was a seventeen-year-old coupon clerk named Art Linkletter, who later became a famous television personality. Another was a twenty-year-old assistant in a brokerage house, Everett Sloane, who developed into a distinguished movie and television character actor.

By 2:10 P.M., with 13,838,000 shares already traded, prices were plummeting so fast that even brokers on the floor could not keep track of the situation. Mistakes multiplied as everyone reached the breaking point. One customer was sold out twice. Orders to sell were stacked up so high in brokers' offices that clerks fell two hours behind in the mere task of telephoning them to the floor. Under this avalanche of selling, accounting systems failed and communications systems ruptured. Many commission houses hired boys just to untangle telephone cords on trading tables. One firm thought it had gone bankrupt, only to learn later than an exhausted clerk had made a mathematical error. Women workers fainted and were sent home. One male employee passed out but was revived and put back to work again. After the close of trading one broker found a big wastebasket of orders he had forgotten to process in the excitement.

In commission houses in other big cities across America, people with wet hands stood pale and trembling, hovering over ticker tape machines like relatives at the bedside of a rich uncle. Widows—who had speculated with the insurance money left them by their dead husbands. Chorus girls—who had skimped on hosiery to play the market. Furniture sales-men—who had thrown their life savings at the feet of the golden bull. Now, because the ticker was so tardy, they could not be sure just how much they had lost. Every new quota-tion they saw could be one or two hours late; maybe more. All realized, though, that they were being wiped out, and each reacted in terms of his own temperament. Some were stunned, speechless. Others babbled hysterically. A few, struck by the absurdity of a world gone mad, laughed dry and mirthless laughs.

In Providence, Rhode Island, a coal dealer dropped dead of a heart attack while watching the ticker in his broker's of-fice. In Kansas City an insurance man, eyeing the quotations in the Kansas City Club, shouted, "Tell the boys I can't pay them what I owe them!"—and fired two shots into his chest. Down in the Antarctic a member of Admiral Richard Byrd's expedition announced cheerfully that he had been wiped out but could not think of a better place to be without a cent to his name. . . .

At 3 P.M. the ringing of the bell ended the most disastrous day in the history of the New York Stock Exchange. For a split second, brokers froze on the floor like ballet dancers completing a frenzied whirl. Then in slow motion, they low-ered their heads and arms to trudge with weary steps through torn slips of paper carpeting the floor like dry au-tumn leaves.

Assessing the Damage

The ticker, more than two and one-half hours late, finally caught up with quotations at 5:32 P.M. Only then did everyone learn the official figure of the volume of trading on the biggest exchange in the land: A record-breaking 16,410,030 shares had traded hands. This figure was not to be exceeded for thirty-nine years, not until the year 1968. More than 16,000,000 sales? Why, this was more than triple the volume once considered a fabulously big day in the market.

And what of prices? The industrial average had fallen 70 ¾ points during the day, then recovered 40⅞ during the last-minute surge of buying. Westinghouse had opened at 131, dropped to 100, rallied to 126. American Can had started at 130, sunk to 110, risen to 120. United States Steel, for which Richard Whitney had bid 205 the previous Thursday, fell to 167 in the course of the day but closed at 174. Prices for the day were down a general average of 24⅝. A majority of stocks had become thoroughly demoralized. . . .

How much money was lost? No one knows for sure, not even to this day. The very question is pointless, for it was not just money that was lost but arbitrary values with no roots in reality. Additionally, mistakes were made in bookkeeping, some sales were not recorded and other trading took place outside the walls of organized exchanges.

After the catastrophe of October 29 stock prices continued to sink, although fewer shares were traded. Prices finally plunged to their lowest point on November 13, 1929. . . .

In its issue of October 30, 1929, *Variety* printed this immortal headline:

WALL ST. LAYS AN EGG

A stricken America lay back exhausted.

The Aftermath of the Crash

William K. Klingaman

The 1929 stock market crash helped to trigger the Great Depression, a severe economic downturn that lasted ten years. Quickly spreading from the United States to Europe, the depression caused immeasurable human suffering, putting millions of people out of work, shaming jobless fathers in the eyes of their wives and children, and impressing deep psychological scars—including a lasting memory of poverty and a desperate concern with economic security—on an entire generation. In the United States it sharply altered the political balance between the parties, putting Democrats firmly in control of the White House for two decades and of Congress for most of that time. It also expanded the role of the U.S. government. By greatly reviving a generation's interest in socialism and communism (which seemed like possible remedies to the woes of the 1930s) the depression helped pave the way for the anti-Communist repression of the 1950s.

In the following excerpt William K. Klingaman, author of *1929: The Year of the Great Crash* and *The Encyclopedia of the McCarthy Era*, depicts the United States at the start of the depression and discusses the lasting worldwide consequences of the crash. As Klingaman points out, the depression was of great use to Adolf Hitler in his rise to power. By discrediting and destabilizing Germany's Weimar Republic, the depression helped the Nazis seize control of the government. By weakening the economies of France and England, it prevented them from rearming against a resurgent Germany. Thus, the economic collapse that began in 1929 helped bring about one of the greatest cataclysms in human history—World War II.

In the summer of 1930, President Herbert Hoover greeted a delegation of American clergymen who had come to the White House to urge him to initiate an expanded federal public works program. "You have come sixty days too late," Hoover told them. "The depression is over."

If Hoover truly believed what he said, he was either a fool or a blind man. Between the summer of 1930 and the spring of 1933, the economies of the United States and the nations of western Europe spun ever more swiftly downward into the numbing misery of the Great Depression. The national income of the the United States plummeted from $88 billion in 1929 to $40 billion in 1932–33. The output of American factories declined by 50 percent; automobile production fell to 20 percent of its 1929 high. In the depths of the depression, American steel mills were operating at 12 percent of capacity, and the production of pig iron stood at its lowest point since 1896. Banks failed with increasing and horrifying frequency across the nation: 659 banks went under in 1929; 1,352 in 1930; and 2,294 in 1931. Stronger banks refused to help their weaker brethren, and when the federal government finally provided relief (in the form of loans from the Reconstruction Finance Corporation) to the troubled financial community, bankers kept nearly all the proffered funds tucked away safely in their vaults—to stave off bankruptcy after fearful depositors withdrew their savings—instead of lending them out to get the economy moving again. But still the panic-stricken run on the banks continued.

Prices on the New York Stock Exchange struck rock bottom on July 8, 1932, a day when a mere 720,278 shares were bought and sold. When the dust finally settled, the Dow Jones industrial average, which had peaked at 452 in September 1929, had slid all the way down to 58. U.S. Steel fell from 262 to 22, General Motors from 73 to 8, and Montgomery Ward from 138 to 4. Anaconda Copper, too, landed in the basement at 4, and a share of the ill-starred Blue Ridge investment trust could be had for 63¢. Investment in stocks and bonds tumbled from $10 million in 1929 to $1 million in 1932.

Following a severe drought in the summer of 1930, the

misery and despair of the American farmer reached previously unimagined depths. Farm income fell from $12 billion to $5 billion. Wheat prices declined from $1.05 a bushel in 1929 to a paltry 39¢ three years later; cotton went from 17¢ a pound to 6¢; and corn from 81¢ to 33¢ a bushel. Sheriffs endeavoring to foreclose on farms with unpaid mortgages were greeted by hostile armed mobs of farmers. "They are just ready to do anything to get even with the situation," a Farmers' Union spokesman told a Senate investigating committee. "I almost hate to express it, but I honestly believe that if some of them could buy airplanes they would come down here to Washington to blow you fellows all up. . . . The farmer is naturally a conservative individual, but you cannot find a conservative farmer today."

Between 1929 and 1932, employers slashed factory wages from $12 billion to $7 billion; the average weekly wage dropped from $25.03 to $16.73. Unemployment reached 6 million by the end of 1930, and kept climbing until a staggering 12.8 million workers—25 percent of the total labor force—were jobless in the spring of 1933. Someone compared the heartbreaking unemployment figures in the industrial cities of the north with the British casualty lists at the Somme [a World War I battle resulting in an estimated 500,000 British casualties], "so awesome as to become in the end meaningless, for the sheer statistics numbed the mind": 1 million people out of work in New York City; 50 percent of the Cleveland labor force idle; 80 percent out of work in Toledo; 660,000 unemployed in Chicago, where Al Capone financed a soup kitchen that provided 120,000 free meals to the jobless in the space of just six weeks. Henry Ford, on the other hand, pompously proclaimed that the depression was a "wholesome thing in general"—"It's a good thing the recovery is prolonged," Ford said, "otherwise the people wouldn't profit by the illness". . . .

The Wrong Remedies

As tax revenues declined, state and local governments slashed spending and reduced their already inadequate public works programs. Hoover stubbornly refused to engage in large-scale deficit spending to pump more money into the economy (indeed, when it appeared that the federal budget would post a deficit in 1932, Hoover actually asked Congress to increase taxes), nor would he permit the federal government to provide direct relief for the unemployed. "He made what was probably the last stand for a type of society and government that is gone," wrote journalist Tom Stokes a decade later, "the sort, as he had pointed out, that had given him the opportunity to battle his way to the top." To Herbert Hoover, a poor boy and orphan who had struggled and fought for everything he had gained, it was unthinkable to condone any sort of government initiative that might erode the individual's freedom of action or sap the initiative and vitality of the American spirit. He insisted that self-help and voluntary assistance on the part of the local community—what he liked to refer to as "the American way"—were sufficient to alleviate the worst elements of the economic catastrophe. . . .

Nor could the stolid Hoover project even the image of decisive action that might have inspired the American public to break through the vicious cycle of fear, despair, and deflation that carried the nation ever deeper into a seemingly bottomless abyss. "I have no Wilsonian qualities," he admitted dolefully to a friend. By the autumn of 1932, the Great Engineer had become a forsaken object of ridicule and derision, an austere, uncaring, cold-hearted shell of a man hidden away behind the iron gates of the White House. . . .

The British Response

Like Herbert Hoover, Britain's [Prime Minister] Ramsay MacDonald was a self-made man, and so was MacDonald's chancellor of the Exchequer, the acerbic Philip Snowden. And like the American President, they refused to adopt unorthodox schemes of economic stimulation to pull their nation out of the deepening depression. "A well-balanced budget is not a luxury which is to be avoided," Snowden tartly informed Churchill in 1930. "It is a necessity which is to be provided for." And so Parliament dutifully raised taxes by £47 million in 1930 in a futile effort to balance the budget. By 1931, the economic situation had deteriorated to such a point that MacDonald felt compelled to invite the two opposition parties to form a coalition—the National government—which naturally intensified the drift to the right. Unemployment benefits were slashed (despite the fact that 1.5 million workers were jobless), public works were postponed, and military salaries were cut (provoking a strike by a company of sailors), but the devastating deflationary spiral continued until Britain finally, and most reluctantly, was forced to abandon the gold standard in late 1931.

The Rise of Hitler

In Germany, the government of Chancellor Heinrich Brüning adopted a similar policy of reducing expenditures and raising taxes. This classic and chilling remedy succeeded only in increasing unemployment to six million. Sparked by the failure of the Austrian *Kreditanstalt* in May 1931, the German banking system collapsed altogether, touching off a chain reaction of failures in financial institutions throughout Europe and the United States. [Germany's president, Paul von] Hindenburg appealed to Washington for help in postponing Germany's international obligations. Prompted by Hoover, who was primarily (and quite properly) concerned about the effects of the financial crisis on the United States, the Allies grudgingly consented to a moratorium on reparations [payments owed to the Allies under the terms of the treaty that ended World War I] and war debts payments [on loans taken out by the government during World War I]. Although this "standstill agreement"—which the French deliberately sabotaged shortly after it was signed—was originally intended to form a temporary stopgap, international commercial arrangements had been thrown so completely out of whack by the depression and the ensuing tariff war (aggravated by the United States' infamous Smoot-Hawley Tariff of 1930) [a protectionist measure that worsened the depression by restricting trade] that payments on both reparations and war debts were never resumed. . . .

By 1932, nearly 40 percent of the German work force was unemployed. Brüning responded by tightening the screws further, relentlessly cutting prices, wages, and benefits. In

May, Hindenburg requested Chancellor Brüning's resignation. He replaced him with the aristocratic Franz von Papen, who immediately ordered new elections. . . . The Nazis employed the economic crisis to expand their representation in the Reichstag [German parliament]. After several successive cabinet failures, Hindenburg (who had been overwhelmingly reelected to the presidency of the republic) finally—and very reluctantly—asked Hitler to take the reins of government in January 1933. Within months, Hitler had effectively deprived Hindenburg of all powers and assumed dictatorial control of Germany himself.

He took a desperate, confused nation and remade it in his own perverted image. Power was centralized in the hands of the Fuehrer and his inner circle of lieutenants; in the name of

---

The Wall Street Crash and the Great Depression

Did the 1929 stock market crash cause the depression of the 1930s? The experts have never managed to agree on this question. Economist John Kenneth Galbraith argues that at the very least, the crash made an important contribution to the severity of the Great Depression.

Any satisfactory explanation of the events of the autumn of 1929 and thereafter must accord a dignified role to the speculative boom and ensuing collapse. Until September or October of 1929 the decline in economic activity was very modest. . . . Until after the market crash one could reasonably assume that this downward movement might soon reverse itself, as a similar movement had reversed itself in 1927 or did subsequently in 1949. There were no reasons for expecting disaster. No one could foresee that production, prices, incomes, and all other indicators would continue to shrink through three long and dismal years. Only after the market crash were there plausible grounds to suppose that things might now for a long while get a lot worse.

John Kenneth Galbraith, *The Great Crash: 1929.* Boston: Houghton Mifflin, 1988.

the National Socialist revolution, storm troopers seized the offices of the state governments and arrested anyone who protested; all vestiges of an independent labor movement vanished as trade union leaders were thrown into concentration camps along with dissident politicians, religious leaders, and intellectuals; fulfilling his cherished dream of supremacy as head of the Ministry of Enlightenment and Propaganda, Joseph Goebbels ruled the German press, radio, and movies as an unchallenged dictator. Hitler then embarked on a furious campaign of public works, rebuilding Berlin and revitalizing the nation's transportation system, adding over a thousand miles of new roads and doubling the capacity of the railways. Most important, he found ways to circumvent the Versailles Treaty [the treaty ending World War I] restrictions on the size and power of the German armed forces, and when he could no longer hide his intentions he openly broke the restrictions and dared the Allies to challenge him.

Under the impetus of this massive spending program and a vast expansion in social services, the German economy—freed of the burden of reparations payments—revived and reasserted its natural primacy in Europe. And then the German military machine carried the national resurgence into new territories, assuaging the painful memories of 1919 [the Treaty of Versailles, which many Germans including Hitler considered humiliating]. Between 1933 and 1941, the Third Reich nearly doubled in size, from 180,976 to 323,360 square miles; by the end of 1941, the Reich governed 106 million people, a vast increase from the 65 million of 1933. By the time he was fifty-two years old, Hitler was the most powerful man in the world. . . .

The Rise of Roosevelt

On July 1, 1932, on the fourth ballot at the Democratic National Convention in Chicago, Governor Franklin Delano Roosevelt received his party's presidential nomination, defeating rivals Al Smith, Owen Young, Congressman John Nance Garner, and Newton Baker, an internationalist attorney who had served as secretary of war in Woodrow Wilson's cabinet. Embittered by his defeat at the hands of his former protégé, Smith (who had earlier denounced Roosevelt's innovative state unemployment relief program with the sarcastic comment "This is no time for demagogues") stormed out of the convention hall and petulantly refused to release his delegates, thereby preventing a nomination by unanimous consent.

Four months later, after a strenuous if not particularly edifying campaign in which prohibition, and not the depression, was the most controversial issue, Franklin D. Roosevelt (supported by substantial financial contributions from [financier and presidential adviser] Bernard Baruch and Joseph P. Kennedy [Boston financier and father of John F. Kennedy]) captured the White House in a stunning but hardly unanticipated landslide that matched Hoover's defeat of Smith four years earlier. Roosevelt swept all but six states, winning 22,800,000 votes to Hoover's 15,750,000.

Although the new President succeeded in restoring the invaluable blessings of hope to the anxious American public, and though he did launch desperately needed programs of direct federal unemployment relief that mitigated the most damaging human effects of the economic catastrophe, Roosevelt's inauguration in March 1933 did not immediately dispel the black clouds of depression that stubbornly hung over the nation. Nor did the New Deal, with its contradictory impulses and frequently chaotic administrative style, ever succeed in restoring the United States to full economic health. Not until 1939–40, when the Roosevelt administration—facing fascist aggression on the continent of Europe and in the Far East—launched a substantial rearmament program that pumped vast sums of federal funds into the economy, did the last enduring effects of the Great Crash disappear.

Appendix of Documents

Document 1: Jesus as a Business Leader

The go-getter society of the 1920s valued salesmanship, business acumen, and professionalism. Advertising executive Bruce Barton became a spokesman for these values when he wrote The Man Nobody Knows, *a bestselling reinterpretation of Jesus as a business executive, excerpted below.*

The little boy's body sat bolt upright in the rough wooden chair, but his mind was very busy.

This was his weekly hour of revolt.

The kindly lady who could never seem to find her glasses would have been terribly shocked if she had known what was going on inside the little boy's mind.

"You must love Jesus," she said every Sunday, "and God."

The little boy did not say anything. He was afraid to say anything; he was almost afraid that something would happen to him because of the things he thought.

Love God! Who was always picking on people for having a good time, and sending little boys to hell because they couldn't do better in a world which he had made so hard! Why didn't God take some one his own size?

Love Jesus! The little boy looked up at the picture which hung on the Sunday-school wall. It showed a pale young man with flabby forearms and a sad expression. The young man had red whiskers. . . .

Jesus was the "lamb of God." The little boy did not know what that meant, but it sounded like Mary's little lamb. Something for girls—sissified. Jesus was also "meek and lowly," a "man of sorrows and acquainted with grief." He went around for three years telling people not to do things. . . .

The little boy was glad when the superintendent thumped the bell and announced: "We will now sing the closing hymn." One more bad hour was over. For one more week the little boy had got rid of Jesus.

Years went by and the boy grew up and became a business man.

He began to wonder about Jesus.

He said to himself: "Only strong magnetic men inspire great enthusiasm and build great organizations. Yet Jesus built the greatest organization of all. It is extraordinary."

The more sermons the man heard and the more books he read the more mystified he became.

One day he decided to wipe his mind clean of books and sermons.

He said, "I will read what the men who knew Jesus personally said about him. I will read about him as though he were a new historical character, about whom I had never heard anything at all."

The man was amazed.

A physical weakling! Where did they get that idea? Jesus pushed a plane and swung an adze; he was a successful carpenter. He slept outdoors and spent his days walking around his favorite lake. His muscles were so strong that when he drove the money-changers out, nobody dared to oppose him!

A kill-joy! He was the most popular dinner guest in Jerusalem! The criticism which proper people made was that he spent too much time with publicans and sinners (very good fellows, on the whole, the man thought) and enjoyed society too much. They called him a "wine bibber and a gluttonous man."

A failure! He picked up twelve men from the bottom ranks of business and forged them into an organization that conquered the world.

When the man had finished his reading he exclaimed, "This is a man nobody knows.

"Some day," said he, "some one will write a book about Jesus. Every business man will read it and send it to his partners and his salesmen. For it will tell the story of the founder of modern business."

Bruce Barton, *The Man Nobody Knows*. Indianapolis: Bobbs-Merrill, 1924.

Document 2: The Merchandising of Radio

Radio was an exciting new technology in the 1920s. The public was enraptured by it, and merchandisers and advertising executives were aware of its potential as an advertising medium. In 1925 the Curtis Publishing Company (publisher of the most successful weekly magazine of the 1920s, the Saturday Evening Post*), sponsored a marketing study of the radio industry.*

Radio has probably grown more rapidly than any other industry grew in its initial years. From sales figures of about $2,000,000 in 1920 it increased, according to trade estimates, to $350,000,000 in 1924 and it is estimated that it will attain a volume of $500,000,000 in 1925. From 60,000 receiving sets with one or more tubes in 1922 it grew, according to trade estimates, to 3,700,000 sets by

January 1, 1925. The first broadcasting to attract attention was the election returns of 1920. By December, 1922, 576 stations were in operation. By June 1, 1925, most of the more densely populated sections of the United States were within 100 miles of a radio station, and a belt of more powerful stations extended across the continent from coast to coast.

The reasons for this rapid growth are primarily four:

1. Radio made a stronger appeal to the imagination than did any other merchandise. The thought that the very room in which one sits is filled with music from distant cities and that any of this may be made audible gave a thrill to a world that thought it had grown blasé to invention and to entertainment.

2. Manufacturing and financing facilities, such as never before had been offered a new industry, were placed at the service of radio. During the [First] World War and the period following, plant equipment was created in excess of demand. Accumulations of capital were seeking investment. The thoughts of investors turned to the early days of the automobile industry—the fortunes won in that industry stimulated imagination; the fortunes lost were forgotten.

3. Advertising held a more important place in public confidence than at the beginning of any other great industry. The past six years of great advertising volume evidences a public that reads advertising and buys advertised merchandise. Public favor for advertised products, dealer interest in advertised lines, knowledge of advertising copy, experience in methods of merchandising through advertising, made possible as never before at the inception of an industry quick and effective presentation of the product to the public.

4. The talking machine had prepared the way by creating a demand for good music in the home.

The radio market is permanent. Broadcasting met an unexpressed yearning of the human heart, the desire to hear that which the world is saying at the time the world is saying it. When broadcasting was launched, something was given the public which cannot be taken away. Who will do broadcasting? Who will pay for broadcasting? These are secondary to the prime fact: The American public will have broadcasting.

Charles Coolidge Parlin, *The Merchandising of Radio*. Philadelphia: Curtis, 1925.

Document 3: The Menace of Chain Stores

In the 1920s, chain stores like A&P, Kroger, and Woolworth (the original "five-and-dime" store) expanded immensely. Able to order goods in mas-

sive quantities, chain retailers had enormous bargaining power and were able to put smaller stores out of business. In the pamphlet excerpted here, an advertising agency describes the growth of chain stores in the United States.

Chain stores are merely *big* stores with multiple outlets.

The big downtown store, by reason of its central location, its prestige, and its aggressive preselling to the consumer, is able to bring its customers to it. The chain stores take the store to the customer.

The chain store is fundamentally sound. Multiple retail outlets and high-pressure selling give volume. Volume gives advantageous buying power and commensurate selling advantages. Size gives opportunity for economical operation and efficient management. The chain stores have matched the mass production of the modern manufacturer with *mass distribution.*

Most retailers, in spite of their rising gorge [fear] at the aggression of the chains, secretly cherish the ambition that some day, when they get their one store on a highly profitable basis, they can take the surplus and open another store in another neighborhood. It is the best way to grow big. If one store is profitable, ten stores will yield ten times the profit.

The whole trend of business in the past two decades has been toward consolidation and the amalgamation of smaller units into bigger ones. In the terrific competition of modern selling, the larger units can compete successfully with each other. But the little fellow is unmercifully squeezed in the battle of the giants. . . .

In Chicago there were 50 chain groceries ten years ago. Today there are more than 1,200—and the number is increasing daily.

In Philadelphia twelve years ago the chain stores handled about 10 per cent. of the retail grocery business of the city. Today they handle more than 65 per cent. of it.

Ten years ago there were 600 chain stores in New York. Now there are 6,500 chain groceries (more than 30 per cent. of all the grocery stores in New York), and they did more than $250,000,000 business last year. That was more than 65 per cent. of the retail food business in the city.

The chains are not growing in the big cities alone. The Great Atlantic and Pacific Tea Company—the "A&P"—operates in many smaller cities and ruins the peaceful sleep of many a local merchant who has grown gray in the service of his community. In 1916 there were 2,800 A.&P. stores; in 1920, 4,500; in 1922, 6,800—and now more than 10,000. The Kroger chain of grocery stores did a business of $90,000,000 last year. . . .

Nor is the grocery business the only one in which the chains are rapidly annexing the lion's share. Drug chains are less numerous, but in their communities they are just as powerful, just as aggressive and successful.

In 1900 there were just 25 chain drug stores in the United States. Now there are more than 2,000—and they transacted 20.6 per cent. of all the retail drug business in the United States in 1923, according to the Harvard Bureau of Business Administration.

There are 48,713 drug stores in the United States. The chains number only four per cent. *Yet this four per cent. of the stores do more than a fifth of the total business!*

The Menace of the Chains. Indianapolis: Mills Advertising, 1924.

Document 4: A Flapper's Appeal to Parents

Flappers were young women of the World War I era and 1920s who broke free from social conventions. They bobbed their hair, wore short skirts, and socialized more freely with men than preceding generations of women had. The following excerpt was written by a flapper in 1922 appealing to the older generation to understand the struggles of a postwar youth.

If one judge by appearances, I suppose I am a flapper. I am within the age limit. I wear bobbed hair, the badge of flapperhood. (And, oh, what a comfort it is!), I powder my nose. I wear fringed skirts and bright-colored sweaters, and scarfs, and waists with Peter Pan collars, and low-heeled "finale hopper" shoes. I adore to dance. I spend a large amount of time in automobiles. I attend hops, and proms, and ball-games, and crew races, and other affairs at men's colleges. But none the less some of the most thoroughbred super-flappers might blush to claim sistership or even remote relationship with such as I. I don't use rouge, or lipstick, or pluck my eyebrows. I don't smoke (I've tried it, and don't like it), or drink, or tell "peppy stories." I don't pet. And, most unpardonable infringement of all the rules and regulations of Flapperdom, I haven't a line! But then—there are many degrees of flapper. There is the semi-flapper; the flapper; the superflapper. Each of these three main general divisions has its degrees of variation. I might possibly be placed somewhere in the middle of the first class.

I think every one realizes by this time that there has been a marked change in our much-discussed tactics. Jazz has been modified, and probably will continue to be until it has become obsolete. Petting is gradually growing out of fashion through being overworked. Yes, undoubtedly our hopeless condition is improving. But it was not for discussing these aspects of the case that began this article.

I want to beg all you parents, and grandparents, and friends, and teachers, and preachers—you who constitute the "older generation"—to overlook our shortcomings, at least for the present, and to appreciate our virtues. I wonder if it ever occurred to any of you that it required brains to become and remain a successful flapper? Indeed it does! It requires an enormous amount of cleverness and energy to keep going at the proper pace. It requires self-knowledge and self-analysis. We must know our capabilities and limitations. We must be constantly on the alert. Attainment of flapperhood is a big and serious undertaking!

"Brains?" you repeat, skeptically. "Then why aren't they used to better advantage?" That is exactly it! And do you know who is largely responsible for all this energy's being spent in the wrong directions? You! You parents, and grandparents, and friends, and teachers, and preachers—all of you! "The war!" you cry. "It is the effect of the war!" And then you blame prohibition. Yes! Yet it is you who set the example there! But this is my point: Instead of helping us work out our problems with constructive, sympathetic thinking and acting, you have muddled them for us more hopelessly with destructive public condemnation and denunciation. . . .

We are the Younger Generation. The war tore away our spiritual foundations and challenged our faith. We are struggling to regain our equilibrium. The times have made us older and more experienced than you were at our age. It must be so with each succeeding generation if it is to keep pace with the rapidly advancing and mighty tide of civilization. Help us to put our knowledge to the best advantage. Work with us! That is the way! Outlets for this surplus knowledge and energy must be opened. Give us a helping hand.

Ellen Welles Page, "A Flapper's Appeal to Parents," *Outlook*, December 6, 1922.

Document 5: The Dangers of Too Much Mother Love

Americans in the 1920s vested a naive faith in the opinions of experts, especially those with scientific credentials. One such highly lauded expert was John B. Watson, who established the psychological school of behaviorism. He claimed that mothers who hug and kiss their children harm them. However, there was no experimental data to support his assertion. Psychologists today recommend plenty of interaction and physical affection between parents and children.

Once at the close of a lecture before parents, a dear old lady got up and said, "Thank God, my children are grown—and that I had a chance to enjoy them before I met you."

Doesn't she express here the weakness in our modern way of bringing up children? We have children to enjoy them. We need to express our love in some way. The honeymoon period doesn't last forever with all husbands and wives, and we eke it out in a way we think is harmless by loving our children to death. Isn't this especially true of the mother today? No matter how much she may love her husband, he is away all day; her heart is full of love which she must express in some way. She expresses it by showering love and kisses upon her children—and thinks the world should laud her for it. *And it does.*

Not long ago, I went motoring with two boys, aged four and two, their mother, grandmother and nurse. In the course of the two-hour ride, one of the children was kissed thirty two times—four by his mother, eight by the nurse and twenty times by the grandmother. The other child was almost equally smothered in love.

But there are not many mothers like that, you say—mothers are getting modern, they do not kiss and fondle their children nearly so much as they used to. Unfortunately this is not true. I once let slip in a lecture some of my ideas on the dangers lurking in the mother's kiss. Immediately, thousands of newspapers wrote scathing editorials on "Don't kiss the baby." Hundreds of letters poured in. Judging from them, kissing the baby to death is just about as popular a sport as it ever was, except for a very small part of our population.

Is it just the hard heartedness of the behaviorist—his lack of sentiment—that makes him object to kissing? Not at all. There are serious rocks ahead for the over-kissed child. . . .

The infant child loves anyone who strokes and feeds it. . . .

To understand the end results of too much coddling, let us examine some of our own adult behavior. Nearly all of us have suffered from over-coddling in our infancy. How does it show? It shows as *invalidism.* . . .

There is a sensible way of treating children. Treat them as though they were young adults. Dress them, bathe them with care and circumspection. Let your behavior always be objective and kindly firm. Never hug and kiss them, never let them sit in your lap. If you must, kiss them once on the forehead when they say good night. Shake hands with them in the morning. Give them a pat on the head if they have made an extraordinarily good job of a difficult task. Try it out.

In a week's time you will find how easy it is to be perfectly objective with your child and at the same time kindly. You will be utterly ashamed of the mawkish, sentimental way you have been handling it.

John B. Watson, "The Dangers of Too Much Mother Love," *Psychological Care of Infant and Child*. New York: W.W. Norton, 1928.

Document 6: Attorney General A. Mitchell Palmer on the Red Menace

In 1919 an unknown anarchist exploded a bomb on the doorstep of U.S. attorney general A. Mitchell Palmer. In response, the outraged attorney general launched a series of illegal roundups of suspected "reds" (a term that included both Communists and anarchists). In this excerpt Palmer defends his actions.

In this brief review of the work which the Department of Justice has undertaken, to tear out the radical seeds that have entangled American ideas in their poisonous theories, I desire not merely to explain what the real menace of communism is, but also to tell how we have been compelled to clean up the country almost unaided by any virile legislation. Though I have not been embarrassed by political opposition, I have been materially delayed because the present sweeping processes of arrests and deportation of seditious aliens should have been vigorously pushed by Congress last spring [1919]. The failure of this is a matter of record in the Congressional files.

The anxiety of that period in our responsibility when Congress, ignoring the seriousness of these vast organizations that were plotting to overthrow the Government, failed to act, has passed. The time came when it was obviously hopeless to expect the hearty cooperation of Congress in the only way to stamp out these seditious societies in their open defiance of law by various forms of propaganda.

Like a prairie-fire, the blaze of revolution was sweeping over every American institution of law and order a year ago. It was eating its way into the homes of the American workmen, its sharp tongues of revolutionary heat were licking the altars of the churches, leaping into the belfry of the school bell, crawling into the sacred corners of American homes, seeking to replace marriage vows with libertine laws, burning up the foundations of society. . . .

Upon these two basic certainties, first that the "Reds" were criminal aliens and secondly that the American Government must prevent crime, it was decided that there could be no nice distinctions drawn between the theoretical ideals of the radicals and their actual violations of our national laws. An assassin may have brilliant intellectuality, he may be able to excuse his murder or robbery with fine oratory, but any theory which excuses crime is not wanted in America. This is no place for the criminal to flourish, nor will he do so so long as the rights of common citizenship can be exerted to prevent him. . . .

My information showed that communism in this country was an organization of thousands of aliens who were direct allies of Leon Trotzky [a leader of Russia's Bolshevik revolution]. Aliens of the same misshapen caste of mind and indecencies of character, and it showed that they were making the same glittering promises of lawlessness, of criminal autocracy to Americans, that they had made to the Russian peasants. How the Department of Justice discovered upwards of 60,000 of these organized agitators of the Trotzky doctrine in the United States is the confidential information upon which the Government is now sweeping the nation clean of such alien filth. . . .

It has been [implied] by the "Reds" that the United States Government, by arresting and deporting them, is returning to the autocracy of Czardom, adopting the system that created the severity of Siberian banishment. My reply to such charges is that in our determination to maintain our government we are treating our alien enemies with extreme consideration. To deny them the privilege of remaining in a country which they have openly deplored as an unenlightened community, unfit for those who prefer the privileges of Bolshevism [communism], should be no hardship. It strikes me as an odd form of reasoning that these Russian Bolsheviks who extol the Bolshevik rule should be so unwilling to return to Russia. The nationality of most of the alien "Reds" is Russian and German. There is almost no other nationality represented among them. . . .

It is my belief that while they have stirred discontent in our midst, while they have caused irritating strikes, and while they have infected our social ideas with the disease of their own minds and their unclean morals we can get rid of them! and not until we have done so shall we have removed the menace of Bolshevism for good.

A. Mitchell Palmer, "The Case Against the Reds," *Forum*, 1920.

Document 7: Ku Klux Klan: Defender of Americanism

The Ku Klux Klan was revived in 1915 and become a highly visible presence in the early 1920s, with an estimated membership of between 2 and 4 million. In September 1925, an article declaring the Klan "un-American" appeared in Forum, *a well-regarded magazine of the time. In the De-*

cember 1925 issue Forum *respectfully printed a rebuttal by Hiram Wesley Evans, a former Texas dentist who was at that time "emperor" and "imperial wizard" of the Klan. Although most Americans disapproved of the Klan, its racist ideas were widely held, as Evans points out in his article.*

It is hard to answer criticisms of the Ku Klux Klan directly and categorically, because what the Klan needs is not so much defense as explanation. Most attacks have been deliberately unfair and so misleading that reply is impossible. . . .

In the case of the Klan that main issue is usually missed because the men who make the criticisms have lost contact with the deeper emotions and instincts which, far more than their brains, control the majority of men. Our "intellectuals", particularly, in the process of becoming intellectualized, have cramped their emotional perception to such an extent that they are crippled, like a bird-dog that has lost the sense of smell. They, therefore, are quite nonplussed when confronting a "common" man, and cannot understand his mind, his actions, or the causes for which he fights. . . .

There is no possibility of trying to prove the soundness of the Klan position, or of the controlling instincts and beliefs of the common people of American descent, to any of those who insist on measuring either by the purely theoretic philosophy of cosmopolitanism: of universal equality in character, social value, and current rights. I will not attempt to argue about that doctrine. Science does not support it, and certainly the average American does not believe it. Our attitude toward the Orientals proves this, no matter what our oral professions may be, as well as does our treatment of the Negro. . . .

We Americans all deny equality to ten millions of our own citizens; deny it with facts and in fact, if we do not deny it by argument. The idea itself, however it may be glossed over and given theoretic acceptance, is actually abhorrent in practise to the American mind. And in fact, actual social equality between whites and any other race is not practised to any important extent anywhere on earth. Facts prove the idea unworkable. This beautiful philosophy, therefore, the Klan will not argue about. It merely rejects it, as almost all Americans do.

Neither will we argue at all about the questions of white supremacy. In that case, even, we do not propose to permit any argument to avail. We may be intolerant in this, but we will not delude other races into looking forward to privileges that will, in truth, be forever denied. The Klan looks forward to the day when the union of a white person with one of any other race will be illegal in every State of the Union, and when the question of social supremacy will have been settled on a much safer basis than that of racial mongrelization.

With people who hold the cosmopolitan view of these two things we cannot have useful discussion; there is a gulf between our minds.

Hiram Wesley Evans, "The Klan: Defender of Americanism," *Forum*, December 1925.

Document 8: H.L. Mencken on William Jennings Bryan

The following excerpt is from an obituary of William Jennings Bryan by columnist H.L. Mencken. Bryan was a Populist statesman and fundamentalist hero. He died in 1925, soon after acting as a witness for the prosecution in the trial of John Thomas Scopes for the crime of teaching the theory of evolution in Dayton, Tennessee. The obituary is a good example of Mencken's acerbic prose style, and reflects very clearly the contempt that many city dwellers had for country people in the 1920s.

Has it been duly marked by historians that William Jennings Bryan's last secular act on this globe of sin was to catch flies? A curious detail, and not without its sardonic overtones. He was the most sedulous fly-catcher in American history, and in many ways the most successful. His quarry, of course, was not *Musca domestica* but *Homo neandertalensis*. For forty years he tracked it with coo and bellow, up and down the rustic backways of the Republic. Wherever the flambeaux of Chautauqua smoked and guttered, and the bilge of idealism ran in the veins, and Baptist pastors dammed the brooks with the sanctified, and men gathered who were weary and heavy laden, and their wives who were full of Peruna and as fecund as the shad (*Alosa sapidissima*), there the indefatigable Jennings set up his traps and spread his bait. He knew every country town in the South and West, and he could crowd the most remote of them to suffocation by simply winding his horn. The city proletariat, transiently flustered by him in 1896, quickly penetrated his buncombe and would have no more of him; the cockney gallery jeered him at every Democratic national convention for twenty-five years. But out where the grass grows high, and the horned cattle dream away the lazy afternoons, and men still fear the powers and principalities of the air—out there between the corn-rows he held his old puissance [power] to the end. There was no need of beaters to drive in his game. The news that he was coming was enough. For miles the flivver dust would choke the roads. And when he rose at the end of the day to discharge his Message there would be such breathless attention, such a rapt and enchanted ecstasy, such a sweet rustle of amens as the world had not known since Johann fell to Herod's ax. . . .

His last battle will be grossly misunderstood if it is thought of as a mere exercise in fanaticism—that is, if Bryan the Fundamentalist Pope is mistaken for one of the bucolic Fundamentalists. There was much more in it than that, as everyone knows who saw him on the field. What moved him, at bottom, was simply hatred of the city men who had laughed at him so long, and brought him at last to so tatterdemalion an estate. He lusted for revenge upon them. He yearned to lead the anthropoid rabble against them, to punish them for their execution upon him by attacking the very vitals of their civilization. He went far beyond the bounds of any merely religious frenzy, however inordinate. When he began denouncing the notion that man is a mammal even some of the hinds at Dayton [Tennessee, where the Scopes trial took place] were agape. And when, brought upon [the defending counsel] Clarence Darrow's cruel hook, he writhed and tossed in a very fury of malignancy, bawling against the veriest elements of sense and decency like a man frantic—when he came to that tragic climax of his striving there were snickers among the hinds as well as hosannas.

Upon that hook, in truth, Bryan committed suicide, as a legend as well as in the body. He staggered from the rustic court ready to die, and he staggered from it ready to be forgotten, save as a character in a third-rate farce, witless and in poor taste. It was plain to everyone who knew him, when he came to Dayton, that his great days were behind him—that, for all the fury of his hatred, he was now definitely an old man, and headed at last for silence.

H.L. Mencken, "In Memoriam: W.J.B.," *American Mercury*, October 1925.

Document 9: The Bull Market

In the language of the New York Stock Exchange, a bull market is one in which the average price of stocks is rising and most investors are confident that it will continue to rise. The following was excerpted from an article written a few months before the market crash that ended the prosperity of the 1920s.

Under a round glass globe of the sort that used to cover the wax flowers on grandmother's parlor table, in the years before the nation discovered a broad and easy road to wealth, a small brass mechanism purrs and stutters. Click, click, click. Two little rollers pause just long enough to rub their hands in printer's ink, then beat a light tattoo on the strip of tape that runs through a slit in the side of this glass box and falls to the floor in lazy spirals. Click, click, K N 6½, click, click, click, click, L N P 3½, click, click, U N C 7¾. . . . The rat-tat-tat of these little blows spells out the state of mind with which the nation views the outlook for prosperity from one moment's flurry to the next; and outside the box the white tape runs through eager fingers.

It is a commonplace observation that the last few years have witnessed the development of a bull market in this country like no market the world has ever seen before. One phase of this market may be drawing near its end; one phase of this market may, in fact, have ended in a manner wholly satisfactory to the most impassioned pessimists before these words appear in print; the fact remains that the bull market of 1924 to 1929 is a phenomenon unmatched in the records of this country. It is possible to regard this market merely as another of those recurrent waves of speculative mania which sweep all nations periodically, but useless to look for its precise analogy in the [U.S. president William] McKinley boom of 1897, or the Northern Pacific wave of 1901, or the war flurry of 1915–16, or the post-war boom of 1919, for the reason that none of these markets remotely matched it in vigor or duration. As a rule, they lasted two years or three at most; they never succeeded in forcing trading on the New York Stock Exchange above three hundred and fifty million shares a year; and within reasonable limits they conformed respectfully to the scheme of behavior which the experts had charted for them in advance.

By comparison with these earlier waves of speculation, it should be noted of this last great rush that in 1929 it entered its fifth year; that time and again it confounded the experts and robbed the prophets of their honor; that after sixty months of sensational trading the average price of fifty leading securities soared in February, 1929, two hundred and twenty-eight per cent above their level in October, 1923; and that the volume of trading on the Stock Exchange increased so phenomenally as to smother the record of two hundred and eighty million shares in 1924, with a record of more than a billion shares between March 1, 1928, and March 1, 1929. . . .

There are still men left in the spring of 1929 who do not thumb their way straight to the stock news when they have had one fleeting glance at the first-page headlines in their evening papers, but the number of such men is smaller than in the spring of 1928; and the account-books of every brokerage firm in a broad nation show the names of school-teachers, seamstresses, barbers, machinists, necktie salesmen, gas-fitters, motormen, family cooks, and lexicographers who have taken their first dip in the market in the last two years. The ticker tape runs on. And to a greater extent than ever before in its history the whole country has been buying stocks, selling stocks, trading stocks, assessing profits, covering close margins with fresh capital, and following with increasing interest the broad line in the market-graphs that curves between the lowlands and the Himalayas.

Charles Merz, "Bull Market," *Harper's Monthly*, April 1929.

Document 10: The Wall Street Crash

The Wall Street stock market crash of 1929 lasted from October 23 through October 29. On October 30, the front page of the New York Times *provided its readers with this account of the final disastrous day.*

Stock prices virtually collapsed yesterday [October 29, 1929], swept downward with gigantic losses in the most disastrous trading day in the stock market's history. Billions of dollars in open market values were wiped out as prices crumbled under the pressure of liquidation of securities which had to be sold at any price. . . .

Trading on the New York Stock Exchange aggregated 16,410,030 shares; on the Curb, 7,096,300 shares were dealt in. Both totals fare exceeded any previous day's dealings.

From every point of view, in the extent of losses sustained, in total turnover, in the number of speculators wiped out, the day was the most disastrous in Wall Street's history. Hysteria swept the country and stocks went overboard for just what they would bring at forced sale.

Efforts to estimate yesterday's market losses in dollars are futile because of the vast number of securities quoted over the counter and on out-of-town exchanges on which no calculations are possible. However, it was estimated that 880 issues, on the New York Stock Exchange, lost between $8,000,000,000 and $9,000,000,000 yesterday. Added to that loss is to be reckoned the depreciation on issues on the Curb Market, in the over the counter market and on other exchanges. . . .

The market on the rampage is no respecter of persons. It washed fortune after fortune away yesterday and financially crippled thousands of individuals in all parts of the world. It was not until after the market had closed that the financial district began to realize that a good-sized rally had taken place and that there was a stopping place on the downgrade for good stocks.

The market has now passed through three days of collapse, and so violent has it been that most authorities believe that the end is not far away. It started last Thursday, when 12,800,000 shares were dealt in on the Exchange, and holders of stocks commenced to learn just what a decline in the market means. This was followed by a moderate rally on Friday and entirely normal conditions on Saturday, with fluctuations on a comparatively narrow scale and with the efforts of the leading bankers to stabilize the market evidently successful. But the storm broke anew on Monday, with prices slaughtered in every direction, to be followed by yesterday's tremendous trading of 16,410,030 shares. . . .

Wall Street was a street of vanished hopes, of curiously silent apprehension and of a sort of paralyzed hypnosis yesterday. Men and women crowded the brokerage offices, even those who have been long since wiped out, and followed the figures on the tape. Little groups gathered here and there to discuss the fall in prices in hushed and awed tones. They were participating in the making of financial history.

New York Times, October 30, 1929.

Chronology

1920

January 1: The U.S. census reports a 117.8 million population. For the first time in U.S. history, the urban population exceeds the rural population.

January 2: About twenty-seven hundred suspected anarchists and Communists are arrested in thirty-three cities under orders from Attorney General A. Mitchell Palmer.

January 5: Boston Red Sox star Babe Ruth is sold to the New York Yankees for $125,000—the biggest trade deal in baseball up to that time.

March 26: F. Scott Fitzgerald's novel *This Side of Paradise* is published.

April: George Nathan and H.L. Mencken found the detective-story magazine *Black Mask*. It will introduce the world to the tough-talking American "private eye."

April 1: Five members of the New York State legislature are expelled for being members of the Socialist Party.

April 11: Women's hemlines are now closer to the knee than the ankle.

May 5: Anarchists Nicola Sacco and Bartolomeo Vanzetti are arrested for the murder of a shoe factory paymaster and a guard.

May 19: Members of the United Mine Workers union and detectives hired by the mine operators clash in a pitched gun battle in Matewan, West Virginia. Twelve men are killed.

August 26: The Nineteenth Amendment to the U.S. Constitution (ratified on August 18) is adopted, giving women the right to vote.

September 16: A bomb kills thirty and injures three hundred people on Wall Street. Suspected radicals are arrested and later released, but the perpetrator is never found.

September 17: The American Professional Football Association (later renamed the National Football League) is organized, with Jim Thorpe as the first president.

September 28: Three members of the Chicago White Sox baseball team confess to fixing the 1919 World Series and implicate five others, including "Shoeless" Joe Jackson. The eight men are banned from baseball forever.

October 19: Membership in the Communist Party is ruled grounds for deportation by a New York judge.

October 23: *Main Street*, a novel about small-town life by Sinclair Lewis, is published.

November 2: Republican Warren G. Harding wins the presidency.

November 25: WTAW-AM radio station in College Station, Texas, broadcasts the first live play-by-play of a football game (Texas University vs. Agricultural and Mechanical College of Texas).

1921

February 6: Charlie Chaplin and child actor Jackie Coogan star in a sentimental silent comedy, *The Kid*.

February 17: The U.S. government reports that 9 million automobiles were sold in the United States in 1920.

March 21: The U.S. Congress approves the burial of an unidentified American soldier at the Tomb of the Unknown Soldier, a new monument in Arlington National Cemetery.

June 1: Race riots in Oklahoma cause the deaths of sixty African Americans and twenty-five whites.

September 7: The first Miss America Beauty Pageant is held in Atlantic City.

November 10: At the first American Birth Control Conference, organized by Margaret Sanger, the American Birth Control League is founded.

December 25: President Warren G. Harding commutes the prison sentence of Socialist leader Eugene V. Debs, who had been jailed for protesting World War I.

1922

May 19: The first laboratory transmission of a television signal takes place.

June 11: *Nanook of the North*, Robert Joseph Flaherty's documentary film about traditional Inuit life, premieres.

July 8: Louis Armstrong, a jazz trumpeter from New Orleans, arrives in Chicago and joins King Oliver's band at the Lincoln Gardens.

August 28: The first radio commercial is broadcast over station WEAF in New York City.

September 22: A collection of short stories by F. Scott Fitzgerald called *Tales of the Jazz Age* is published.

November 4: King Tutankhamen's tomb is found by British Egyptologists.

December 30: The *Literary Digest* reports on one of the many fads of the 1920s: a simplified version of the Chinese game mah-jongg. Six books on mah-jongg were published in 1922.

1923

January 27: The Nazi Party holds its first party congress in Munich, Germany.

March 3: Henry Luce publishes the first issue of *Time* magazine.

March 23: The song "Yes We Have No Bananas" is released. Later introduced by Eddy Cantor in the musical revue *Make It Snappy*, it takes the country by storm.

April 18: Yankee Stadium opens in the Bronx, New York.

June 4: Émile Coué, a French pharmacist, comes to the United States to preach his creed of "auto-suggestion." On his advice, millions of people repeat the words, "Every day in every way I am getting better and better."

August 2: Harding dies in office, and Calvin Coolidge becomes president.

October 15: Senate hearings begin on the Teapot Dome corruption scandal involving trusted members of the Harding administration.

December 6: The first radio broadcast of a presidential address occurs.

December 29: Vladimir Zworykin applies for a patent for the iconiscope, a key component in television.

1924

January 21: Soviet leader Vladimir Lenin dies, leaving a power vacuum that will ultimately be filled by Joseph Stalin.

February 3: Woodrow Wilson dies.

February 12: George Gershwin premieres his jazz-influenced composition *Rhapsody in Blue* with the Paul Whiteman Orchestra in New York's Aeolian Hall.

May 19: The first transmission of pictures over telephone wires is publicly demonstrated by Bell Systems' engineers.

May 24: J. Edgar Hoover becomes head of the Bureau of Investigations (later renamed the Federal Bureau of Investigation).

May 26: The U.S. Congress passes the Immigration Restriction Act of 1924, sharply limiting immigration from certain countries and barring virtually all Asians from entering the United States.

June 2: Kleenex, the first disposable tissue, is introduced by the Kimberly-Clark company, initially under the name Celluwipes.

August 5: The comic strip *Little Orphan Annie* premieres in the *Chicago Tribune*.

October 13: *The Navigator*, a silent comedy directed by and starring Buster Keaton, premieres.

November 2: Coolidge is reelected president.

November 9: The first woman governor of a U.S. state, Nellie Tayloe Ross of Wyoming, is elected.

November 11: The New York Stock Exchange breaks trading records with 2,226,226 shares trading hands.

November 27: The first Macy's Thanksgiving Day Parade is held.

1925

January 3: In Italy, Fascist premier Benito Mussolini dismisses parliament and assumes dictatorial powers.

February 17: Harold Ross publishes the first issue of *New Yorker* magazine.

February 18: Floyd Collins, a man trapped in Sand Cave in Kentucky, dies after an eighteen-day vigil. During that time reporters from all over the country have made his plight a national newspaper story.

April 10: F. Scott Fitzgerald's novel *The Great Gatsby* appears.

May 5: John T. Scopes is arrested for teaching evolution in a Tennessee school.

August 8: Approximately forty thousand members of the Ku Klux Klan march on Washington, D.C.

1926

February 27: Chicago business leaders beg the U.S. Senate to investigate organized crime.

April: The first issue of *Amazing Stories*, the first science-fiction magazine, appears on newsstands.

April 5–24: The U.S. Senate holds hearings on the effects of Prohibition. The annual value of alcohol bootlegging in the United States is estimated at $3.6 billion.

May: Evangelist Aimee Semple McPherson disappears; she appears weeks later, claiming to have been abducted and tortured. Blues guitarist Blind Lemon Jefferson records "Long Lonesome Blues."

May 9: U.S. commander Richard E. Byrd and pilot Floyd Bennett are the first to fly over the North Pole in the zeppelin *Norge*.

August 5: John Barrymore stars in Warner Brothers' *Don Juan*, a feature-length movie with synchronized music and sound effects (but no dialogue).

August 6: Gertrude Ederle, the daughter of a New York delicatessen owner, becomes the first woman to swim the English Channel, breaking the previous men's record in the process.

August 23: Silent-movie idol Rudolph Valentino dies, and tens of thousands mob his funeral.

September 18–21: A devastating hurricane hits Florida, killing 372 people, destroying five thousand homes, and putting a serious dent in the Florida land boom.

September 23: Gene Tunney takes the world heavyweight boxing title from Jack Dempsey by a unanimous decision after a ten-round fight.

September 25: Henry Ford introduces the five-day workweek and eight-hour workday at his auto plants.

October: *The Sun Also Rises*, a novel by Ernest Hemingway, is published.

November 29: Duke Ellington records "East St. Louis Toodle-Oo."

1927

January 1: Massachusetts becomes the first state to require auto insurance.

January 17: Commercial transatlantic telephone service between London and New York begins.

February 4: Al Jolson stars in *The Jazz Singer*, the first sound picture with dialogue.

April 25: The first successful long-distance television broadcast is demonstrated.

May–August: A Mississippi River flood covers an estimated 11 million acres from Cairo, Illinois, to Natchez, Mississippi, kills 246 people, forces 700,000 people from their homes, and causes between $200 million and $400 million in damage.

May 20: Charles Lindbergh becomes a national hero when he makes the first solo nonstop transatlantic flight in his monoplane, *Spirit of St. Louis.*

May 27: Henry Ford ceases production of the Model T and plans the introduction of the new Model A.

August 2: President Coolidge announces that he will not run for another term.

August 23: After many appeals, Nicola Sacco and Bartolomeo Vanzetti are executed in the electric chair in Charlestown Prison, Massachusetts.

1928

January 12: The execution of Ruth Snyder, in the electric chair at Sing Sing Prison, is photographed with a hidden camera by a reporter from the *New York Daily News.*

January 30: Eugene O'Neill's play *Strange Interlude* premieres on Broadway.

June 17–18: Amelia Earhart becomes the first woman to fly across the Atlantic.

June 28: Louis Armstrong records "West End Blues."

July 3: The first television sets go on sale. It will be another twenty years before they become a common household item.

July 6: Warner Brothers premieres the first full-length talking film, *The Lights of New York*.

July 30: Two major carmakers, the Dodge Brothers and the Chrysler Corporation, merge.

August 15: Fifteen nations, including the United States, renounce war in the Kellogg-Briand Peace Pact in Paris.

September 19: The first Mickey Mouse cartoon premieres in movie theaters.

November 6: Herbert Hoover defeats presidential candidate Al Smith by a landslide.

1929

January 14: George Gershwin's musical *Strike Up the Band* opens in New York.

February 1: *The Broadway Melody*, a talking picture with music, earns $2 million for MGM.

February 4: Charles Lindbergh starts Central American airmail service.

February 14: Mobsters working for Al Capone kill seven of Bugs Moran's men in a Chicago garage on St. Valentine's Day.

March 26: The New York Stock Exchange sets a record volume of 8.2 million shares traded.

May 16: The first Academy of Motion Picture Arts and Sciences Awards (Academy Awards) ceremony is held. A silent movie about World War I, *Wings*, wins the first Oscar for best picture.

September–December: *The Maltese Falcon*, a novel featuring a private eye named Sam Spade, is serialized in *Black Mask* magazine.

September 3: Wall Street securities reach a record high, with some stocks three times the price they were a year before.

October 18: Thomas Wolfe's novel *Look Homeward, Angel* is published.

October 23–29: The stock market crashes.

November 10: Jazz pianist and future bandleader Count Basie makes his first record, *Blue Devil Blues*, with Walter Page's Blue Devils, in Kansas City, Missouri, for Vocalion Records.

For Further Research

Books

Frederick Lewis Allen, *Only Yesterday: An Informal History of the 1920s.* New York: HarperCollins, 1931.

Sean Dennis Cashman, *Prohibition: The Lie of the Land.* New York: Free Press, 1981.

David M. Chalmers, *Hooded Americanism: The First Century of the Ku Klux Klan.* Garden City, NY: Doubleday, 1965.

John Milton Cooper Jr., *Breaking the Heart of the World: Woodrow Wilson and the Fight for the League of Nations.* New York: Cambridge University Press, 2002.

Malcolm Cowley, *Exiles Return: A Literary Odyssey of the 1920s.* New York: Penguin, 1994.

Anne Douglas, *Terrible Honesty: Mongrel Manhattan in the 1920s.* New York: Farrar, Straus, and Giroux, 1996.

Harold Evans, *The American Century.* New York: Knopf, 1998.

Paula Fass, *The Damned and the Beautiful: American Youth in the 1920s.* New York: Oxford University Press, 1977.

F. Scott Fitzgerald, *Flappers and Philosophers.* New York: Washington Square Press, 1996.

———, *The Great Gatsby.* New York: Scribner Paperback Fiction, 1995.

John Kenneth Galbraith, *The Great Crash: 1929.* Boston: Houghton Mifflin, 1955.

David J. Goldberg, *Discontented America: The United States in the 1920s.* Baltimore: Johns Hopkins University Press, 1999.

Ernest Hemingway, *The Sun Also Rises.* New York: Scribner Paperback Fiction, 1995.

Maury Klein, *Rainbow's End: The Crash of 1929.* New York: Oxford University Press, 2001.

William Leach, *Land of Desire: Merchants, Power, and the Rise of a New American Culture.* New York: Pantheon Books, 1993.

Gerald Leinwand, *1927: High Tide of the Twenties*. New York: Four Walls Eight Windows, 2001.

William E. Leuchtenburg, *The Perils of Prosperity, 1914–1932*. Chicago: University of Chicago Press, 1993.

Roland Marchand, *Advertising the American Dream: Making Way for Modernity, 1920–1940*. Berkeley: University of California Press, 1985.

Michael E. Parrish, *Anxious Decades: America in Prosperity and Depression, 1920–1941*. New York: W.W. Norton, 1992.

Geoffrey Perrett, *America in the Twenties: A History*. New York: Simon & Schuster, 1982.

Cabell Phillips, *From the Crash to the Blitz, 1929–1939*. Toronto: Collier-Macmillan Canada, 1999.

Page Smith, *Redeeming the Time: A People's History of the 1920s and the New Deal*. New York: Penguin, 1991.

Tom Streissguth, *The Roaring Twenties*. New York: Facts On File, 2001.

Wyn Craig Wade, *The Fiery Cross: The Ku Klux Klan in America*. New York: Simon & Schuster, 1987.

Nancy Woloch, *Women and the American Experience*. New York: Knopf, 1984.

Internet Sources

Marilyn Bardsley, "Made in America." www.crimelibrary.com/gangsters_outlaws/mob_bosses/capone/index_1.html. An online biography of 1920s Chicago gangster Al Capone.

Chicago Radio Show 1924. http://xroads.virginia.edu/~UG00/3on1/radioshow/home.htm. A history Web project on the early days of radio, created by students at the University of Virginia.

Encyclopedia.com, "Harlem Renaissance." www.encyclopedia.com/html/H/HarlemR1en.asp. Article on the Harlem Renaissance of the 1920s, with links to articles on various figures in the movement.

Library of Congress, "Prosperity and Thrift: The Coolidge Era and the Consumer Economy, 1921–1929." http://memory.loc.gov/ammem/coolhtml/coolhome.html. Site with links to primary sources from the 1920s.

The Roaring Twenties. http://cvip.fresno.com/~jsh33/roar.html. Links to many sites concerning the culture and history of the 1920s, established by a member of the Roosevelt High School Social Studies Department in Fresno, California.

The Roaring Twenties and the Great Depression. http://users. snowcrest.net/jmike/20sdep.html. Links to sites concerning the 1920s and the 1930s, sponsored by Amazon.com.

"Roaring Twenties: History in the Key of Jazz," excerpted from *Jazz: A History of America's Music.* www.pbs.org/jazz/time/time_ roaring.htm. Web page associated with a PBS television documentary on the development of jazz. Contains analysis as well as audio samples of early jazz.

Jennifer Rosenberg, "Flappers in the Roaring Twenties." http:// history1900s.about.com/library/weekly/aa022201a.htm. Article from a full-length twentieth-century history sponsored by About.com and the History Net.

Paul Sann, *The Lawless Decade: A Pictorial History of the Twenties.* www.lawlessdecade.net. Site devoted to twenties ephemera and nostalgia, based on a book of the same title.

Smithsonian, "In Ponzi We Trust," December 1998. www. smithsonianmag.com/smithsonian/issues98/dec98/ponzi.html. Abstract of a *Smithsonian* magazine article about one of the famous get-rich-quick schemes of the 1920s.

———, "The Madness That Swept Miami," January 2001. www. smithsonianmag.si.edu/smithsonian/issues01/jan01/miami.html. Abstract of a *Smithsonian* magazine article about the Florida real estate boom during the 1920s.

Temperance and Prohibition, 1997. http://prohibition.history.ohio-state.edu. An online history maintained by the History Department of Ohio State University.

Index